William Friedkin: Interviews

Conversations with Filmmakers Series
Gerald Peary, General Editor

William Friedkin
INTERVIEWS

Edited by Christopher Lane

University Press of Mississippi / Jackson

The University Press of Mississippi is the scholarly publishing agency of
the Mississippi Institutions of Higher Learning: Alcorn State University,
Delta State University, Jackson State University, Mississippi State University,
Mississippi University for Women, Mississippi Valley State University,
University of Mississippi, and University of Southern Mississippi.

www.upress.state.ms.us

The University Press of Mississippi is a member
of the Association of University Presses.

First printing 2020

∞

Library of Congress Cataloging-in-Publication Data

Names: Friedkin, William, interviewee. | Lane, Christopher, editor.
Title: William Friedkin : interviews / edited by Christopher Lane.
Other titles: Conversations with filmmakers series.
Description: Jackson : University Press of Mississippi, 2020. | Series:
    Conversations with filmmakers series | Includes index.
Identifiers: LCCN 2019053440 (print) | LCCN 2019053441 (ebook) | ISBN
    9781496827098 (hardcover) | ISBN 9781496827081 (paperback) | ISBN
    9781496827104 (epub) | ISBN 9781496827074 (epub) | ISBN 9781496827111
    (pdf) | ISBN 9781496827128 (pdf)
Subjects: LCSH: Friedkin, William—Interviews. | Motion picture producers
    and directors—United States—Interviews. | BISAC: PERFORMING ARTS /
    Individual Director (see also BIOGRAPHY & AUTOBIOGRAPHY / Entertainment
    & Performing Arts)
Classification: LCC PN1998.3.F75 A5 2020 (print) | LCC PN1998.3.F75
    (ebook) | DDC 791.4302/33092 [B]—dc23
LC record available at https://lccn.loc.gov/2019053440
LC ebook record available at https://lccn.loc.gov/2019053441

British Library Cataloging-in-Publication Data available

Contents

Introduction

Claustrophobia and irrational fear are two elements that interest me as
a filmmaker. I'm drawn to people who are thrown together in a tense
situation, with no escape. . . .

—WILLIAM FRIEDKIN

William Friedkin represents one of the last great true American auteurs, helping to
define and shape what would become known as the Directors Era. Friedkin would
strike box office gold with two of the biggest films of the seventies, *The French
Connection* (1971) and *The Exorcist* (1973). His subsequent films would experience
varying degrees of critical and box office success. Upon their original release many
of these films received somewhat tepid reviews or poor box office receipts, or
experienced some sort of controversial backlash. With time and ensuing rereleases,
though, many of these same films have gone on to find new audiences, and upon
further review and critical analysis are now rightly considered masterpieces of
cinema. Friedkin is no stranger to controversy, or hard work, often outspoken,
always opinionated, with a wry and devilish sense of humor—and an absolute
willingness to speak his mind unabated. And much like the players who populate
his body of work, Friedkin continues to march forward always searching for truths
and meaning, innately self-aware that he as well as most of his films deal in one
way or another with the inherent conflict or struggle found within each and every
one of us, or as he eloquently states, "the thin line between good versus evil."

The interviews and articles curated in this book boldly shine an intricate light
on the filmmaker who is completely unabashed and freely answers questions in a
verbose and expository way that only someone with the confidence of a superstar
could possibly do. This collection of interviews begins with an American Film
Institute seminar conducted in the 1970s, just shortly after his second blockbuster
film was released, and on display is a self-assured storyteller whose desire to push
the limits of the medium sometimes outweighed his need to fit in. The American
Film Institute (AFI) considers Friedkin one of their premier directors and conducted
a series of seminars and interviews beginning in the 1970s and continuing through
the 2000s. In 1974, Friedkin addresses a crowd and panel of interviewers gathered
at the AFI and weighs in on a number of subjects, sharing insight to his unique

and rather unconventional meteoric rise through the television studio path of his early days while still in Chicago.

"I would probably still be working in live TV if I hadn't been fired from every station for which I worked," he exclaimed when asked how he got started in the industry. Friedkin recounts being unceremoniously fired for nothing more than just being the youngest guy on staff during a round of budget cuts, and then again from another station after going $6500 over budget on his first documentary film after promising to do the piece for under $500. But Friedkin would have the last laugh because the little documentary, *The People vs. Paul Crump* (1965), would garner much praise and attention—even winning the prestigious Golden Gate Award, the grand prize at the San Francisco International Film Festival. As Friedkin shares in the interviews in this book, there the film was seen by David L. Wolper who was producing a string of documentaries at the time. Impressed, Wolper would offer Friedkin a job with his company if he was to ever find his way out to Los Angeles.

The early AFI seminar explores much of Friedkin's career to that point starting with the early Chicago television days and working through his progression to feature films including *Good Times* (1967), *The Night They Raided Minsky's* (1970), and *The Birthday Party* (1970). The in-depth interview explores the psyche of Friedkin and his early development as an artist, with Friedkin relating a story of how "when I was much younger, I used to make up stories and scare the little girls in my neighborhood. Really. I have vivid memories of making up these outlandish stories that would drive these little girls to tears, and the more response I got out of them the scarier would be these fantasies that I would make up" (AFI, 1974), hinting at the somewhat unorthodox methods of direction he would later employ—striving to elicit some sort of response from those around him. These candid comments lend themselves to the frame of mind and development of Friedkin as he ventured into the visual storytelling arena.

Friedkin would take Wolper up on his offer and moved to Los Angeles, where he would find himself further developing and pushing his understanding of his craft continuing with a series of documentaries and television movies. He was young and brash and full of bravado but very much still honing his skills on the job, and as Friedkin candidly shares with the audience at the seminar, "Every time you pick up a camera, you learn."

Friedkin relates a story that could have only unfolded as it did with the swagger of a supremely confident and cocksure artist mixed with exuberant youth. In 1965, the young director was offered an opportunity to direct "Off Season," an episode of *The Alfred Hitchcock Hour*. Friedkin remembers aggravating the great director when Hitchcock asked about Friedkin's lack of tie on set, remarking "usually our directors wear ties" and then turning and leaving before Friedkin could explain his crime. A few years later after winning the Directors Guild Award for *The French*

Connection, the elated yet ever-defiant Friedkin recalls: "I had on a rented tuxedo with one of those snap-on bowties, and I walked down the center steps instead of to the side and I went right over to Hitchcock's table and I had this award. And I snapped my tie at him. And I said to him, "How do you like the tie now, Hitch?"

William Friedkin touches on and shares insight into a great many of his early accomplishments including his first real venture into the world of established Hollywood feature filmmaking. This came as the director of *Good Times* (1967) starring musical sensations Sonny and Cher. When referring to working with Sonny Bono, Friedkin suggests that Bono might be the only real "genius" he's ever truly encountered. The film cleverly spoofed many of Hollywood's classic movie scenes throughout the ninety-one minutes that highlighted the duo's unique onscreen comic chemistry—foreshadowing their hugely popular television show that would follow some years later. The film ultimately proved to be a failure—no doubt as the counterculture audience by this time would have been tuning out the likes of Sonny and Cher. But the film would get Friedkin noticed by Blake Edwards who would ask him to direct the feature version of the television series *Peter Gunn*. Things were beginning to really fall into place for Friedkin, the ball was rolling. Unfortunately, *Peter Gunn* never materialized, not for Friedkin anyway, as his sharp tongue would get the better of him. He recounts the incident, "And I read the script and I hated it, really hated it. I didn't really know what to say to Blake because I wanted to do the picture, but not that picture. So, I went back to see Blake and I said, 'Blake, I really hate this script. As a matter of fact, I think it's the worst piece of shit I ever read in my life.'" His contemptuous yet direct criticism of the "piece of shit" would win over the writer, who broke into hysterical laughter upon the review. The writer was William Peter Blatty, and he would remember Friedkin's unedited and frank honesty.

Within a very short time Friedkin was beginning to make a name as a go-to low-budget "art house" director, known for films like *The Night They Raided Minsky's* (1968) which Friedkin now admits he's "divorced" from as the film was "over his head," and he "frankly made the picture because it was an opportunity to make a feature film for a large company; and like many filmmakers my early steps were not always inspired," he shared with Ralph Appelbaum in a 1979 interview for *Films and Filming*. He would follow it up with *The Boys in the Band* (1970), a ground-breaking film exploring homosexual themes set in the Upper East Side of New York City in the 1960s. Showcasing the talent of a skilled artist, capable leader, and inspired storyteller, Friedkin tells Gerald R. Butler of *Film Quarterly* (1975) that he was "inspired" by cubist art that he had seen while visiting the Museum of Modern Art in New York City during the time he was making *The Boys in the Band*, and as he explains it "I was really struck by this notion of attempting to break free from what was essentially a restriction of the art form. And it occurred to me that this was a challenge offered by the motion picture medium." The *Film Quarterly* interview offers much debate and back and forth on the norms of filmmaking, as Friedkin also shares his thoughts about those that would choose to comment on and criticize the medium of film, holding nothing back.

The reader truly gets the sense that Friedkin wasn't necessarily satisfied with being thought of as a mere art house master. And these conversations provide real insight through intimate dialogue suggesting that the formative early years of documentary film work helped equipped Friedkin with a truly unique perspective and tools with which to relate his stories. These helped inspire him to create richer and far more textured films that not only strived to capture the current sociopolitical environment of the day but also straddled the line of what was socially acceptable, allowing him to explore and further push psychological boundaries. So, in 1971, William Friedkin unleashed his gritty police thriller *The French Connection*. Many of the interviews in the anthology touch on various aspects of the development and success of *The French Connection*, as it would turn out to be a pinnacle and defining moment in Friedkin's career. The film explores what Friedkin refers to on several occasions throughout these interviews as the "thin line," and in the 2003 AFI seminar he examines this topic thoroughly in regard to this film. Pointing out that this time the "thin line" suggests the subtle line "between the policeman and the criminal, the thin line between good and evil" and how closely the two are related. This driving force attracts Friedkin to stories such as *The French Connection*: "that is the theme that attracts me—my belief that there's good and evil within all of us. I don't make films about heroes and villains. Each person, with rare exception, has both things going on at all times" (AFI, 2003). We see this simple truth, this theme, explored over and over again throughout Friedkin's career.

The French Connection proved to be a critical success and ultimately amass five Oscars at the 1972 Academy Awards, including Best Picture, Best Director, and Best Actor in a Leading Role awarded to Gene Hackman, despite, as revealed within these conversations, not being Friedkin's first choice. In fact, in the 1990 AFI seminar Friedkin describes Hackman's inclusion as being "my last choice" and holding no punches goes on to suggest "he bored the shit out of me." Some would argue Friedkin deserved the Best Director award for turning the relatively unknown lead into an actor of note.

This new-found success would put Friedkin squarely into the conversation with an old acquaintance, author William Peter Blatty, for what would turn out to be *The Exorcist*, a film based on his best-selling novel of the same name. Blatty wanted Friedkin for *The Exorcist*, but the studio was hesitant to allow the relatively new director to helm the epic horror film and already had another director in mind. In a *Venice Magazine* interview conducted by Alex Simon in 1997, Friedkin explains the process and the events leading to how he eventually landed the role of directing *The Exorcist*. He discloses quite simply and matter-of-factly, "Bill felt he could communicate with me. So, I got that picture because of Blatty. . . . I understand they had to pay off [Mark] Rydell since they had a deal with him" (Simon, 1997).

The 2014 *Hollywood Reporter* interview by Stephen Galloway describes in detail the casting process for the film, which proved extremely difficult as at least two thousand girls came out for the role of Reagan. Eventually it would be Linda Blair's brazen honesty and clever remarks when asked about the potentially controversial masturbation scene that would ring true for Friedkin and set the young actress apart, earning the trust of the director who cast the twelve-year-old immediately upon meeting her. "I knew that she could handle this material with a sense of humor," recounted Friedkin. He would round out the cast with Ellen Burstyn, Max von Sydow, Jason Miller, and an actual man of the cloth, Father William O'Malley. Friedkin would push the boundaries not only of narrative filmmaking and the genre but of actual production techniques and would go to extreme lengths to create the proper look and feel of the film; the production, which was scheduled for eighty-five days, ultimately took a grueling 224 to complete.

The Exorcist opened in December 1973 to mixed reviews ranging from "instant classic" to "trash." However, some of the more renowned critics like Roger Ebert saw the phenomenon brewing and gave the film four out four stars (RogerEbert. com, December 26, 1973). One film critic remarked *The Exorcist* was "the scariest film he had ever seen," and another said, "it will scare the shit out of you." Friedkin had succeeded at creating a somewhat claustrophobic, authentic, and powerful film, which was destined to become a horror classic with such craft and artistry as to get it recognized by the Academy of Motion Picture Arts and Sciences. At the 1974 Oscars, *The Exorcist* would receive twelve nominations, making it the first horror film ever to receive a nomination for Best Picture. Unfortunately, the film would lose to *The Sting* (1973) that year, ultimately only receiving an award in two categories—Best Sound and Best Adapted Screenplay. In the 1975 interview with Bartlett for *Film Quarterly*, Friedkin talks extensively about his disappointment with the Oscar loss. However, we gain great insight into the audio techniques employed as Friedkin does talk about his process for audio and the uniquely ground-breaking method for the sound design for this and many other films throughout his career.

In that same interview, Friedkin recounts how he was approached by Charlie Bludhorn of Paramount Pictures, to join with colleagues Francis Ford Coppola and Peter Bogdanovich to form a director-run production company, aptly named the Director's Company. The three powerhouses would be given carte-blanche to produce *any* film they so wanted, provided the budget remained below $3 million. Only three films actually came to fruition, Bogdanovich's *Paper Moon* (1973) and

Daisy Miller (1974) and also Coppola's *The Conversation* (1974). Coppola approached Friedkin (after Bogdanovich rightly passed) with the script for *Star Wars* (1977). Friedkin declined the fantasy film, choosing to make his own film *Sorcerer* (1977) instead. With little interest or a real commitment, Friedkin soon parted ways without ever completing a film for the company. Soon after, the Director's Company folded altogether.

Throughout these interviews, regardless of which decade they were conducted in, Friedkin steadfastly admits his favorite film of his professional career remains *Sorcerer*. Alex Simon reminisces with Friedkin about his self-proclaimed masterpiece in the 2013 *Hollywood Interviews* article. The film starred *Jaws* lead Roy Scheider, along with a truly international cast. And this time Friedkin took the reins of the project and both produced and directed this existential thriller that pushed production costs increasingly upward with a skyrocketing budget starting at $15 million and finishing with over $22 million in expenditures. The 1979 *Films and Filming* interview describes how *Sorcerer* was a disappointment at the box office, only gaining a return of $5.9 million and landing Friedkin in hot water with coproduction companies Universal Pictures and Paramount Pictures. Many felt that the very film Friedkin passed on, *Star Wars*, contributed to the defeat of *Sorcerer* as the aforementioned film was released at roughly the same time as Friedkin's flop. However, in recent years *Sorcerer* has been revisited through various rereleases, and now many critics and cinephiles believe the film represents a truly missed masterpiece of cinema that stands the test of time. Shortly after this perceived setback Friedkin made another attempt at the genre with the crime thriller *The Brink's Job* (1978); this also failed to find its audience.

The *Cineaste* article written in 1980 portrays the level of controversy facing his next project, *Cruising* (1980), which was based on the Broadway play of the same name. *Cruising* starred Al Pacino and dealt with a police officer who dives into the world of the New York gay and S&M scenes while on the hunt for a serial killer who had been targeting the homosexual community. The title *"Cruising"* played on the double meaning of the police patrol cars that were cruising the roads and the gay men who cruised for sexual encounters. Friedkin explains that he had no intention on commenting on the gay scene itself but rather found it to be an intriguing backdrop to the story he was trying to tell. The article explores how the filming of the movie was fraught with controversy and often impeded by protestors. The movie was poorly received by critics but had moderate success at the box office, an example of yet another Friedkin film that many have re-examined favorably over the years through various rereleases, also along the way gathering a dedicated cult following.

Soon after *Cruising*'s release, William Friedkin suffered a minor heart attack. He spent several months in rehabilitation for a genetic heart defect. Filmmaking for Friedkin became more and more infrequent throughout the eighties and nineties, and Friedkin's films still struggled to find an audience. An exception was *To Live and Die in L.A.* (1985), which pleasantly reminded audiences and critics of Friedkin's abilities and previous successes. In 2000, *The Exorcist* was theatrically rereleased for a whole new generation along with extra footage. The limited release earned over $40 million in the United States alone and put Friedkin back in the conversation of critics and film lovers. Friedkin's involvement in the rerelease seemed to reinvigorate him, and soon Friedkin was back working in Hollywood with a current line-up of talent like Tommy Lee Jones, Samuel L. Jackson, and Guy Pearce, with the release of *Rules of Engagement* (2000).

Sven Mikulec of *Cinephilia and Beyond* gets Friedkin to open up about a trip to the theater in 2004 where he met playwright Tracy Letts. The introduction led Friedkin to begin work on his newest mind-bending film, *Bug* (2007). Although up against giants like *Spider-Man 3*, *Pirates of the Caribbean 3*, and *Shrek 3*—*Bug* still managed to rank fourth in its opening weekend of "most-watched films." At age seventy-six William Friedkin debuted *Killer Joe* (2011), another film penned by Tracy Letts. The film was released in only seventy-five theaters worldwide but still managed an impressive $3.5 million in just two months. Of the fourteen film festival nominations around the world, *Killer Joe* earned seven wins, proving that the public still has an appetite for William Friedkin's unique on-edge brand of storytelling. In fact, 2013 marked the release of William Friedkin's memoir, *The Friedkin Connection*, and the presentation of the Lifetime Achievement Award at the Cannes Film Festival.

In the 2014 *Hollywood Reporter* interview conducted by Stephen Galloway, Friedkin talks about his growing distaste for the current state of cinema, compelling Friedkin to start to explore the greater possibilities and artistic freedoms that can be found in long-format storytelling. He has begun developing some of his previous works like *To Live and Die in L.A.* and *Killer Joe* into television series.

The *Rolling Stone* interview from 2018 discusses Friedkin's release of *The Devil and Father Amorth* (2018)—a documentary exploring the life of Father Gabriele Amorth, a Vatican-approved exorcist. Still always searching for truth and meaning and still exploring the thin line between good and evil found in man, Friedkin set forth to document an actual exorcism, stating "I'm convinced that Father Amorth was authentic" and admitting to being absolutely terrified during the actual exorcism. In *The Devil and Father Amorth* Friedkin documents the priest performing exorcisms atop the Scala Sancta steps in Rome. He parallels this with the steps in *The Exorcist*. He describes trying to scale the steps from *The Exorcist* in his senior years saying, "I tried it last week here, and it almost claimed my life. I actually had the thought on the last landing that it would not only be fitting but poetic for me to die on these steps."

In his eighties, Friedkin is still a fascinating and intense filmmaker, still always outspoken, still sometimes controversial, never at a loss for an opinion, and still proving that he is a serious force to be reckoned with.

A Note from the Editor

The very nature of editing a collection of conversations such as this means the inevitability of repetition. And as even the great William Friedkin noted, "it's hard not to repeat yourself, there's only so many things one knows and can talk about." Yet for the purpose of this unique anthology I have made my best attempt to eliminate blatant reiterations and retellings so that the reader of this book can, without a doubt, gain valuable insight to the thoughts and process of one of cinema's true masters through Friedkin's own words. These interviews and conversations appear unedited, save punctuation corrections and the omission of the aforementioned retellings, which should allow for a candid and concise impression of the filmmaker William Friedkin as he was from 1974 to 2018.

This collection would not have been possible without the generous participation, help, and guidance of a great many people. I would like to acknowledge all the authors, interviewers, and publications who have provided their articles, materials, and hard work. I have taken great care to ensure all are credited accordingly. This includes Ralph Appelbaum, Alex Simon, Sven Mikulec, and Ian Johnston for your graciousness and generosity. I'd also like to thank Mike Pepin at the American Film Institute for not only providing access and assistance throughout this process but also for pointing me in the right direction of some very interesting supplementary seminars. Thanks also goes out to other publications that have participated in this anthology including *Rolling Stone*, *Literature Film Quarterly*, *Cineaste*, and the *New York Times*. Thank you to the representation of Mr. Friedkin for taking the time to answer my inquiries. Additionally, my sincere appreciation and gratitude to the University Press of Mississippi and especially Emily Snyder Bandy, the wonderful assistant to the director, for her patience, correspondence, kindness, and guidance. As well the series editor, Gerry Peary, and the project editor, Valerie Jones, for their help in editing this manuscript. Thanks for your assistance in transcribing, Joe Smith and Andrew Moir. Lastly, I'd like to thank my research assistant, Michelle Long, for the long hours, late nights, diligent eye, and loving support.

CL

Chronology

1935   On August 29, William Friedkin is born to Ukrainian parents Rachael and Louis Friedkin in the suburbs of Chicago, Illinois, USA.

1951   Friedkin graduates high school early due to social promotion. He begins working in the WGN-TV mailroom in Chicago.

1953   At age eighteen, begins directing live television shows for WGN-TV.

1962   Begins directing TV documentaries, including *The People vs. Paul Crump*, which is instrumental in the commutation of Crump's death sentence. The film wins the Golden Gate Award at the San Francisco Film Festival. His success gets him noticed by producer David L. Wolper.

1965   Friedkin heads west to Los Angeles where he gets a job directing television with an episode of Alfred Hitchcock's *The Alfred Hitchcock Hour*. The episode is titled "Off Season." He also directs *The Bold Men*, a TV documentary movie.

1966   Directs a TV documentary movie titled *The Thin Blue Line*.

1967   Friedkin meets with Sonny Bono and is asked to direct the upcoming Sonny and Cher movie *Good Times*, spoofing several other Hollywood films, which Friedkin admits is "unwatchable." The film is released in May.

1968   Friedkin begins directing "art-house" and low-budget films including the feature film *The Birthday Party*, which is described as a "comedy of menace" and is based on a play Friedkin saw by Harold Pinter, who would also pen the screenplay. The film is released on December 9. December 28: Releases feature film *The Night They Raided Minsky's*, based on the fictional account of the invention of the striptease in 1925. The film directed by Friedkin is produced by Norman Lear.

1969   Begins relationship with Kitty Hawks, daughter of director Howard Hawks.

1970   Friedkin directs the feature film *The Boys in the Band*, developed from the off-Broadway play of the same name. The film revolves around gay characters and was touted as a step forward for queer cinema. It is released on March 17.

1971   Friedkin directs his first major commercial and critical success, released on October 7, *The French Connection*. The film depicts two New York Police narcotics detectives on the tail of a drug ring with French ties. The film features a car chase that is often voted one of the best all-time cinematic chase sequences.

1972   Ends relationship with Kitty Hawks and begins relationship with Australian dancer and choreographer Jennifer Nairn-Smith. February 6: Wins three Golden Globes after four nominations for *The French Connection*. Friedkin wins for Best Director and Best Picture. April 10: *The French Connection* wins five out of eight awards it's nominated for at the Academy Awards. Friedkin wins Best Director and Best Picture, making him the youngest director to ever win the Best Director award and the first rated-R film to ever be nominated, let alone win, Best Picture.

1973   December 26: Releases feature film *The Exorcist*.

1974   *The Exorcist* is nominated for seven Golden Globes and on January 26 wins four including Best Picture and Best Director for Friedkin. *The Exorcist* is nominated for ten Academy Awards including Best Picture and Best Director; only wins for Best Adapted Screenplay and Best Sound Mixing. First horror film to ever be nominated for an Academy Award.

1975   Releases documentary film *Fritz Lang Interviewed by William Friedkin*, a film featuring William Friedkin on camera speaking with Fritz Lang, the director of *M* and *Metropolis*.

1976   November 27: Son with Jennifer Nairn-Smith, Cedric Friedkin, is born. Ends relationship with Jennifer Nairn-Smith.

1977   February 8: Marries French actress, director, and screenwriter Jeanne Moreau, best known for her appearance in Francois Truffaut's *Jules et Jim* (1962). June 24: Releases feature film *Sorcerer* based on film *Wages of Fear*. Friedkin produces and directs the film starring Roy Scheider. The film is released roughly the same time as *Star Wars*, contributing to its commercial failure.

1978   December 8: Releases feature film *The Brink's Job* based on the real-life heist in 1950 where over $3 million was stolen. Friedkin shot the film on location in Boston where the original robbery took place.

1979   Divorces Jeanne Moreau.

1980   February 8: Releases feature film *Cruising* amidst threats and complaints from the homosexual communities in America who tried to shut down production of the film, which they deemed exploitive and inaccurately representative of their culture.

1982   Marries English actress, model, and singer Lesley-Anne Down. August 30: Jack Anthony Friedkin (Jackson) is born to William and Lesley-Anne.

1983   November 4: Releases feature film *Deal of the Century*. The comedy film is directed by Friedkin and stars *SNL* alum Chevy Chase, and *Alien* star Sigourney Weaver.

1984   April: Directs short music video for Laura Branigan titled "Self-Control."

1985   August 5: Files for divorce from Lesley-Anne Down and begins brutal custody battle over son Jack. October 18: Friedkin-directed episode segment of *The Twilight Zone* titled "Nightcrawlers" airs. November 1: Friedkin writes, directs, and releases feature film *To Live and Die in L.A.* which was cowritten by a former US Secret Service operative and tells the story of the lengths two Secret Service agents would go to catch a known counterfeiter. Directs and appears in short film *Putting it Together: The Making of a Broadway Album*.

1986   July 27: Directs and airs TV movie *C.A.T. Squad*.

1987   June 7: Marries American journalist Kelly Lange. September 11: Writes, directs, produces, and releases feature film *Rampage* about a serial killer who drinks blood based on paranoid delusions.

1988   May 23: *C.A.T. Squad: Python Wolf* airs on television. The film is written and directed by Friedkin. Daughter Kelly (Snyder) is born to William Friedkin and Kelly Lange.

1990   April 27: Returns to his horror roots and releases feature film *The Guardian* which Friedkin cowrites based on the novel *The Nanny* by Dan Greenburg.

1991   June 26: *The Guardian* is nominated for three Saturn Awards, including Best Horror Film. July 6: Marries first female studio executive Sherry Lansing (former CEO of Paramount Studios and president of 20th Century Fox).

1992   June 27: Directs and airs "On a Deadman's Chest," episode segment of *Tales from the Crypt*.

1994   September 9: Releases feature *Blue Chips*, a basketball-based film starring Nick Nolte. September 9: Directs and airs "Jailbreakers" episode of *Rebel Highway*.

1995   October 13: Releases erotic thriller feature film *Jade*.

1997   August 17: Directs and airs TV movie *12 Angry Men*.

1998   Directs Alban Berg's opera *Wozzeck* in Florence, Italy, with Zubin Mehta conducting.

2000   April 7: Releases war-based feature film *Rules of Engagement* starring Tommy Lee Jones and Samuel L. Jackson.

2002   Stages two productions for the Los Angeles Opera, *Il Tabarro* and *Suo Angelica*.

2003   March 14: Releases feature film *The Hunted*.

2006   Directs *Salome* opera in Munich, Germany.

2007   May 25: Releases feature film *Bug* written by Tracy Letts based on his play. May 29: Directs and releases documentary short film "The Painter's Voice." December 6: Directs and airs episode of *CSI: Crime Scene Investigation* titled "Cockroaches."

2009   April 2: Directs and airs episode of *CSI: Crime Scene Investigation* titled "Mascara."

2011   Friedkin teams up with Tracy Letts again and on September 8 releases feature film *Killer Joe* starring Matthew McConaughey and Emile Hirsch.

2012   March: Directs Viennese opera *The Tales of Hoffmann* at Theater an dier Wien in Vienna, Austria.

2013   April: Publishes and releases memoir entitled *The Friedkin Connection*. August/September: Is presented with the Lifetime Achievement Award at the 70th Annual Venice International Film Festival.

2017   April 28: Releases the documentary *The Devil and Father Amorth* at the Venice Film Festival.

Filmography

THE PEOPLE VS. PAUL CRUMP (1962)
WBKB Channel 7
TV documentary
Director: **William Friedkin**
Producer: Sterling "Red" Quinlan
Cast: Major James Harris, Mary Alice Harris
52 minutes

THE BOLD MEN (1965)
David L. Wolper Productions
TV documentary
Director: **William Friedkin**
Producer: Julian Ludwig, Sam Farnsworth, Mel Stuart
Writer: Don Bresnahan
Cast: Van Heflin
60 minutes

THE ALFRED HITCHCOCK HOUR: OFF SEASON (1965)
Shamley Productions
TV series, episode
Director: **William Friedkin**
Producer: Gordon Hessler, Norman Lloyd
Writer: Robert Bloch, Edward D. Hoch
Cinematography: John F. Warren
Editing: Douglas Stewart
Cast: Alfred Hitchcock, John Gavin, Richard Jaeckle, Tom Drake
50 minutes

PRO FOOTBALL: MAYHEM ON A SUNDAY AFTERNOON (1965)
American Broadcasting Company/ David L. Wolper Productions
TV documentary
Director: **William Friedkin**

Producer: **William Friedkin**, Harvey Bernhard, Bert Gold, Mel Stuart
Writer: Bernard Wiser
Cast: Van Heflin (narrator)
60 minutes

TIME LIFE SPECIALS: THE MARCH OF TIME (1965–1966)
David L. Wolper Productions
TV documentary series, 9 episodes
Director: **William Friedkin**
Producer: Alan Landsburg, Irwin Rosten, Jack Haley Jr., William Kronick, Nicolas Noxon, William T. Cartwright, Mel Stuart
Writer: Arthur Bramble, James L. Brooks, William Kronick, Alan Landsburg, Nicolas Noxon, Irwin Rosten, Bud Wiser
Cast: William Conrad (narrator), Henry Fonda (narrator)
60 minutes

THE THIN BLUE LINE (1966)
American Broadcasting Company/ David L. Wolper Productions
TV documentary
Director: **William Friedkin**
Producer: **William Friedkin**, Bert Gold, Mel Stuart
Writer: **William Friedkin** (story), David H. Vowell, Bud Wiser
Cast: Van Heflin (narrator)
60 minutes

GOOD TIMES (1967)
American Broadcasting Company/ Motion Pictures International
Feature film
Director: **William Friedkin**
Producer: Steve Broidy, Lindsley Parsons
Writer: Tony Barrett, Nicholas Hyams
Cinematography: Robert Wyckoff
Editing: Melvin Shapiro
Cast: Sonny Bono, Cher, George Sanders, Norman Alden, Larry Duran
91 minutes

THE BIRTHDAY PARTY (1968)
Palomar Pictures International/ American Broadcasting Company
Feature film
Director: **William Friedkin**

Producer: Max Rosenberg, Edgar J. Scherick, Milton Subotsky
Writer: Harold Pinter
Cinematography: Denys N. Coop
Editing: Antony Gibbs
Cast: Robert Shaw, Patrick Magee, Dandy Nichols
123 minutes

THE NIGHT THEY RAIDED MINSKY'S (1968)
Tandem Productions
Feature film
Director: **William Friedkin**
Producer: George Justin, Norman Lear
Writer: Arnold Schulman, Sidney Michaels, Norman Lear
Cinematography: Andrew Laszlo
Editing: Ralph Rosenblum, Pablo Ferro
Cast: Jason Robards, Britt Ekland, Norman Wisdom, Forrest Tucker, Elliott Gould,
Jack Burns
99 minutes

THE BOYS IN THE BAND (1970)
Leo Films/ Cinema Center Films
Feature film
Director: **William Friedkin**
Producer: Matt Crowley, Dominick Dunne, Robert Jiras, Joe Allen
Writer: Matt Crowley
Cinematography: Arthur J. Ornitz
Editing: Gerald B. Greenberg, Carl Lerner
Cast: Kenneth Nelson, Frederick Combs, Cliff Gorman, Laurence Luckinbill
118 minutes

THE FRENCH CONNECTION (1971)
Philip D'Antoni Productions/ Schine-Moore Productions/ Twentieth Century Fox
Feature film
Director: **William Friedkin**
Producer: Phil D'Antoni, G. David Schine, Kenneth Utt
Writer: Ernest Tidyman
Cinematography: Owen Roizman
Editing: Gerald B. Greenberg
Cast: Gene Hackman, Fernando Rey, Roy Scheider, Tony Lo Bianco
104 minutes

THE EXORCIST (1973)
Hoya Productions/ Warner Brothers
Feature film
Director: **William Friedkin**
Producer: William Peter Blatty, Noel Marshall, David Slaven
Writer: William Peter Blatty
Cinematography: Owen Roizman
Editing: Norman Gay, Evan A. Lottman
Cast: Ellen Burstyn, Max von Sydow, Lee J. Cobb, Linda Blair, Jack MacGowran, Kitty Winn
122 minutes

FRITZ LANG INTERVIEWED BY WILLIAM FRIEDKIN (1975)
Feature documentary
Director: **William Friedkin**
Cast: **William Friedkin**, Fritz Lang
140 minutes

SORCERER (1977)
Film Properties International/ Paramount Pictures/ Universal Pictures
Feature film
Producer: **William Friedkin**, Bud S. Smith
Writer: Walon Green
Cinematography: Dick Bush, John M. Stephens
Editing: Robert K. Lambert, Bud S. Smith
Cast: Roy Scheider, Bruno Cremer, Francisco Rabal, Amidou
121 minutes

THE BRINK'S JOB (1978)
Dino De Laurentiis Company/ Universal Pictures
Feature film
Director: **William Friedkin**
Producer: Dino De Laurentiis, Ralph B. Serpe
Writer: Walon Green
Cinematography: Norman Leigh
Editing: Robert K. Lambert, Bud S. Smith
Cast: Peter Falk, Peter Boyle, Allen Garfield, Warren Oates
104 minutes

CRUISING (1980)
Lorimar Film Entertainment/ CiP Europaische Treuhand AG
Feature film
Director: **William Friedkin**
Producer: Jerry Weintraub, Burtt Harris
Writer: William Friedkin
Cinematography: James A. Contner
Editing: Bud S. Smith, M. Scott Smith
Cast: Al Pacino, Paul Sorvino, Karen Allen, Richard Cox
102 minutes

DEAL OF THE CENTURY (1983)
Warner Brothers/ Dream Quest Images
Feature film
Director: **William Friedkin**
Producer: Bud Yorkin, Jon Avnet, Paul Brickman, David Salven, Steve Tisch
Writer: Paul Brickman
Cinematography: Richard H. Kline
Editing: Jere Huggins, Ned Humphreys, Bud S. Smith
Cast: Chevy Chase, Sigourney Weaver, Gregory Hines
99 minutes

THE TWILIGHT ZONE: NIGHTCRAWLERS (1985)
Persistence of Vision Films/ CBS Entertainment Production
TV series, episode segment
Director: **William Friedkin**
Producer: Philip DeGuere, Harvey Frand
Writer: Philip DeGuere, Robert R McCamm
Cinematography: Bradford May
Editing: Jere Huggins
Cast: Scott Paulin, Robert Swan, Exene Cervenka, Sandy Martin, Joey Sotello,
James Whitmore Jr.
45 minutes

TO LIVE AND DIE IN L.A. (1985)
SLM Production Group/ New Century Productions/ United Artists
Feature film
Director: **William Friedkin**
Producer: Irving H. Levin, Samuel Shulman

Writer: **William Friedkin**, Gerald Petievich
Cinematography: Robby Muller
Editing: M. Scott Smith
Cast: William Peterson, Willem Dafoe, John Pankow, Debra Feuer, Dean Stockwell, Robert Downey
116 minutes

C.A.T. SQUAD (1986)
NBC Productions
TV movie
Director: **William Friedkin**
Producer: **William Friedkin**, Cynthia Chvatal, David Salven
Writer: Gerald Petievich
Cinematography: Robert D. Yeoman
Editing: Bud S. Smith, M. Scott Smith
Cast: Jack Cortese, Jack Youngblood, Steve James
97 minutes

RAMPAGE (1987)
De Laurentiis Entertainment Group
Feature film
Director: **William Friedkin**
Producer: **William Friedkin**, David Salven
Writer: **William Friedkin**
Cinematography: Robert D. Yeoman
Editing: Jere Huggins
Cast: Michael Biehn, Alex McArthur, Nicholas Campbell, Deborah Van Valkenburgh
97 minutes

C.A.T. SQUAD: PYTHON WOLF (1988)
NBC Productions
TV movie
Director: **William Friedkin**
Producer: **William Friedkin**, David Salven
Writer: **William Friedkin**, Robert Ward, Gerald Petievich
Cinematography: Guy Defaux
Editing: Jere Huggins
Cast: Jack Cortese, Jack Youngblood, Steve James
93 minutes

THE GUARDIAN (1990)
Universal Pictures/ Nanny Productions
Feature film
Director: **William Friedkin**
Producer: David Salven, Joe Wizan
Writer: Stephen Volk, Dan Greenburg, **William Friedkin**
Cinematography: John A. Alonzo
Editing: Seth Flaum
Cast: Jenny Seagrove, Dwier Brown, Carey Lowell
92 minutes

TALES FROM THE CRYPT: ON A DEADMAN'S CHEST (1992)
Home Box Office (HBO)/ Tales from the Crypt Holdings
TV series, episode segment
Director: **William Friedkin**
Producer: Robert Zemeckis, Gilbert Adler, Richard Donner, Walter Hill, Joel Siler,
David Giler, Michael Hirsh
Writer: Larry Wilson
Cinematography: Rick Bota
Editing: Robert DeMaio
Cast: Tia Carrere, Yul Vazquez, Paul Hipp
29 minutes

BLUE CHIPS (1994)
Paramount Pictures
Feature film
Director: **William Friedkin**
Producer: Michael Rappaport, Wolfgang Glattes, Ron Shelton
Writer: Ron Shelton
Cinematography: Tom Priestley Jr.
Editing: Robert K. Lambert, David Rosenbloom
Cast: Nick Nolte, Mary McDonnell, J. T. Walsh
108 minutes

REBEL HIGHWAY: JAILBREAKERS (1994)
Drive-in Classics/ Showtime Networks/ Spelling Films International
TV series, episode
Director: **William Friedkin**
Producer: Lou Arkoff, Debra Hill, Willie Kutner

Writer: Debra Hill, Gigi Vorgan
Cinematography: Cary Fisher
Editing: Augie Hess
Cast: Sean Whalen, Adrien Brody, Talbert Morton
76 minutes

JADE (1995)
Paramount Pictures/ Robert Evans Company
Feature film
Director: **William Friedkin**
Producer: Gary Adelson, Craig Baumgarten, Robert Evans, William J. McDonald, Joe Eszterhas
Writer: Joe Eszterhas
Cinematography: Andrzej Bartkowiak
Editing: Augie Hess
Cast: David Caruso, Linda Fiorentino, Chazz Palminteri
95 minutes

12 ANGRY MEN (1997)
MGM Television
TV movie
Director: **William Friedkin**
Producer: Terence A. Donnelly
Writer: Reginald Rose
Cinematography: Fred Shuler
Editing: Augie Hess
Cast: Jack Lemmon, George C. Scott, James Gandolfini
117 minutes

RULES OF ENGAGEMENT (2000)
Paramount Pictures/ Seven Arts Pictures/ Munich Film Partners & Company
Feature film
Director: **William Friedkin**
Producer: Scott Rudin, Adam Schroeder, James Webb, Richard D. Zanuck
Writer: James Webb, Stephen Gaghan
Cinematography: William A. Fraker, Nicola Pecorini
Editing: Augie Hess
Cast: Tommy Lee Jones, Samuel L. Jackson, Guy Pearce
128 minutes

THE HUNTED (2003)
Lakeshore Entertainment/ Alphaville Films
Feature film
Director: **William Friedkin**
Producer: Richard Hawley, James Jacks, Ricardo Mestres, Sean Daniel, Marcus Viscidi
Writer: David Griffiths, Peter Griffiths, Art Monterastelli
Cinematography: Caleb Deschanel
Editing: Augie Hess
Cast: Tommy Lee Jones, Benicio Del Toro, Connie Nielson
94 minutes

BUG (2006)
Lions Gates Films/ L.I.F.T. Production/ DMK Mediafonds International/ Inferno Distribution
Feature film
Director: **William Friedkin**
Producer: Kimberly Calhoun Boling, Michael Burns, Gary Huckabay, Michael Ohoven, Malcolm Petal, Andreas Schardt, Jim Siebel, Holly Wiersma
Writer: Tracy Letts
Cinematography: Michael Grady
Editing: Darrin Navarro
Cast: Ashley Judd, Michael Shannon, Harry Connick Jr.
102 minutes

CSI: CRIME SCENE INVESTIGATION: COCKROACHES (2007)
Jerry Bruckheimer Television/ CBS Paramount Network Television/ Alliance Atlantis Productions
TV series, episode
Director: **William Friedkin**
Producer: Dustin Lee Abraham, Jerry Bruckheimer, Steven Felder. David Rambo
Writer: Dustin Lee Abraham
Cinematography: James L. Carter
Editing: John Ganem
Cast: William Petersen, Marg Helgenberger, George Eads
44 minutes

CSI: CRIME SCENE INVESTIGATION: MASCARA (2009)
Jerry Bruckheimer Television/ CBS Paramount Network Television

TV series, episode
Director: **William Friedkin**
Producer: Dustin Lee Abraham, Jerry Bruckheimer, Steven Felder, David Rambo
Writer: Dustin Lee Abraham
Cinematography: Nelson Cragg
Editing: Augie Robels
Cast: Laurence Fishburne, Marg Helgenberger, George Eads
60 minutes

KILLER JOE (2011)
Voltage Pictures/ Picture Perfect Corporation/ Worldview Entertainment/ ANA Media
Feature film
Director: **William Friedkin**
Producer: Nicholas Chartier, Scott Einbinder, Christopher Woodrow, Vicki Cherkas, Molly Conners
Writer: Tracy Letts
Cinematography: Caleb Deschanel
Editing: Darrin Navarro
Cast: Matthew McConaughey, Emile Hirsch, Thomas Haden Church
102 minutes

THE DEVIL AND FATHER AMORTH (2017)
LD Entertainment
Documentary
Director: **William Friedkin**
Producer: **William Friedkin**
Writer: **William Friedkin**, Mark Kermode
Cast: Gabriele Amorth, Robert Barron, **William Friedkin**
68 minutes

William Friedkin: Interviews

Harold Lloyd Master Seminars with William Friedkin

American Film Institute / 1974

From AFI's Harold Lloyd Master Seminars, January 9, 1974 © 1974, courtesy of American Film Institute.

American Film Institute: Ladies and gentlemen, I'd like you to meet Mr. William Friedkin. Do you want to make any opening statement about your work?

William Friedkin: No, I think the work is its own reward. It speaks for itself. You might be curious as to how I got started. I started in television in Chicago. I started in the mailroom of a television station and—

AFI: Which one?

Friedkin: WGN in Chicago and I let everybody there down because they all thought I'd take over the mailroom one day, because I was one of the best mailroom guys they ever had. Live TV was just happening and there were all kinds of dramatic and musical and variety shows, and I thought I would probably make a career out of live television. I started in the mailroom as I say, then became a floor manager, which is like an assistant director in films. I was directing by the time I was seventeen. I did about two thousand live TV shows in about eight years and I would probably still be working in live TV if I hadn't been fired from every station for which I worked.

AFI: Why?

Friedkin: Once I got fired because I was the youngest guy on the staff and they had to make a cut in the staff and so they fired the guys who were young and single and I was the youngest and the singlest. Then I used to get in trouble a lot at a couple of these stations in Chicago and I used to try a lot of things and sometimes after sign-off, a couple of the cameramen and I used to go to the sound stage and fool around and just experiment with things. We used to try some stuff and the chief engineer would come in the studio and see us playing with his cameras and his

3

equipment and say, "What is this? You can't do that. It's not in the deck." So, I got fired. Three stations. I figured I had to do something, so I came out to Hollywood and became a movie director.

AFI: Just like that?

Friedkin: Sort of . . . pretty much. l did a documentary film in Chicago which I was sort of pretty proud of. It was called *The People vs. Paul Crump* and it was about a black man who was on death row for twelve years at the Cook County Jail. It was the first film I ever made. I learned how to make this film by doing it. I did it as a kind of court of last resort for this fellow, who was on trial for murder and going to the chair and the film was instrumental in the governor of Illinois commuting his sentence to life imprisonment, but I knew nothing at that time about how to make a film at all. I was a live television director and I went into an equipment rental house in Chicago and I asked a guy named Jack Baron to show me how to load a camera and show me how to take sound and fortunately for me, the Arriflex camera had just hit. It had just come to Chicago, the Arriflex 16. I mean it might have been some lousy piece of equipment and I never would have learned anything had I learned on an old Bolex or something, I don't think I would have really come up with as much technical information that afforded me so much later as I did. The Arriflex had just come into Chicago. This was 1959. And he showed me how to work it, and also the Nagra tape recorder had come in and he showed me how to operate a Nagra and an Arriflex. Another guy and I went out and made this movie. And we didn't know anything about how you get it together. We went out and we shot things that we thought would be good, but then we didn't realize that that was on negative we were working with, so we were cutting it. Along the line, we kept learning certain things like sync sound. We had no idea how you got a sync signal on—well, you've all been through it. I went through it only in the making of this documentary. The money was put up by the local ABC station in Chicago and they said, "Can you make this one-hour documentary?" which they didn't really want to make, but I really wanted to make it. And I went and did a big selling job on it and they said, "Can you make it for $500?" I said, "Absolutely." You know, there's no way you could make this for $500. It cost about $7,000. They went crazy and I got fired from there. But that won the San Francisco Film Festival award and Dave Wolper saw it and he hired me and that's how I came out here.

AFI: What was the first movie you did?

Friedkin: It was called *Good Times* with Sonny and Cher. It was 1966. And I think it was seen by eleven people in Topanga Canyon. I'd like to have the right to it now though. But I was doing these documentaries for Wolper, and Sonny Bono had a hit record and we met, and he said, "Hey, we got a guy who wants to put up some money to make a movie. Would you like to direct it?" I said, "Sure." He said, "Can you make it for $500?" He said can you make it for some incredible thing which we couldn't make it for, but we made it anyway and it died, had a short, happy life. *The Night They Raided Minsky's* was my second picture and then *The Birthday Party*, *Boys in the Band*, [*The*] *French Connection*.

AFI: How did you become interested in suspense? That seems to be in almost all of your movies in one way or another.

Friedkin: When I was much younger, I used to make up stories and scare the little girls in my neighborhood. Really. I have vivid memories of making up these outlandish stories that would drive these little girls to tears, and the more response I got out of them the scarier would be these fantasies that I would make up. But then, I guess the pictures that had the most effect on me when I was younger were suspense films, like *Wages of Fear*. I don't know if any of you ever saw that or *Diabolique* by the same director, Clouzot. And those two pictures really had a great influence on me. Then I went to work for Hitchcock later after all these documentaries. As a matter of fact, I did the last *Alfred Hitchcock Hour* ever made. My contract with Hitchcock consisted of him coming on the set on my first day of shooting. He was there to film his introduction to the series and God, I was really terrified because he was this great director and he came up to me and he stared at me and he said, "Mr. Friedkin, you're not wearing a tie." And I said, "No, no." And I wasn't, either. He said, "Usually, our directors wear ties." I thought he was putting me on, but he was absolutely straight and that's all he ever said to me. So, I mean I've used that advice in all my suspense films ever since. But that's the only contact I had with Mr. Hitchcock. I loved *Psycho*, you know, and I sort of studied, went to school on *Psycho*. By that I mean I've seen it thirty times. It's terrific.

AFI: It's our main picture here.

Friedkin: I'm sure. It's just great. I figured because of *Psycho*, I could get away with a lot in this [*The*] *Exorcist*. I figured he had about forty-five minutes in *Psycho* where absolutely nothing happened. It's a dull sort of story, but the audience is so expectant. The audience knows that they're coming in to see this horrific suspense film and they're not getting it. They're getting edgy and then suddenly, he whacks them with it and boom, you've got them in your back pocket. So, I figured what I'm going to try and do is make this [*The*] *Exorcist* go on for about an hour with nothing happening and then see how long I could pull the string. Really, I was very conscious of that, have been for quite some time. I've wanted to make a film where I could do that, and all the circumstances have to be right. I mean obviously I'm not Hitchcock. So, people come in to see a film by the guy who directed *Good Times* or something, they're not going to be scared. But I had this book which I knew scared a lot of people, so I figured this is it. This is it. I'm going to go for that effect here and just see. And it's working pretty good that way.

AFI: I saw *The Exorcist* in Westwood. The sound was very, very loud. Was that meant to be that way?

Friedkin: Yes, that's how I want the sound, very loud. I figured it took me three months to get the sound track. It might as well be loud. As a matter of fact, I have set the sound level in each of the theaters where the picture is playing, in the twenty-four opening engagements. I've set the sound level and the light level on the screen, which I'll get into a little bit with you because it really turns out to be, I find, the most engrossing if not interesting part of filmmaking and that's seeing what happens to the picture after you make it because no matter what you hear, the projectionist has final cut always. You've got to set the sound and light levels and take a hard line policy and make sure you get what you want now at the National Theatre; we're setting the faders on twelve on the projectors. The manager at the National told me that he had gotten some complaints, that it was a little too loud, could we set it at eleven? So, I said, because I liked this manager, he's a terrific guy, he really knows his audience, I said, "Could we sit in the last row on opening night and listen to it at eleven?" And it was okay. I could hear everything, so I've taken it down a little. But periodically, I call him up and say, "Maybe you ought to put it on twelve tonight." You know, if it's raining or something, I figure maybe there won't be too many people in the house, kick it up a little. So, he kicks it up and he calls me and says, "We got some complaints." So, I say, "Put it back to eleven." But you'd be amazed. The standard generally for how much light you're supposed to have on the screen is 15 percent Lamberts. Most of the theaters in the country run anywhere from three to twelve. So that it's almost impossible to have your picture seen in some of the best theaters in the country the way you shot it. What we did on *The French Connection* and *The Exorcist* is we had some people go around. On *The Exorcist*, I've got the best people doing it. On *The French Connection* we sort of improvised it and all took turns showing up in all the theater where the picture shows before the picture opens and setting the light level and the sound level in the theater. In the case of some theaters, we replaced the screen. In the Gopher Theatre in Minnesota, the guy who we sent out said, "This damn thing is playing across the street from a whore house and a porno movie parlor, number one. Number two there's potholes in the screen." So, I called up the head of distribution and he said, "How's it coming?" I said, "Well we'll have twenty-three prints ready, not twenty-four." I said, "The Gopher Theatre in Minnesota is not getting a print." He said, "Why not?" I said, "Potholes in the screen." He said, "They put up a $100,000 for the picture." I said, "Fine. They can put up $5,000 and replace the screen." So, we replaced the screen for them and billed them for it. Cinema 1 in New York which is a very good theater, very good house, the guy checked the theater out for me and called me back and said, "I wouldn't play a Randolph Scott western in here." He said, "The stuffs running out of focus. The lenses are shot." So, we replaced the lenses on the projectors at Cinema 1.

AFI: You mean you replaced them as part of your expense or their expense?
Friedkin: We replaced them at our expense. At the end of the run, they can either buy the lenses or go back to the crap that they're using for their next picture.

AFI: Did you know you were going to do *The Exorcist* when you read it?
Friedkin: Yes, absolutely. I read it and I thought, this is pretty powerful stuff here. I mean, this is scary stuff. It'd make a good movie.

AFI: How did you go about getting it then?
Friedkin: Well, I called up Bill Blatty, who I knew. He wrote *The Exorcist*. He and I met about six years ago. Blake Edwards asked me to direct the film of *Peter Gunn*, which was a television series, that Blake had on TV and I had done *Good Times* which nobody had seen, but the word was out that it was a good picture. You'll find in Hollywood the word gets out. Usually it's somebody on the public relations staff of the picture who puts out the word, but the word was out that *Good Times* was a hot picture. It turned out to be a dog as we all know, but Blake Edwards heard that it was a good picture and he wanted a young whatever—and I was a young whatever—to direct *Peter Gunn*. We met, we liked each other, and I was interested in doing *Peter Gunn* and so I came in and I had a meeting with Blake and he already had a script and I had never worked from a script before in my life, except I did this *Hitchcock Hour* which had a script of sorts, and the Sonny and Cher movie was totally adlibbed, no script. Now here he gives me a script on *Peter Gunn* and I took it home and I thought, "Jesus, what a great opportunity. I'm in the big time now and I'm going to direct." And I read the script and I hated it, really hated it. I didn't really know what to say to Blake because I wanted to do the picture, but not that picture. So, I went back to see Blake and I said, "Blake, I really hate this script. As a matter of fact, I think it's the worst piece of shit I ever read in my life." And I never had directed anything really and Blake is a really fine director and he was a little stunned by what I had to say and pushed a button on his desk and he said, "Oh, really? Is that your comment?" I said, "Yeah." He said, "Well, I'd like you to give it to the fellow who wrote the script. He's sitting in the other office." And in came Bill Blatty. And Bill was this kind of nervous guy. He had a facial tic and he was sort of nervous and he needed money and he came in and sat down and Blake said, "Bill Friedkin, this is Bill Blatty. He's read your script. Why don't you tell him what you think of it?" Well, I didn't temper my comments too much, but

after I said it, Bill Blatty broke into hysterical laughter and he said, "You know, you're absolutely right. It really is a rotten script and nobody around here has had the guts to say it." Well, he was finished off the picture and Blake went on and made the film and—

AFI: Did he rewrite the script?

Friedkin: I don't know. I don't know who did or if anyone—I haven't seen the picture, but it was made. Bill and I sort of kept in touch over the years and we'd just talk on the phone or I'd run into him on the street or at the racetrack or something. I saw *A Shot in the Dark*, which he did, which I thought was terrific, but then we'd talk a little and then I was in postproduction on *The French Connection* and I started reading *The Exorcist* and it really wiped me out, I thought it was great. I called him up, said, "This'd make a great picture. I'd love to do it." He said, "That's terrific." He said, "Warner Bros. just paid me $640,000 for the rights. I'll tell them you're interested."

AFI: Could you talk a little bit about the problems that you had with the special effects in *The Exorcist*?

Friedkin: The whole thing was a problem. Well, the cold room. In the old days when they wanted breath to show in a room, they used to go down to the Glendale ice house and build a stage. Well, the Glendale ice house doesn't exist anymore. So, in order to show breath on a set consistently you have to refrigerate the room. In other words, you have to build the set literally in the inside of a refrigerated cocoon. Which is what we had to do. The set was balanced. We shot this thing in New York in the section known as Hell's Kitchen, on 54th Street, on F & B Ceca's stage. I built the entire house, the interior, two stories and a staircase and all kinds of rooms on the first floor, two bedrooms on the top floor, and a trap door leading to the attic. And then we had a separate stage on which we built the little girl's bedroom, which was a refrigerated cocoon to encompass the little girl's bedroom and the hallway which was a duplicate of the little girl's bedroom on the other stage, because I wanted to have shots of people coming down the hall and in one, in the same shot, you'd see no breath in the hallway and they open the door and suddenly the breath comes out in the room. So, the hall was not refrigerated, the bedroom was. The entire bedroom set, four walls with a removable ceiling, was built inside a cocoon, which was able to take the cold down to ten below zero. At the end of each day's shooting, we had to turn the air conditioning on to build it up for tomorrow morning's shooting, because we'd get in and it would start at ten below and after the lights went on and we'd be shooting for four or five hours, it would go up. It would go up sometimes to 25° and sometimes to 35° and there'd be no more breath in the room, so we'd have to stop shooting, build the cold up some more, turn off the lights. The entire set was balanced on a bowling ball, which permitted us to rock it back and forth when we wanted to. The bed—there were three different beds which did three different things. One bed went one way, another bed bounced up and down, and another bed just went sailing up into air. And there were three different weight devices for the various effects on the bed, but that was largely a question of error and trial.

AFI: How did you do the levitation?
Friedkin: There are a few things I don't want to discuss. One is the levitation and the other is how the head turns around. Because—this stuff gets reprinted and it gets sent around. I would tell you individually. But I know that these very wonderful accounts of these seminars get printed and sent around the country and some guy at a news desk in Miami will read it and put it in the paper about how we made the head turn around and it will limit people's enjoyment. You know, some guy will sit there and say, "You know how they did that?" And it's over. So, there are a couple of things that are pretty basic about how we did it. The levitation was not basic nor was the head turn and I'd like to sort of leave that, but I'll answer anything else.

AFI: Well, what about the make-up?
Friedkin: The make-up took four hours. The little girl's make-up took four hours every morning and Max von Sydow's make-up took four hours every morning.

AFI: Did you have a big problem with matching?
Friedkin: Yes, matching was a problem. But Dick Smith, who did the make-up, made various pieces from molds, which he was able to use over and over again. He made several thousand pieces. The make-up had to be torn off at the end of every day's shooting and started over every day—obviously. The same thing with von Sydow, and it had to be specially treated make-up for Iraq, because all those scenes in Iraq were shot in temperatures of 120 to 130 degrees. We were able to shoot from six o'clock in the morning in Iraq to nine o'clock in the morning and that was it. Because after ten o'clock in the morning, it went up to 130 degrees in the shade. And at ten o'clock in the morning, von Sydow would peel off his make-up and the sweat would literally pour out from behind his make-up. So, it had to be tested in New York against crumbling in the cold and it had to be completely redesigned for the extreme heat.

AFI: What was it about his make-up that took so long?
Friedkin: He's totally transformed. Von Sydow is forty-four years old. He doesn't have a line in his face. And he's playing a man in his late sixties, seventies if you

will. His hands are entirely made up. All of his face, his hair had to be colored every morning, because it's a very dangerous thing to dye a man's hair. It can ruin the hair, just kill the roots. So, we had to experiment with the exact kind of coloring that would match every day and it doesn't match. The hair doesn't match from scene to scene in the picture. It's very difficult under different lighting conditions.

AFI: How did you work out the problems with the little girl taking on the devil's voice? Was it played back every day? Because the scene was perfect.
Friedkin: No, she mouthed all of those things. She had to give me a guide track. And for a long time, I thought I would use the guide track. I did a lot of experimentation with electronic distortion of her own voice and I took a lot of time and went through a lot of experiments, before I decided what to do with the voice. Briefly, most of her voice is replaced by Mercedes McCambridge, but some of her voice is her own and what it is that the stuff that's the most effective was recorded in sync to the little girl's own dialogue, into a microphone as well as into a Motorola speaker. The mixer is on a very tinny old Motorola speaker and is between the speaker and the mike and setting a different balance for each line. The thing was literally postsynced line for line. Sometimes I would change the balance between the Motorola speaker and the microphone. Sometimes a little more Motorola, sometimes a little more mike. But we experimented with every damn thing imaginable. At one point, we went back to New York where a guy had an idea to feed the dialogue into a timpani drum head and adjust the skin of the drum to the words and re-record that. So that the drum was bending the sound, making it go . . . in a strange way and I did all of that and I wasn't satisfied that it had enough of a sense of reality about it, so I kept experimenting, and finally, the most effective thing I came up with was straight Mercedes McCambridge plus the Motorola feedback, which gives it that harsh abrasive quality, but the most effective thing about it is the way she's reading it, the dramatization she gives it. Now in addition to that, a lot of those sounds that are not verbal, but vocal, the growling stuff, I got that idea from having heard a cassette recording of an actual exorcism that was done in Rome by the Roman Catholic official exorcist, Father Luigi Novarisi. I got a tape through the Jesuit Provincial of New York of Father Novarisi, Monsignor Novarisi, exorcising a fourteen-year-old boy in Italian and the sounds on this tape are the sounds I duplicated with Mercedes for the little girl, the growls and stuff. In order to get those, the way you hear them, what we did in many cases was we pitched the sound or varied the speed. In a few cases, I did that with Linda Blair's own voice. In some cases, I did that with my own voice. Again, it was a question of trial and error, error and trial mostly. There is no set pattern. It's all a question of taste, and what I tried to do is arrive at something that I thought was going to be pretty believable given the conditions. Now going back

to the classic symptoms of possession, they all involve this business of complete personality change, physical change, obscenities, supernatural occurrences; the characteristic always in a young person, male or female, is that the voice becomes deeper, matured beyond its years and somewhat emphysemaic. The key word was emphysemaic. The wonderful wheeze sound that those of you who have seen the picture hear on the track is Mercedes McCambridge. She smokes heavy. It sounds like she has three or four different screaming animals in her throat. We recorded that very close up and then made a loop out of it, a long loop. And just after I dubbed in the voice, you see, there was something wrong and I said, "Jeez, this doesn't play. It looks like a dub job." Then it occurred to me that I had to keep that demon presence alive, even when it wasn't talking, and that's when we decided to put that looped wheeze in there.

AFI: So, during the dialogue sequences, the distortion had to be induced during the actual looping?

Friedkin: That's right. All Linda Blair did was mouth the words as best she could. Some of her stuff was very good. But it's very important to indicate . . . You see, there are times in the film when it quickly goes back and forth between the girl herself and the demonic voice. So, I knew if I was going to delineate that, I had to not be able to use Linda Blair's own voice. I had to use another voice to indicate the personality transformation. Now I decided to go with a woman's voice. When I started the picture, I didn't think about that. I thought I'm just going to get a good ballsy, masculine voice to do this thing. But it then occurred to me that if I could get a female voice that had a masculinity to it, it would be all that much more believable. That's why it works. Mercedes McCambridge is one of the best actresses in this country and whatever effectiveness the voice has is in large part due to the way she dramatized it.

AFI: How much of *The French Connection* did you shoot as you planned?

Friedkin: I'll tell you what happens to me. I plan these things so damned carefully. One day I'll send my notes over here and let you look at both. Every shot is laid out. I get to the set and I work it out. I always use a viewfinder. I use a viewfinder off a camera. I don't like those director finders. I take the viewfinder off the camera and I hold it up and I move around and generally I see something through there that's beyond my wildest imaginations. So generally, before I shoot a scene I'll take the finder and walk around and just, you know, move around and just stand there until something feels right. I try desperately to not just move the camera for its own sake but to this date, I've not been successful in achieving that one hundred percent. There's still some moves in there that don't mean anything. Each picture I make I'm trying not to move the camera; let the actors move and follow them.

AFI: What about the chase scene in *The French Connection*, did you storyboard that?
Friedkin: It was pretty close to everything I had written.

AFI: Did you get an idea for music at the time?
Friedkin: No, when I cut the chase in *The French Connection*, I used—

AFI: Did you do that yourself?
Friedkin: Yes. I used a track from Santana called "Black Magic Woman." I cut that whole chase scene to "Black Magic Woman." I didn't put any music in it in the picture. There's not a note of music in the chase. I just cut it to that tempo. There's like nice, sliding, long sort of guitar trills and licks and the thing sort of moved along nice to that and then there's some hard stuff and it slows down. But I had "Black Magic Woman" in mind when I shot that scene. The final cutting of it really happened out of a number of shots in that chase scene. On one Bill Hickman and I—he was the stunt driver—he and I got in the car. I operated the camera inside and I had a camera on the front bumper of the car. I said to him—I had been building Hickman up to this for weeks—I said, "Hickman, you have no guts. You're chicken-shit. You need a couple of drinks to drive good." I kept getting under his goat. And he said, "I'll tell you what. I'll show you some driving if you get in the car with me." So, I got in that car and he went for twenty-six blocks with just the siren on top of the car. We broke every stop light. We went through everything. We went in and out of lanes. There was no control. At all.

AFI: That was pre-arranged.
Friedkin: It was not pre-arranged. It was shot at speed. Both cameras. Most of the POV shots in *The French Connection* are made up of those two cuts made on that one run.

AFI: You mean you broke the law?
Friedkin: In New York City, if you drive like that, they don't pay too much attention.

AFI: Are your notes storyboards or floor plans?
Friedkin: No, what I do is first I make sketches and from those sketches I write out in longhand a complete verbal description of every single shot in every sequence. I have those mimeographed, those notes mimeographed, and duplicated by the assistant director to everybody concerned with the scene. And they all either two or three days in advance have a copy of my notes so they all know what I want. They all have an idea from reading this thing what the cutting sequence is. But again, I see an entire picture in my head before I do it. And then, like a novelist, I set out and

write a visualization instead of prose—narration and dialogue, I write out a visual novel of the movie. The thing that like throws me though is like a year or two later, I'm in the shower and a shot or a scene comes to me of the way I should have done the thing and it's better than the way I did it. For example, not long ago, I had a whole different idea for the ending of *The French Connection*, which I think is better than the one I have and I would give almost anything to go back and reshoot it.

AFI: What is it?

Friedkin: I was in the shower and I thought, God, what a great ending it would be to see two junkies sitting on the East River at seven o'clock in the morning on a wintry day, nodding off on the East River and a barge is going along on the East River, dumping all this heroin, all this shit into the East River, which is what they were doing at the time with all the confiscated stuff that had reached its final disposition in court. Whenever a court case was closed on this junk, they would take it out and dump the bags in the East River. Now as we all know, a lot of bags didn't get dumped. They got sold back onto the market, but police procedure was to dump this stuff, and that image of these two guys, just nodding out, seeing $32 million worth of heroin in the East River early in the morning I thought it would have been the most—I mean it reminded me of *The Treasure of the Sierra Madre*, which I thought would have been a gas. And if I could, I'd shoot it tomorrow. It's a lot of prints to correct.

William Friedkin Interview

Gerald R. Barrett / 1975

From *Literature/Film Quarterly* 3, no. 4 (Fall 1975). Reprinted by permission.

Gerald R. Barrett: I want to say at the outset that I'll try not to duplicate questions and discussions the reader could find in your other interviews.
William Friedkin: Well, it's hard not to repeat yourself, there are only so many things one knows and can talk about.

Barrett: I have a few things to talk about that I don't think you have previously discussed in an interview.
Friedkin: Good. And I have a couple of new things I want to talk about.

Barrett: What are they?
Friedkin: I'm sure they'll come out naturally during our conversation.

Barrett: How is *The Exorcist* doing these days?
Friedkin: *The Exorcist* is right now, after eight months of release, the fourth-highest-grossing film of all time. It will eventually be the all-time top-grossing film. In America, so far, it has grossed $65 million in profits, and the estimate for the foreign market is another $40 to $50 million.

Barrett: What are you doing these days?
Friedkin: I've worked on *The Exorcist* from beginning to end, and it took three years. The end was last week. I just finished doing all the foreign versions of the film. I did Italian, German, and French dubbed version and supervised all the subtitled versions too. Japanese . . . Spanish . . .

Barrett: Sounds tedious.
Friedkin: I don't mind when I see the checks! That kind of thing is the hard work of direction that people don't think about.

Barrett: What's the most important part of direction?

Friedkin: It changes at different points in the making of the film. Initially, the more important decision you make is to decide what story you're going to tell. There's no decision more important than that. Because the commercial cinema, in which I work, is a storytelling medium. It's not necessarily a medium for . . . well, it isn't at all a medium for documentary purposes. It's strictly a medium of entertainment. And the other aspects of it, if there are any, come as a kind of by-product of the audience experiencing the story. So, the most important decision I make as a filmmaker is to decide what story I'm going to do. There's nothing more important than that . . . ever.

Barrett: And after you select your story?

Friedkin: Once that's decided, it then becomes a matter of translating the story into details, it becomes a matter of how I'm going to tell it. And the next most important elements are the casting and the people who are going to work on the film.

Barrett: What's the relationship between you, your cast, and your script?

Friedkin: After I know who's going to act in the film and who's going to work on it—I pretty much take things by osmosis. The way I work is pretty well set. I don't change my style of work from one film to another. I prepare very carefully. I communicate what I have in mind to everybody on the picture, immediately. Either with diagrams, drawings, or written explanations of everything that I have in mind. While I'm shooting I constantly try to achieve as much spontaneity as possible. Which is to say, I try to work with actors who are free to throw away the script. Who, like me, work on a script as hard as they need to, and then disregard it and just *become* the character.

Barrett: How do you get your cast to *become* the characters they play?

Friedkin: I try to cast people based on one inherent quality: intelligence. I don't care how good an actor is, or how good his performances have been, when I talk to him, in my initial meetings up front, I try to gauge intelligence. And I don't mean bullshit artists. I don't mean a guy who's going to tell me what I want to hear, but real intelligence and the ability to understand what the story's about on very deep levels so that one can disregard all those levels, not have to play them.

Barrett: I'm not sure I follow that.

Friedkin: Take, for example, the Vincent Price horror films. Everything is played on the surface level. Personality, behavioral, thematic facets are so clearly understood by those people that they try to play every level and leave none to the imagination.

That's why all the looks are arch, that's why everything is overemphasized. I try to deemphasize all that old theatrical stuff, because you find that the camera has a tendency to reflect further than the mirror does. The camera has the tendency to magnify facets of human behavior and to suggest many more things than are there. It's like putting a pebble into the water, and from it flow all the many waves. So, I cast people who are capable of understanding and then disregarding all the very deep levels. I also believe in casting to physical types in the sense that if I'm doing a film, let's say, about a boxer, I'm not going to have the part played by someone who slouches around, looks like he's never been in a gym.

Barrett: You say that your actors are free to throw away the script?

Friedkin: I work on the scripts very long and very carefully,, and by the time I get onto the floor, I never use them. I throw them out, just throw them out, and the actors do the same. I will rehearse extensively with actors on a scene, and then I'll say, "Do you remember all that stuff? Okay, now throw it all out, and do it your way!" Then we start messing around with it. Around 98 percent of all the dialogue in the last two pictures was the actors' invention. Occasionally, someone in the writing process comes up with a line that is, shall we say, comparably memorable. And so, we'll keep that particular line. Because it seems to be a good button on the scene, or a good way to come into the scene; but in the middle of a scene, all of the stuff is the actors living out their roles. And then I work as a kind of road guide, a tourist guide, making sure that they don't wander off onto byways that will lead them nowhere. Because the main thing you have to know as a director is where the hell you're going with this thing. Whereas, the actor may not: the actor comes in and does piecework, really; he has no real knowledge of how his performance is going to be ultimately used, nor control over the ultimate use of his effort.

Barrett: What about the others who work on the film?

Friedkin: Same is true for all of the other creative people who contribute. Camera, sound, lighting, wardrobe, whatever. Film is probably the most collaborative medium of communication there is. They all have their ideas about what their particular area should contribute, but none of them really know, ultimately, not only how it is going to be used, toward what end, but what's going to be used of what they've done. So, they're all out there giving 100 percent all of the time. Whereas, I may have in the back of my mind, let's say, that I might not even make use of wardrobe detail for somebody who's in the background in a scene. And I might not even use the scene! I shoot a lot of scenes, you know, that never get into the picture. Sometimes I'll say, "Don't worry about that detail," and the person in charge of wardrobe will say, "What do you mean?" I'll say, "It's okay, don't worry about that." And the people who know me, who have worked with me more than once, know what that means by now. Whereas, at another time, I'll be a total stickler for authenticity, because I have a gut feeling at the time that that particular shot or scene has got to find its way into the ultimate picture. But I do encourage everybody to cut loose once I'm convinced that they share my vision about what the hell we're supposed to be doing.

Barrett: Do you give your cameraman and the various technicians the same freedom to improvise on the floor as you do your actors?

Friedkin: No. But one of the things I would suggest to anyone who wanted to make films is that you should visualize the entire film in your head before you make it. You've got to see the entire film in your head. Once you can do that, then you can go out and start changing it. If you've ever seen Picasso paint as I have, or if you look carefully at his finished work, you see that he constantly alters the image. Somewhere in his head he knows what he wants. Meanwhile, he gets on the canvas and starts transposing, and scratching out, and drawing over and painting over. You can do that if you have a clear vision of what you want to achieve. You can't do that if you're out there just messing around. You can't go out there on the floor with a crew and start improvising with technicians unless you're independently wealthy and you're financing the project yourself. You certainly can decide that this angle is better than that angle, or that you should be twenty feet closer instead of further away, or that you should be on a long lens rather than a wide lens; but, at the time, you can't change everything and say, "We should be pointing that way instead of this way." Or everybody shows up at seven in the morning to shoot the scene and you say, "This should be a night scene, what the hell are we doing here. I'm going back to bed, see you tonight at eight." That kind of improvisation is just masturbatory. But within the give and take of selecting the frame, choosing just the right kind of light, selecting what should be excluded or emphasized in the frame, what details should be pointed up from in the background, all of that has a great element of improvisation to it; and it's very collaborative in the sense that others you are working with are contributing to it. Very often the script girl or the cameraman or whoever will say, "What would happen if you did this?" There are a lot of things in films that I have directed that were provided by people I worked with. With respect to my cameraman and soundman, I encourage them to go off and be very interpretive while always remembering that the important thing is to tell the story. Everybody has to realize that what we're all there for is not to jerk off, you know, or to experiment to find a new form, but to tell the story as simply as possible. And that, strangely, is one of the toughest things there is to do—to make oneself tell the story simply. Because, when you first start out and learn that you can handle the camera, you know what the lenses can do, you know what different microphones are capable of, you know what you can do with different lights, light used either as a sidelight or a backlight, or a full front light or whatever; at the beginning when you're learning these technical things, the tendency is to demonstrate your knowledge of them and to put them up front in a film. That's something I still haven't mastered; it's a very strenuous task to keep technique totally absent from the storytelling.

Barrett: How long has it taken you to master the techniques of the medium itself?

Friedkin: It wasn't until I was making *Boys in the Band* that I really knew what I was doing with the film. I had no real idea about technique or how to really use the medium until something happened that sparked my thinking: I was in New York making *Boys [in the Band]* and I wandered into an exhibit of cubist painters at the Museum of Modern Art. I was really struck by the quality of those early paintings. I had not previously read anything about the cubists . . . I later did. I was struck by how those painters, working in a two-dimensional medium, were able to suggest an object in motion and an object seen from all sides at once. I was really struck by this notion of attempting to break free from what was essentially a restriction of the art form. And it occurred to me that this was a challenge offered by the motion picture medium, too; where, again, you could only show height and width. And the secret of using the camera is to create the illusion of depth where there really is no depth. For example, most scenes shot by most beginning directors are shot pretty flat. The audience observes the scene pretty much as if it were watching actors on the stage, in profile, talking to each other, with very little suggestion of depth. It occurred to me that I was not really using the medium in my films to that point. *The French Connection* was the very first film in which I was able to try out my ideas. Take something as simple as showing a car in motion. The standard method might be to cut from one angle to another to show the progress of the car. But it occurred to me that it might be extraordinarily more interesting to show person and object head-on. coming toward the camera, and let the camera pan them as they move laterally past so that we have a side view, and then let the camera hold and continue to show the object as it continues in the distance and we see it from the rear. Just that simple use of montage within the frame, itself, which is possible only in the film medium, is something that was never taught and never learned except by a kind of osmosis while observing the cubist paintings. I tried out such notions in *The French Connection* and I feel that it's the first film I made where I really used the medium. And that was quite recent, in 1971. I've only made one film since, so my ideas are very much formulative. Every picture I've made has been both an adventure and an education. I've not only learned more about the use of the medium, but I've learned about subjects I've come in contact with that I wouldn't have known about if I weren't a filmmaker.

Barrett: Getting back to the idea of creative collaboration, how much freedom do you give to your editor?

Friedkin: None, really. I go into the room and edit the film. I mark up the stuff on my own and then the editor goes in and does that actual physical work. My recent editor was allowed to edit a trailer on his own, but that's the farthest I've gone. To me editing is more exciting, more interesting, more discovery prone, more important than any other facet of filmmaking. You can, literally, blow a good film in the cutting room, or make a film better than it is, or ruin stuff that was well-shot to begin with—you can just ruin it. I find that the attitude in the cutting room that works best for me is to be merciless. I've reached the point now where I don't have to psyche myself to do it; I just view the stuff as total shit; I divorce myself from the guy who directed it. I become another person, in effect. You literally have to split yourself in two at that point. And you have to forget about all of the troubles that you had getting that shot, all the difficulties you had in achieving that performance on take twenty-eight, or whatever it was, and say, "This doesn't work. This doesn't make it! And not only doesn't it make it, but it's holding up the flow of the stuff that does, and it has to go. . . . So, all of the beautiful sunsets go, and everything else. But more than that, you know, not just great shots, but whole sequences that you thought were crucial if not vital to the film. When the editing process begins and takes on a life of its own, the footage becomes another film. And all of the planning and preparation, everything that you did leading up to that, is so much grist for the mill. Editing is the most exciting part of filmmaking for me. I would be an editor full-time if I could make as much money at it, if I could live the same lifestyle, as I do by directing.

Barrett: Since we're on the subject of cutting, did you have final cut on *The French Connection* and *The Exorcist*?

Friedkin: Mm-hem. Which isn't to say that I didn't solicit opinion and advice from a variety of people, I did, and I had a lot of very helpful advice. But I've never had a film, except for *The Night They Raided Minsky's*, that ever went out in any way except the way I cut it. The first film I made was *Good Times* with Sonny and Cher. I'm not advertising it; it had been quietly put to rest some seven years ago, and now television has brought it back from the dead. But right from the very first film, when I didn't have it contractually at all, as imperfect, shall we say . . . my choice of adjectives . . . as imperfect as *Good Times* is, it's all my cut. I did it.

Barrett: Well let me ask you this: Why do you have final cut and so many directors do not?

Friedkin: First of all, because I know what I'm doing in the cutting room, and many other directors don't know and don't care. It's a place they don't want to go;

it has great mysteries. And some people have built careers on directing films and never chancing to investigate the mysteries of editing. And I love editing, as I said. Secondly, if you make a film that goes out and works in its initial engagements, nobody comes around and tries to recut it. It's when you make a film like *Isadora*, the biography of Isadora Duncan . . .

Barrett: The Reisz film?

Friedkin: Karel Reisz directed it, and I thought it was terrific at the time. It went out and died; so, immediately a committee at Universal took it over and recut it by the numbers. One said, "I saw eight people yawn at this part," and another said, "I saw fourteen people fall asleep at that part," and so they yank that out and they continue to recut it. Recutting, generally speaking, happens when a film goes out and bombs in its initial engagements. There are other situations, of course, where the guys running the studio are so egomaniacal that they say, "I'm going to cut this picture." But now, myself and others have it in our contracts that those guys . . . for example, when I make a film, I deliver a can of film to the studio. I have nothing to do with the studio. They don't see the rushes, they don't talk to me, advise me, buy me a cup of coffee, discuss the sports pages with me . . . nothing. We make a deal. I go out and make a movie, I hand them a can of film, they say, "Thank you very much."

Barrett: But you're unlike many directors in that you get involved in distribution.

Friedkin: I give my advice on that but I don't get in too deeply in their bailiwick, although I have turned a lot of ad campaigns around, as well as a little bit of distribution. And on the first-run engagements of *The Exorcist*, I literally checked the theaters where the film was going to play. The projection equipment, the sound equipment, everything. And then, that's it. Then I go off and do something else. I must say, however, that if *The Exorcist* had gone out and bombed, it would have been recut. There would have been nothing I could do about it.

Barrett: You're a part owner of a film company too, aren't you?

Friedkin: Yes, the Director's Company, but it's a production company; Warners does the distribution. I'm in it with Peter Bogdanovich and Francis Coppola. I have yet to make a film through the company. Coppola did *The Conversation* and Bogdanovich did *Paper Moon* and *Daisy Miller*. *Daisy Miller* has proved to be a bomb at the box office. We'll be lucky if it gets back its $1 million production cost, not to mention its $1 million advertising budget and another million spent on prints, legal fees, and the like.

Barrett: Now that's one aspect of the system that puzzles me. How can some directors make one expensive bomb after another and still continue to make films? For example, take Robert Altman and Ken Russell. I enjoyed *McCabe and Mrs. Miller*, *Images*, *The Savage Messiah*, and *The Music Lovers*, but the mass public didn't. In fact, except for *McCabe*, neither did the critics. How are such filmmakers allowed to continue to lose money?

Friedkin: The trick is to make a smash film and get someone to sign you to a long-term contract. Altman made *MASH* and Russell made *Women in Love*. That, incidentally, is the way some think Otto Preminger has spun out his career.

PART II (On Critics)

Barrett: I'd like to summarize central portions of Pauline Kael's *New Yorker* article of August 5, 1974, because so much of it seems to be about you. She writes about "slam-bang" films that appeal to illiterate audiences in underdeveloped countries, "visceral" pictures that numb an audience and prevent a mass response to true film artists who are less blatant. She claims that people get "pummeled and deafened" by *The French Connection*, and *The Exorcist* is a "debauch" that delivers in much the same way as a porn flick. Such films, she feels, debase the viewer with their "philosophical nihilism" and leave them soiled. She goes on to claim that saturation publicity and the producers' treatment of a film as a piece of goods leads the mass audience to believe that best-selling junk is better than less publicized poor-selling works of film art. She asserts that film students are being taught to worship the director who makes the buck and suggests that directors should take over the business end of their films. She says that the industry's worship of films that are "crude and insensitive" could kill film as an art form. She believes that films such as *The French Connection* and *The Exorcist* indicate a lack of belief in the good taste of the audience. She concludes by pointing to you and George Roy Hill as directors who can work within the system, and feels that "the system works for those who don't have any needs or aspirations that are in conflict with it: but for the others—and they're the ones who are making movies—the system doesn't work anymore and it's not going to." What is your response to all of this?

Friedkin: Well, number one, I read the article because I was asked to respond to it by the *Los Angeles Times*. That was why I read it. As an article, I found it thick, and muddle-headed, and almost impossible to plow through. For somebody in the field, its conclusions are both simpleminded and wrongheaded. As a practical matter, the person who wrote it has an enormous contempt for the audience. The person who wrote it condemns the audience out of hand for what they choose as opposed to what they do not choose and is contemptuous of the audience for choosing X instead of Y, for choosing a hot dog sandwich instead of a cheese soufflé or a beef

Wellington. This is, you know, fair enough: anyone can do this. If you have access to print, or any medium of communication, you can impose your taste on other people, and if they're watching, or reading, or listening, they have to pay attention. This is the case with Kael's piece. But I know a couple of things about her that are not apparent to the people who read her. First of all, she tried to do an interview with me on three occasions, and I refused to do so because I feel that the *New Yorker* is an elitist magazine and it is trying to foster an idea about the medium in which I work that is contrary to the facts about that medium. And she did a book on Orson Welles's *Citizen Kane* in which she attempted to discredit Welles's contribution to it and to say, without ever bothering to interview Orson Welles, that he didn't write the script, that somebody else did. And I did an interview in New York at the time of the book's publication, with Johnny Carson or somebody like that, wherein I brought this out. I pointed out that she only interviewed anyone with an anti-Welles point of view and so attempted to discredit him. So, there is a personal history that I have with her.

The other thing is people *never* attend a movie in such numbers as when they go to see a hit because they hate the picture. There is only one reason that a movie becomes a hit, one reason, only. It's not publicity, it's not hype, it's not advertising, because I can give you example after example of films like *Lost Horizon* that were heavily advertised, two or three times the advertising budget of *The Sting* and *The Exorcist*, that didn't even return the negative costs. The only thing that causes people to go to the movies is word of mouth. People come out and say whatever they say. They could say, "I hated the thing, but you've got to see it!" or "It's disgusting, it's the most disgusting thing I've ever seen!" And this causes you to go. But generally, I must say, take your own experience, do you generally go to something that somebody tells you is "disgusting" and "horrible"? Not me! If somebody told me that there was a ten-car crash outside, I, personally, wouldn't feel called upon to go out and see it. If somebody came in here and said, "Fifteen bodies are sprawled on the street," I wouldn't be interested. I wouldn't want to see it. So, I don't for a minute believe that people go to see *The Exorcist* because they hear it's disgusting. *The Exorcist*, which is, right now, the third all-time moneymaking film in only seven months in release, is third because people want to see it. Now, you can say, if you don't like the film, you can then say that those people who do are "stupid, cheap, low-brow, and prefer hot dogs to beef Wellington; they're idiots!" And to a large extent you'd be right! But you could never work for the audience and feel that way. Where I take exception to Pauline Kael is that I don't draw the line between chamber music and Guy Lombardo. I don't prefer Guy Lombardo's music at all. I don't listen to it, but I don't condemn it out of hand. I don't say that because I find it sterile and simplistic and crude it's wrong! And I don't accuse Guy Lombardo of being a fascist or a racist or a purveyor of shit! I honestly believe that he's doing the best he can, and he's doing it because people are into it! And if they weren't into it and loving it, he wouldn't be out doing it. At the same time, it would be a terrible wrong for Sviatoslav Richter to go out and do "A-One, A-Two-A," or for Pierre Boulez to make it part of the repertory of the New York Philharmonic.

It's difficult to explain this, but a large part of what people like Kael do is to do, to a large extent, what I attempt to do and that's move people emotionally. And very often by overstating the case. I am not saying that there is nothing valid in Kael's piece. I am saying that working in the field, as I do, I find nothing valid in it, personally. I find that her suggestion that the filmmakers named in the article should band together and form a distribution co-op is addressed to filmmakers who, with rare exceptions, have never had a successful film. Bob Altman has had one successful film out of ten, and he goes public with his works the same as I do. For example, take *California Split*, it opened at the same theater *The Exorcist* did, with the same amount of advertising, no more, no less, and the people took their choice. Now, you can say, "Well the people are idiots!" Well, that's possible, but I just don't believe that people go to see a movie because they hate it. I do not, as Miss Kael does, reject those audiences that do not respond to the same things I do. I disagree with them, but I don't reject them or condemn them. I don't feel that Kael is a very good film critic or a very good person. A good film critic, like James Agee, who was a great critic, never denounced something that he didn't like. He either chose not to write about it, or he criticized it in a way in which the criticism was always positive and optimistic. He never condemned out of hand the people who made the film. Such an attitude is humanistic. The film journalism that prevails today is antihumanistic, it's the kind of film journalism where you condemn those people you disagree with. If you don't like his films, Peckinpah is a fascist! So-and-so a racist! This kind of character assassination does far more harm than any of Sam Peckinpah's movies. His movies are dealing with fictional people in fictional circumstances. When Kael called Peckinpah a fascist, she was dealing with a real person and a real reputation. And whatever else Peckinpah may be, he is not a fascist. And he had no response to her at all. As I have said, you can't sue, you can't get equal time, you can't get equal space. As Willie Loman said in *Death of a Salesman*, "It comes with the territory." Any kind of success, to whatever degree, fosters an extraordinary amount of criticism. On the other hand, I must admit that I prefer this kind of adversary journalism to the kind of ass-kissing crap that goes on. More people get away with murder in the press, be they politicians or filmmakers, because of mindless praise. And you get more junk stuff being praised because of this cult business, which I totally discourage and don't believe in. I'd rather see something like Kael's piece than the auteur stuff. I think it's much more interesting and provocative. I wish there was more of it.

Barrett: I can understand that the problem of negative criticism would get to be a drag for the director, but most critics are locked into deadlines and in too many cases are forced to review films they don't like. Andrew Sarris, the auteurist, has talked to this. He sometimes has a choice, either to be negative or not write and not get paid.

Friedkin: Well, I don't respect Sarris. I've gotten good reviews from him, but he writes for such a *small* intellectual elite and he has misinterpreted everything I've ever done. *Totally* destroyed it. Sarris, you know, bends everything through the prism of his own demi-consciousness, and whoever reads him is stuck with him. I really don't want to talk about it because I don't want to encourage it.

There are two schools of film criticism. One is represented by the kind of mindless person who sits and types out a summary of the film, usually incorrect, as a factual resume of what's in the story. It's like reducing *Hamlet* to its plot; it becomes soap opera. Take a guy like Archer Winston writing for the *New York Post*. His whole review will be a summary of the plot. Why bother to see the movie? The other kind, like Kael or Sarris, take a film that somebody has written, photographed, directed, whatever, and they use it as a springboard for their own ideas on the film industry, the state of the world, the crisis in the sugarcane industry. And their ideas have nothing to do with the film. The art of film criticism has declined to minus ten since James Agee's death. One only has to read the collected reviews of Agee to see what I mean. Occasionally, someone comes in from outside, like Norman Mailer has, and writes a really fantastic piece of film criticism. But I haven't really read film reviews in three or four years, so I don't know what's going on at present.

Barrett: A few new critics are coming into their own. Molly Haskell, for example.

Friedkin: Molly Haskell is, to me, no better and no worse than any of the rest of them. The same with Judith Crist, whom I know very well: she's a close personal friend, but we never talk about films, ever. Because . . . I frankly think she doesn't know a god-damned thing about films! There are no reviewers whom I respect today. Based on what the public relations people tell me, every film that I made got between 70 and 80 percent good reviews. But I don't read them. I gave up reading reviews when I realized that there was nothing to learn from them. The reviewers were not telling me anything that I could use to improve my work or my ability to communicate with audiences. And that's all I really care about.

Barrett: Have you ever been interviewed by Rex Reed?

Friedkin: Several times.

Barrett: I might have known, but I've never read his books.

Friedkin: Neither have I, so I don't know if they're there or not.

Barrett: He seems like a nice enough guy, but I don't think he knows much about reviewing. Would you agree?

Friedkin: Rex Reed has his peculiarities, but he's okay. I particularly like someone like Charles Champlin, who is in the Agee tradition, someone who concentrates on the films he likes and writes about them. But, as I said, I question the value of the whole business. I know that some critics like me and they'll always write a good review and some don't like me and they'll write a bad review no matter what I do. Hostile journalists are depressing. I particularly remember this one person who came in with an ax to grind and was abrasive from the very beginning. I insisted that she get a tape recorder, record the interview, and give me the tape for my information. She did so reluctantly. Later, she called up and quickly read the interview to me over the phone. It was like another world; she distorted what I had said into something that meshed with her imaginative view of me that had led to her initial hostility. I called up her publisher and played the interview for him and he killed the piece.

Barrett: That's a real waste; being forced to spend your time killing distortions.

Friedkin: I don't usually worry about interviews: they'll distort you if they want to and you can't do much about it; but this was so obvious that I had to do something about it.

Barrett: What did you think about the decision to give the Academy Award for best picture of 1973 to *The Sting* rather than to *The Exorcist*?

Friedkin: Naturally, I was disappointed for a few days. But I do believe in the Academy Awards as a standard, as the best prevailing standard that the motion picture industry has to honor those films that it believes are meritorious. Now, they don't always make the right decision, but you'll generally find over the years . . . generally, that those films that have won the Academy Award are those films that have appealed to most of the audience[s] and most of the critics.

Tense Situation: William Friedkin in an Interview with Ralph Appelbaum

Ralph Appelbaum / 1979

From *Films and Filming,* March 1979. Reprinted by permission of Ralph Appelbaum.

Right now, the director of *The French Connection, The Exorcist,* and last year's *Sorcerer,* is putting the finishing touches on what may be his most claustrophobic film: *Brink's,* the true saga of seven men who joined forces—at least temporarily—to rob the Brinks Company in Boston of $2.7 million in 1950. It took the police and FBI six years and $29 million to finally bring the case to its conclusion, in what Friedkin describes as the classic case of "disorganized" crime. Starring in the picture are Peter Falk, the leader of the gang of misfits, and Warren Oates, Peter Boyle, and Paul Sorvino.

Last year, he directed the powerful but critically neglected *Sorcerer,* which was loosely based on Clouzot's *Wages of Fear.* Roy Scheider, Bruno Cremer, and Francisco Rabal starred in the film about four desperate men who have to transport two truckloads of highly volatile nitroglycerin over treacherous terrain.

The following interview took place in Friedkin's spacious suite of offices in the Producers' Building at Universal Studios. In his office, now quiet due to the completion of [*The*] *Brink's Job,* Friedkin, looking much younger than his actual thirty-nine years (possibly due to his exuberance and boyish charm), was eager to talk about *Brink's,* big-budgets, studios, critics, and *Sorcerer.*

Ralph Appelbaum: Could you go into the genesis of *Brink's,* your latest film?
William Friedkin: A number of years ago, Paramount asked me if I would make the film. I was definitely interested because the Brinks robbery was an extraordinary event of my youth. It was the kind of thing that in a strange way inspired young guys of my generation. I was about eleven years old when it happened. And it was fascinating that the robbery was pulled off in a matter of minutes, nobody got hurt, nobody was killed, and it took the FBI six years to break the case, which

they did at extraordinary expense and without ever really recovering the money. So, it was the closest thing in my time to the perfect crime. I was fascinated by the kind of people who would put the time and effort into something like stealing a large sum of money.

So, when Paramount came to me, I was interested but unavailable, and had to pass. It turns out that Paramount was involved with Dino De Laurentiis who has commissioned Noel Behn to write a book based on the facts of the case. He has access to the robbers who were still alive, and they gave him their story. A couple of years later De Laurentiis took it to United Artists and they asked me if I could do it, but I was still unavailable. I later learned that John Frankenheimer has started the picture, and a couple of friends of mine were going to work on it. As a matter of fact, Lou DiGiaimo, the fellow who has been working with me as a casting director for four or five pictures, was going to cast it. And they were supposed to start shooting about a week from the time I got a call in the South of France, where I was with my wife.

It was from Mr. De Laurentiis, asking if I would be interested in doing *Brink's* and I said: "Jesus, I thought you were going to start that picture next Monday." And he said, "No, there's been a problem, would you read the material and let me know if you're still interested?" I didn't get into what the problem was at the time, but I read the scripts that they had—they had a number of scripts—and I read Noel Behn's book which I hadn't read up to that point. The scripts I thought were just bad, totally unproduceable in my opinion. It turns out that's what the problem was for De Laurentiis; he had put a lot of time and money into several scripts that he did not want to produce.

I flew back to New York to tell him there was no way I could take those scripts and make them work; that if he wanted me to do the film he would have to start over from scratch, with a writer of my choice. He agreed and I set to work with Wally Green. We moved to Boston and we interviewed all the people we could who were involved with the case, including the four robbers who still survived. We visited various locations that figured into the story and out of that we developed our own approach, which is completely different from what Frankenheimer was going to make.

RA: How did your approach differ from the other scripts?
WF: We approached it as a kind of farce, and they were making a film that was, in my opinion, a routine caper, with no discernible attitude towards the robbers. This was not a reflection on Frankenheimer, who I feel is really a fine filmmaker. I read the final script and I don't know how much he has to do with it or if he was even happy with it himself; I doubt it. But the approach in the early scripts was just kind of banal caper film; ours is a story not of organized crime and a brilliant caper, but

of disorganized crime and its farcical forces of the establishment, which was not only the Brinks company but the FBI as well. Their reputation as crime-busters was enhanced by the facts that they broke the Brinks case but that was a sham; the robbers were known to most of the police officers and wise-guys in Boston the day after it happened—but it took the FBI six years to break the case and they spent $29 million on it, because J. Edgar Hoover was convinced that it was a conspiracy between the Communist Party and organized crime. So, they were off in the wrong direction. It's a classic story of misdirection and of things not being as they seem.

RA: How accurate is what you put on the film to the events that really happened?
WF: No film of two hours' duration can be accurate. It's always an impression. *The French Connection* is an impression of what happened, because you can't be accurate in two hours, dealing with a story whose principal lines stretched out across twelve years and involved many hundreds of people. There's no way to deal dramatically with the thousands of incidents that go into a story like that. Any two-hour film or three- or four-hour film is an impression; this is my impression of the events surrounding the Brinks robbery.

RA: In terms of shooting, did you go to the actual locations?
WF: For the most part, I shot the entire film in Boston. That's another thing that differed from the original approach. The original idea was to build sets in Hollywood. I felt that there was a particular aura about doing it in Boston. I felt that its story has a historical significance. It's not one of the brighter moments in American history, but it is memorable, I think because of the time and place in which it happened. I couldn't film on all of the exact locations because in cases they had been torn down or the neighborhood drastically changed. But, for the most part it was filmed in the actual locations. We shot in the Brinks building, where the robbery took place. That building is about to be torn down or converted into something else, but we were able to refurbish it exactly as it was at the time of the robbery, interior and exterior.

RA: Was it difficult to recreate the period of the fifties?
WF: No. It exists there. In that particular neighborhood, which is one of the reasons I felt we could do it there, the character of the place hasn't changed. It's an Italian neighborhood. It's a very close, inbred place, and it's beautiful. It's an incredible cityscape that hasn't changed since the time it was built. Prince Street it's called. Prince Street in the North End.

RA: Most of your films have been shot on location rather than in studios. Is that a conscious decision on your part?

WF: Yeah, I don't like filming in studios. I don't like the whole atmosphere of a studio, and I don't like the atmosphere that we have to create on a real location. The minute the lights go up and all that stuff, you've got to fight hard to maintain whatever fantasy of reality you're trying to recreate.

RA: But isn't that easier to do on location?
WF: It depends. Anything's easier to do on a sound stage. Anything. You have control over the elements, you're not going to hear unwanted traffic noises; you're not going to have power failures which you constantly get on location. Now in a studio, obviously you don't get the same flavor. I couldn't have filmed *The French Connection* on a sound stage and have the same film. I did most of *The Exorcist* on a stage, but in New York, not in Los Angeles. But that picture couldn't have been done in a real house, because there was so much time spent in the house that, I mean, the seasons would have changed out the window when they weren't supposed to. That picture had to be done on set. *Brink's* didn't have to be done on location, but I thought it would be richer and more significant if we could capture the look and sounds of Boston.

RA: After the actual robbery, the criminals became celebrities, local and national heroes . . .
WF: Yes. What these guys did almost immediately entered the realm of American mythology.

RA: Why do you think that was?
WF: The period in which it happened. It happened in 1950 and America was just coming out of a kind of lull. The end of the World War II was a dull time in America. The elation of victory has expired; the country was about to enter a period of hypocrisy and oppression, vis-à-vis the McCarthy era. And that period, 1950, was kind of a breather; it was a lull in American history. It was a time in which very little was happening. We weren't at war anywhere; the economy was good, nobody was uptight, adults weren't intimidated by the youth culture; rock and roll hadn't happened yet.

It was a very dull, passive time and this robbery burst on the consciousness of America like a bombshell. Then too, that period was the beginning of the modern rise to prominence of the media. The Brinks job was a natural-born media event. It got nationwide headlines; the headlines were as large as the declaration of war, or the death of a president. It got full newsreel and network radio coverage. And that was because of the time in which it took place. If that happened today it would [just] be another heist. The fact that it was executed so smoothly, that it seemed to be the work of master criminals, captured the imagination of the country.

RA: Throughout the history of films, audiences have been able to root for the criminal if he's shown in a good light. Your last film *Sorcerer* was not a success, and I was wondering if one of the reasons for that could have been the fact that your lead characters were killers?

WF: Possibly. I'm sure the post-mortems as to why it didn't work will go on for years. I don't know why. I mean, the ultimate reason why it didn't make it is because the audience rejected it. People don't send me letters and tell me why they don't like a film of mine, as a rule. But I must say that I had more mail favorable to that film than any other film I've ever done. And yet it was a failure. And I don't have the answer other than that people couldn't get behind it.

I don't think it has anything to do with the fact that it was based on *Wages of Fear*, because most people in this country don't know what that is. I think the time in which it came out was bad for a film that was basically looking on the downside, and a film that ended with an act of betrayal. It came out in a period when *Star Wars* was sweeping the country and the mood of the movie-going public had swung quite away from what I was trying to do with *Sorcerer*. Timing has a lot to do with the acceptance of a film. I don't know whether these pictures of mine or anyone else's that make it are really good or bad. I happen to like *Sorcerer*; it's my favorite of all the films I've made.

RA: Visually, it was breathtaking. I think people sometimes forget, or don't realize, how hard it is to achieve a certain look.

WF: I tried to make a film that was primarily using visual language, filmic language, and not dialogue to advance the story. And I think this bothered people in a way, in that they got very little help with the characters; the characters didn't spend a lot of time talking about themselves; they just did things. Generally, the films that make it have a lot of dialogue.

RA: Another constant complaint one heard about the film was the amount of money it cost. What's your feeling about that?

WF: Yes, that's true. When the cost of a picture becomes a determining factor as to whether or not it has any merit, the picture is going to lose out. On the other hand, people in the media have a right to ask: "Why is it that studio or filmmaker had to spend so much money to make that film?" It's a quandary, because there was no money squandered on *Sorcerer*; it was a difficult film to make, everybody knew it was going to be difficult. Its physical problems were unpredictable: the nature of the weather. There were two droughts in two countries where I was filming that dried up the riverbeds that I needed to shoot the bridge sequence. We had a hurricane that washed away one of the sets; and the living conditions were terrible. Some of the areas we were in had no living facilities, so we had to build camps. So, yes it may have been a folly to make an investment like that, but the money was spent trying to get the picture right.

There seems to be a school of criticism in this country that is oriented towards the *Wall Street Journal* approach. I must say that I admire a film that is made for very little money and works; but that's not my criticism for wanting to see it or not. And yet we have a media today that is obsessed with such things, not because they really are watchdogs for the public, but because it's an easy approach for a journalist to take. Generally, when I do an interview with a journalist who knows nothing about the film you're talking about, or films in particular, he'll say: "Well, how much did it cost?" If you go to Cleveland or some towns around this country and do an interview with reporters or guys on radio or television, generally, "Who are the stars, and how much did it cost?" [are] the first two questions, no matter what the picture is; it might be a picture that was made for a few thousand dollars and stars nobody, but the question is generally, "What's the story about?" Because the interviewer doesn't have to do any homework. You're going to have tell him the story, who's in it, how much it cost. That's fifteen minutes right there for the average guy to talk about his movie. It's very seldom that a journalist understands or cares enough about the film to get beyond that.

I remember seeing reviews on television where somebody would say *"Star Wars* is a great film and it only cost $10 million," as if that matters. It cost what it should have cost. There are a lot of mistakes made by filmmakers and studios in terms of how much to invest in a film, but if it works, if the film is good and if its aims are realized, generally the public will respond; and they don't care how much it costs. The studios are no happier about their small pictures that don't work than they are about their big ones that don't work. I'm sure Universal is extremely unhappy that *Sgt. Pepper* is not doing business. But I would think that everything they spent on it was to try and make it better. When the result appears and it's overwhelmingly rejected, then some people say, "Well, they did the wrong thing." But that's hindsight.

RA: But isn't it true that their break-even point would be much lower if it cost less?
WF: There's usually no middle ground today. It's success or failure. There's generally no break-even. These studios aren't in business to invest a million dollars in a film and make two hundred thousand profit on it. For every *Rocky* that comes along and costs a million dollars and makes forty million profit, you've got twenty others that cost a lot and make a lot, or cost a lot and make nothing.

RA: It seems to me that studios are willing to pour a lot of money into what they feel will be potential blockbusters. The small film seems to have disappeared.
WF: Oh, I think there are a lot of so-called small movies. The idea of a small

movie is no longer . . . I mean, a million dollars today is a small movie, because of inflation, because of continuous raises in the pay scales for everybody working in the industry. So a small movie is a million dollars, and there are very few pictures that can be made for that. But there are a number of pictures in the range of $2.5–$3 million, which is considered a small investment today. *Midnight Express* comes to mind, *Days of Heaven*. These are films that were made on relatively low budgets, and I think they're going to be successful enough to warrant a continued investment in more personal films that don't quite cost so much. I think there are quite a few of those in the planning stages, more than in recent history.

RA: Prior to doing *Sorcerer* you directed two of the most successful films in the history of movies: *The Exorcist* and *The French Connection*. Do you think that no matter what film you did, it couldn't live up to what the people would expect, because of those two successes?
WF: I don't think so. No. I think that every film comes and goes on its own terms. I'm not talking about the handful of people in the media who are concerned about such things; I'm talking about the public. The public generally doesn't know who the hell made the film.

RA: I'm sure that in those two cases they knew who the filmmaker was.
WF: But they don't really care: they go to see a movie. The overwhelming thing that brings people into the theaters is word of mouth. Somebody sees a picture they like, they go out and tell other people to see it. And if they don't like a film they say, "Eh, you don't have to see this," or don't go back themselves to see it again. No, I don't feel that my reputation had anything to do with the success or failure of *Sorcerer*. I know it got generally unfavorable press, which surprised me—and bothered me. I suppose if it had got better press it might have done more business. The attacks on it, in many cases, were vitriolic, along the lines of "it was a sin to make," that kind of thing.

RA: But it was a remake?
WF: There was a lot of that.

RA: But your film deviates quite radically from the original.
WF: Yes, it does. The only thing I wanted from the original *Wages of Fear* was the premise. Four men sitting on a load of dynamite, which I thought was a marvelous premise that could be updated, and I thought people would want to see such a film. To a large extent they didn't, and I was wrong; that's the bottom line. But I love the film, and I don't think of it as a remake at all, and I don't really compare it to Clouzot's film, which I also happen to love. But I think it's valid for someone

to make a premise (after all, there are only so many premises available), and to credit it and say, "Yes, I'm doing a film based on *Wages of Fear*, but I would like to re-examine this premise and this theme in terms of a different set of characters and a different locale." But people didn't buy it.

RA: It seems to me, though, and other people I've spoken with feel the same way, that once you hit a certain plateau and get too big, too successful, people want to cut you down.
WF: That may be. I'm not really conscious of that. Generally, I just go around and make my films. I don't hang around with the people who are running this town. I know them, I have sort of a nodding acquaintance with them, and I imagine that there are some who resent success, but I don't really encounter that, at least not directly. There are a lot of people running studios that I don't respect. Not at every studio, but the kind of people who would tend to cut you down . . . are you talking about studio heads, media people?

RA: I would say for the most part media people.
WF: Yes. But generally my films have failed or succeeded without too much help from the media. *The French Connection* got generally good reviews, but *The Exorcist* got generally bad reviews, and was enormously successful with the public. Other films I've made got very good reviews but didn't do well. *Sorcerer* got uniformly bad reviews and very little box-office. So, it's clear that the media didn't love *Sorcerer*, but I don't think that if they loved it, it would have made a difference. There were some critics who are influential who really went out on a limb for it, but overwhelmingly the reviews were bad. And I guess bad reviews can to some extent hurt a picture.

RA: When you start off on a movie, is it the story that attracts you first?
WF: Yeah. Absolutely. But the story is the sum of its parts, which is the theme, the characters, and incidents. That's what the story is. The story doesn't exist in limbo.

RA: I would like to go back to Brinks for a moment. I recall reading that you had experts come in and show Peter Falk how to crack a safe.
WF: Pick locks. A guy was on parole for armed robbery. He's an expert burglar and safecracker.

RA: What about the four surviving Brinks robbers?
WF: They were there, too. I think that having them around and talking about their work and lives was valuable to the whole cast. It certainly was to me. It helped to solidify an impression.

RA: What character does Peter Falk play?

WF: He plays a guy called Tony Pino, who was given credit for dreaming the whole thing up. He was a congenial thief, the kind of guy who's known as a "booster." He would "boost" (steal) golf balls, underwear, a pair of socks, a tie, anything. He would not differentiate between stealing a golf ball and stealing a million dollars. He was in on some of the biggest and smallest thefts in the history of the United States, and he was a very funny guy. He ran a funky little diner in the lower-class section of Boston.

RA: Do you use the actual names of the robbers?

WF: Yes.

RA: Were there any legal problems with that?

WF: No; most of the guys not only signed releases with De Laurentiis, but got together, you know, to write the book with Noel Behn, upon which the film is based.

RA: Usually that's done the other way around: the book is commissioned after the movie.

WF: I don't know many cases of a nonfiction book being commissioned with the intent of making a film of it. There had been a lot of bullshit surrounding the Brinks robbery for many years, and these guys had the story and they were reluctant to talk about it for the reason that most thieves don't like to talk about what happened or who did what. But this fella, Ralph Serpe, who was the line producer for De Laurentiis, has some connections in the East Coast underworld that led him to the guys that did the Brinks job, and was really the guy who unearthed these people and got them to talk.

RA: Was there any interference from De Laurentiis in terms of your approach to the material?

WF: No, not at all. I really enjoyed working with him. As a matter of fact, I learned a great deal from him. I think he has the sane approach to filmmaking. Nothing but encouragement, as far as I was concerned. But always with a producer's eye toward practical matters. He's the best producer I've worked with, he has an uncanny sense of story, what works on the screen. I really respect him. I'm not saying he's an expert. Nobody is an expert, or really has the ultimate answers. But I found his opinions enormously valid and helpful.

RA: There were some reports—I don't know whether they were overblown or not—about the negative being robbed . . .

WF: They never stole the negative. Three guys came into the cutting room on the Friday of the last week of shooting. They knocked on the door and used the name of Fred Sidewater, who's one of De Laurentiis's associates who was in Boston. So they had information about our operation. They knew Sidewater's name, which was not a publicized name. I mean, my name was in the papers all over Boston, Peter Falk's name, Serpe's name. But Sidewater's name was never used. So somebody who knew who he was knocked on the cutting room door—using his name to get in—and were let in by the assistant editors, who were then pistol-whipped, bound, and gagged, and these guys took fifteen reels of work-print out of the cutting room. Now it's clear that they had a very good idea, which is: if you steal something from a movie company, you've got something to ransom. But they weren't aware that there was such a thing as a negative, and that in a cutting room you'll never see negative around; the negative's always held back at the lab.

It set us back a little in that we had to reprint these reels, but it was nothing of irreplaceable value to us. It's like if somebody steals your shirt, you have to walk around without a shirt until you buy another one. But it doesn't mean you'll never again have a shirt. And that's what they didn't realize.

Whoever pulled it off was unaware of the difference between a work-print and a negative. They asked for $600,000 and they later came down to $500,000, but by then the FBI was all over our offices and had tapped our phones. And the FBI has them on tape asking for a half-a-million dollars in ransom.

RA: That's incredible.

WF: The fortunate thing was they didn't hurt somebody, because they were obviously crazy brigands.

RA: Could you talk about the casting of Falk and the others?

WF: Very frankly, I couldn't think of anybody else to play the part of Tony Pino. There aren't too many actors around who can play a kind of lower-class, urban hustler as well as Peter Falk, who hasn't been doing too much of that recently. Peter Falk's always been a marvelous and an accomplished actor. He's best known for roles that I don't think represent his best work, such as his television series, which has made him successful and famous. But what interests me is some of the work he did before he got a television series. And it's not easy to cast these parts in *Brink's* because you're dealing with sort of old-world guys that don't exist anymore. I mean today's generation actors are all very contemporary. It would have been difficult to do that picture with say, someone like Travolta or Nolte or Redford, or other really fine actors who I don't think have Peter Falk's sense of comedy and timing. And I'm really pleased with his performance in the picture. The same is true of the entire cast. The people I went after (and in a couple of cases they're total unknowns; in one case a guy who's not even an actor, but he's a character I've known for years) . . . I can't imagine anyone else doing it as well.

RA: Warren Oates is the perfect choice for a criminal.
WF: He's terrific. I must say that Warren Oates gives the best performance in a film that I've ever stood behind a camera and watched. He plays Specs O'Keefe, the guy who ultimately gave testimony to the FBI that broke the case.

RA: And that was eleven days or so before the statute of limitations would have run out?
WF: It was four days.

RA: At what point do you start the story?
WF: It starts with a few brief sequences about twelve years before the robbery, works its way up through 1950, and ends in '56. It's a two-hour film. I haven't made a film that's longer than two hours. I think that's enough time to be sitting there, really. I'm still editing. I'd like to take out maybe another ten minutes if I can. Right now it's an hour and fifty-eight minutes exactly.

RA: Do you tend to shoot more scenes than you actually use?
WF: Yes. I tend to shoot a lot of scenes that eventually wind up to be scaffolding. I mean, I didn't realize it at the time; I thought they were going into the picture. If I knew as much in the production stage as I do later in the editing stage, I guess I could work a lot more economically.

RA: When you're working, are all your shots planned out in advance?
WF: Generally, I have all the shots planned and discussed with everyone on the crew at least several weeks before I get to them. But then I'm flexible enough to change if a better idea comes up on the set. But you can't really go to the set and improvise; you have to know how it's all going to connect.

RA: How close is what's on the screen to what you actually envisioned?
WF: Not very close as a rule. I've never made a film that lived up to my expectations, because you're working with so many different and intangible elements. You're working with a writer, cameraman, art directors; the weather, your own shortcomings as a filmmaker. I imagine that a painter often finds a gap between what he's trying to achieve and what he's actually achieving; but at least he only has himself to deal with in that case. In the case of making a film you've got to go out and not only explain what you have in mind to a great many other people, but

you've got to mold them into an organization that is functioning to bring about what you have in mind, and that's very difficult. And it means being as specific and exact as you can in communicating with other people, and ultimately communicating through them with an audience. And very often you just don't know what you want. If I'm sitting there with a blank piece of paper or a blank canvas, I can try to find what I'm after; but if you're out there with several hundred people on set you've got to do something, and your first instincts about a scene may not be your best.

RA: You once said that you're actually shooting three different movies: the one you conceive, the one you edit, and the one you actually end up with.
WF: I don't know if I said that, but it's pretty accurate. Yeah. What I would really mean to say by something like that is that the film changes through all of its phases in the cutting room. The film takes on a life of its own and begins to dictate to you. With this *Brink's* film I've switched sequences completely around and certain unimportant ones. Or an aspect that I overlooked becomes extremely important. It takes on another personality. It's like a child maturing from conception to youth into adulthood.

RA: Could you please give an example of a scene that was changed or altered in *Brink's*?
WF: There are so many. Well, a sequence that was intended to be used in about the middle of the film, carrying very little weight, is now the ending of the film. It's not the absolute ending of the film. It carries all the weight. And becomes the statement of the film itself: and it's just about thirty seconds of the film that was used in the aftermath of the robbery.

RA: Was there a certain visual look you wanted for the film?
WF: I studied photographs of Boston from the late thirties to the early fifties with Dean Tavoularis, who's the production designer, a brilliant guy, and his crew. We set out to do an impression of that period in Boston. A lot of which still exists. What we tried to do for the most part is simplify the look, not do a complex or overly detailed group of settings. The look probably owes a lot to the paintings of John Sloan and Edward Hopper, who painted bleak cityscapes in the thirties. It's just isolated little touches that gave you the scene. A lot of that, of course, is dictated by what in fact the look of Boston was then—and still is.

RA: Was there ever any thought to doing it in black and white?
WF: No. But I've tried to keep the color very monochromatic. The color has a black and white feeling. Strong primary things that I thought were vital to it are tones and not too many of them.

RA: In retrospect, are you happy with the way *The Exorcist* turned out?

WF: I'm very happy with *The Exorcist*. I love it; I think it's a terrific film. It's a little slow in spots, but it tells a story economically. I think it accomplished what it sets out to do. I love the characters. And it's one of the best stories I've come across. I think it's as good as anything Edgar Allan Poe ever wrote, or any of the masters of the classic horror story. It was a terrific challenge to try and film it. I set out to do it without really knowing in detail how I was going to accomplish it, and I'm very pleased with the end result. I don't like *The Birthday Party* as a piece of filmmaking at all. I think it's inept. I don't think I was completely familiar enough with its nuances and tones, although it's a very good script. But [*The*] *Exorcist* satisfies me on almost every important level. I've had occasion to look at it recently—a friend has it on video-tape cassette, and I hadn't seen it in years—and I'm very pleased with it.

RA: How close was that to what you visualized?

WF: Very close. I mean there are sequences that I think can be better done. I think perhaps a more skillful director could have even done it better, certainly, but I'm happy with what I did with it.

RA: Do you feel that evil was victorious over good in the film?

WF: Not at all. In my opinion it's a film that is pervaded by the presence of God. To me, it poses large forces in mortal conflict with one another. It's a brilliant concept, and though its nuances are not easily understood the broad strokes come across clearly, although I am surprised that a lot of people who wrote about it thought it represented the triumph of evil. It occurs to me that what you bring into a film is what you take away from it. If you come in uptight about a number of things, you're going to leave *The Exorcist* pretty uptight. But I know of instances where it's sent people back to the church; James Cagney told me that his barber for many years saw it and quit his job and entered the church. And I've heard of many such instances.

RA: It's interesting to note that the sequels to both *The Exorcist* and *The French Connection* were enormous box-office disasters.

WF: Well, I think they were misconceived, and I don't think a sequel was possible to either film, other than to try and ring a few extra bucks out of them. I turned them both down. I must say that I haven't seen *The Exorcist II* in its entirety. I saw one sequence which I found appalling. It was so pretentious and yet so dim-witted. It's really an offensive picture. I think that if they had gone to Bill Blatty, who created the original, and asked him to take these themes and try to develop them further, he might have come up with something. It was undoubtedly made by people who did not understand the original material.

As for *The French Connection* sequel: I just feel there is no room in that story for a sequel. It was complete in and of itself, and so what they had was just more of the same, without the car chase. *The French Connection* was, in part, a stripping away of the character of Popeye, this bull elephant, to find a mouse inside; the sequel stripped away an elephant and found another elephant inside. It didn't tell you anything that wasn't in the first story; unlike *The Godfather*, which is really an American saga, *The French Connection* is an incident, and incidents don't lend themselves to sequelization. They were just trying to capitalize on the title, although I think that John Frankenheimer thought he was making a good film, and he got pretty good reviews with it, for the most part. I didn't like it, but I happen to like Frankenheimer and his work. *The Exorcist Part II*, I couldn't even stay to see it all, because I don't respect the guy who directed it. I think he's pretentious, and that he made a pretentious film.

RA: You mentioned the importance of the car chase in *The French Connection*. Do you think that was a key ingredient that made it a success?

WF: It sure is. It was a spectacular scene that people had to see. While I was making it at the time I didn't feel that way. I thought it was pretty good, but I didn't realize it would grab people as much as it did. It's interesting for me to look at it now. I can watch it and still get a kick out of it. I can appreciate it with some perspective now; I was too close to it at the time. You see, when you make a sequence shot like that you approach it shot by shot. There's the problem of making this shot and then the problem of making that shot. One of the most difficult problems was the reaction shots of Gene Hackman. After I made all these point-of-view shots of the car careering wildly through the streets, we had to prove Hackman was in the car, and so there was a whole afternoon spent on just making shots of him looking like he was doing all this. He did part of it, as a matter of fact, but none of it was really that dangerous in the film. It was a question of camera angle, the lens, the lens position, and cutting—all accelerated by the use of sound that pointed things up.

If you run that same sequence without its soundtrack, it won't be half as effective. We sharpened it up pretty good. To me it works as an achievement of editing, and all that constitutes editing, such as sound-mixing.

RA: How long did it take you to shoot the chase?

WF: About three weeks. It was shot in the middle of winter in New York, under fairly difficult circumstances. The problems were to put the chase cars in the middle of crowded traffic. But as I say, there was no one shot that was really hazardous or difficult to make. It was all done shot by shot and I would keep shooting until it looked as good as I thought it could look on camera, and then I'd move on to another shot. And then we brought in all these shots and put them together in a sequence that was very close to what I had in mind when I conceived it.

RA: What attracted you to *The Boys in the Band*?

WF: *The Boys in the Band* was to me a terrific script a great piece of material and I felt it had a lot of comedy and a lot of tension, a good deal of suspense. I was fascinated by the characters. I think the film is less successful that the play was, because on stage the audience presence at the event, the birthday party for this guy, helped to enhance the tension. The play always worked whenever I saw it.

It was a marvelous piece of pure theater, and for me works less well as a film, although I love the performances. On film I find it fairly contrived. But I think it still has something to say to audiences, because wherever it's shown they generally get full houses.

RA: What do you think the picture says that audiences can relate to?

WF: I think they can enjoy the characters and get behind them. I never saw it as outrageous in any sense of the word; I saw it as a love story, about people locked in a tense situation for a given moment in time. That's what *The Exorcist* is, that's what *Sorcerer* is, that's what *Brink's* is. These are claustrophobic films, and I think claustrophobia is an important element in the films I've made. And irrational fear—the fear of the unknown, what might happen; and generally something terrible does happen. A group of people in a tense situation, each deeply obsessed by something—that I guess is what I've been drawn to as a filmmaker. The characters that interest me are obsessed by one thing or another, be it a religious fervor, the pursuit of a criminal, money, fame, recognition, freedom. I'm not looking for themes in my own work, but I guess there are things that come together.

RA: *The Birthday Party* would seem to fit that category too.

WF: It is about five people who are possessed by irrational fear, and take it out on each other. It works well on the stage, but I don't think I enhanced its power on film, or shed any more light on its mysteries. I was moved by *The Birthday Party* on stage. I'm less moved by the film that I made. It's the film of mine that I find the most difficult to watch today. It has a fine script by Harold Pinter, whose mysteries are now reasonably clear to audiences, whereas they seemed befuddled by what he was doing when he wrote it in 1957. Twenty years later it's rather conventional avant-garde theater. And I don't think it should have been filmed, not by me, anyway. I'm not happy with it.

RA: Would you care to comment on *The Night They Raided Minsky's*?

WF: I'm totally divorced from *The Night They Raided Minsky's*. I really didn't understand it when I made it. If I was making it today, I think it would be better, whereas I don't think I can make *The French Connection* or *The Exorcist* any better than I made them. Or *Sorcerer*, in fact. But I think I could have made *The Night They Raided Minsky's* better because I didn't understand it. I was over my head when I did it. It was a terrific opportunity to make a film, but I don't think it works, although I've run into a lot of people who love it. And it has a kind of minor cult status, but I don't like it much. I frankly made the picture because it was an opportunity to make a feature film for a large company; and like many filmmakers my early steps were not always inspired. In some case they are the most inspired. You know, in the case of *Citizen Kane* Mr. Welles never bettered that in my opinion. My early films are disposable.

RA: How did you come to direct *Good Times*, your first film?

WF: I was making these documentaries for Wolper, and Sonny Bono was looking for a young guy who he could communicate with. He had seen a couple of my documentaries and was impressed by them. So, we met, and we liked each other immediately. I thought he was a terrific songwriter and that he was saying things that were very close to young people. And so, we got together and it was a very happy experience for me. I'm pleased with that film.

RA: It's a film whose roots are in the sixties.

WF: A very small corner of the sixties. As soon as the film was released, acid rock came in and wiped out the whole message of Sonny and Cher. The popular song of that period was "Satisfaction, I can't get no satisfaction." And Sonny and Cher were singing about basic emotions that had a long time become passé. So, the film opened to an audience that was rapidly losing interest in Sonny and Cher. They had about a year-and-a-half or two years in the sun and I think that if the film had been released in that period, it would have done better, but it was my first effort at a feature film and I'm not at all disappointed in it. It was made with two people who had absolutely no acting experience, and a director who had never made a feature and whose future was highly questionable, but I can still watch it today and not be embarrassed.

The *Cruising* Controversy:
William Friedkin vs. the Gay Community

Edward Guthmann / 1980

From *Cineaste,* Summer 1980. Reprinted by permission.

Last summer's demonstrations during the production of *Cruising* in New York, and nationwide protests of its release this spring, reflect the growing political power of America's homosexual community. What impact did the protests have on Friedkin's film? The following article examines this and other issues raised by the *Cruising* controversy.

February, 1974. William Friedkin's *The Exorcist* is playing nationally when a story runs in *Rolling Stone* on Ron Nagle, the sound technician responsible for those awful sounds coming from Linda Blair's mouth.

Nagle recorded pigs screaming on their way to slaughter, trapped bees buzzing against the walls of a jar, his girlfriend's palate reacting to raw egg whites, and his dogs, forced into a fight, for *The Exorcist*. Friedkin, as Nagle tells it, loved the effect, and encouraged Nagle to amplify it. Nagle thought it should be more subtle. "It's too loud, too corny," he complained.

"Nothing," Friedkin informed him, "is too corny for me."

Fall, 1975. Friedkin, speaking to a film class at Manhattan's New School, describes his habit of researching his movies firsthand, and recalls going to the Meat Rack, an outdoor sex spot on Fire Island, as a preliminary to filming *The Boys in the Band* in 1969.

"It's a gigantic pit," he tells the crowd, "with two hundred to three hundred guys in a daisy-chain, balling each other in the ass. One guy got real close to me. He said . . ."—and here Friedkin affects a lisp and limp wrist—" . . . 'I think you're cute.' I turned around and got out of there as quick as my legs would take me."

One of the people in the audience is gay activist Arthur Bell, a *Village Voice* reporter. "No wonder your movie was so lousy!" he cries.

Spring, 1979. Friedkin announces plans to shoot *Cruising*, his second major feature with a homosexual theme, on the streets of Greenwich Village. Bell, still smarting from Friedkin's New School flap, and bristling at the thought of another Friedkin distortion of gay life, writes about the above story in a *Voice* column, and he warns against what "promises to be the most oppressive, ugly, bigoted look at homosexuality ever presented on the screen, the worst possible nightmare of the more uptight straight, and a validation of Anita Bryant's hate campaign."

The story of *Cruising*—adapted from a pulp 1970 novel by Gerald Walker, a *New York Times Sunday Magazine* editor—is that of a cop who searches throughout New York's gay S&M underground for a mass murderer who preys on homosexuals. The victims bear resemblance to the young copy (played by Al Pacino), who acts as a decoy to trap the killer.

Friedkin, Bell claims, "is not only playing with a keg of dynamite, he's throwing a match to it." Bell, both hated and adored—but always widely read—in New York's gay community, takes it one step further, and implores his readers "to give Friedkin and his production a terrible time if you spot them in your neighborhood. . . . Owners of gay establishments would do well to tell Friedkin to fuck off when he comes around to film and exploit."

Two weeks later, as many as six gay groups are mobilizing against *Cruising*. They block passage to Friedkin's waterfront production office, blow whistles to disrupt on-the-street filming, harass gay men working as extras with name-calling, intimidation, and anonymous telephone threats. Traffic is stopped on Seventh Avenue; both police and some protestors are injured.

Friedkin responds in a *New York Magazine* interview, "The very violence I am accused of provoking with *Cruising* has already been provoked on the streets." In a feeble attempt to assuage his critics, he claims, "*Cruising* is no more about gays than Woody Allen's *Manhattan* is about New Yorkers. If anything, the film will alleviate the violence against gays in the country. I feel also that *Cruising*, in its portrayal of sexuality, will turn a lot of people on."

"I feel like the Godfather of the gay movement," Bell says. "I put out a contract on Friedkin's movie and I feel confident that it can be stopped."

February 15, 1980. *Cruising* isn't stopped. It opens across the country exactly on schedule. Gay groups, especially in New York and San Francisco, picket the movie theaters where *Cruising* opens, calling the films "a blueprint for the destruction of the homosexual community." Evoking memories of four murders following the showing of *The Warriors* one year before, the group warn that the film will accelerate violence against gays, an already-growing urban problem. But pressure on United Artists, the film's distributor, to withhold it from release is unsuccessful. In San Francisco, vandalism at the tourist-oriented Ghirardelli Cinema results in *Cruising* being rebooked at a dingy Market Street cinema. Two weeks hence, Mayor Diane

Feinstein sends United Artists a $130,450.03 bill for the heavy police protection attending *Cruising*'s San Francisco debut.

May, 1980. *Cruising* has come and gone. There are no murders in its wake, no reports of gay-hating punk gangs swarming from theaters with *Cruising*-inspired venom. The picture is panned by most critics as "hopelessly garbled" and "ambitious"—an "anti-climax," Andrew Sarris claims, in the wake of so much controversy and apprehension. At the box office, it's a "ten-day wonder," according to Hollywood observer and *Village Voice* columnist Stuart Byron. The advance publicity creates an initial rush at the theaters, but once word-of-mouth says it's a dog, people stop going. "U.S. rentals," Byron says, "will in my opinion be no more than $9 or $10 million. When you consider that the advertising, print, and publicity costs were $6 million, you're talking of a return to Lorimar [the 'mini-major' film company that produced *Cruising* after all the major studios nixed it] of $3 or $4 million on a film that cost $8 or $10 million. The potential for revenues from the foreign market is slight," Byron says, "and the chance of a TV sale is nil. Around Lorimar, nobody mentions *Cruising* unless they have to."

Friedkin, apart from enjoying the free publicity that the *Cruising* controversy gave his film, made obvious concessions to those who condemned his project. A disclaimer stating that *Cruising* "is not intended as an indictment of the homosexual world" opens the film, and later, when Pacino goes undercover, his supervising officer (Paul Sorvino) tells him, "This is not the mainstream of gay life. It's heavy leather—S&M—a world unto itself."

Harold Lloyd Master Seminars with William Friedkin

American Film Institute / 1990

From AFI's Harold Lloyd Master Seminars, September 5, 1990 © 1990, courtesy of American Film Institute.

Host: Watching several of your films, and knowing that you come from a documentary background, I'd like you to describe for us just a little bit, how can you give such life and credibility to all of your images: the gestures of your actors, the locations, and everything, is that because of the documentary background simply engrained in you or is there a conscious effort in every single film, directing?
William Friedkin: That's a very good question. I think it's both. The first films that interested me as a filmmaker were documentaries, and the first work that I did in film were documentaries. I started in the mailroom of a television station in Chicago, and I sort of worked my way up to directing live television. I'd never made a film in eight years of doing live TV, but I always wanted to make a film, and there was a live television cameraman at this station in Chicago, his name was Bill Butler, and he and I had this interest in trying to make films. So, we went to the manager of the station. I had this story of a black man on death row who was going to the electric chair, and I had reason to believe that he was innocent of the crime of which he was convicted, that the police had beat a confession out of him. In those days in Chicago, if you were black and accused of a crime, you were just automatically guilty. Didn't matter, trial, there was no Miranda rights. And I knew about this story from the Protestant chaplain at the county jail in Chicago, and I wanted to make a film about this fellow's rehabilitation in prison, and his possible innocence, to save him from the electric chair.

And so, Bill Butler, who had never made any film, he's the cameraman who's since gone on, he made *Jaws* and *One Flew Over the Cuckoo's Nest* and *Grease*, he did *Child's Play*, he's done a lot of good films, interesting work. But we went down to an equipment rental house in Chicago. We went into this place and we said, "We have $6,000 to make a movie for television, and if you teach us how to use your equipment, we'll rent it from you," and that was the only lesson I've ever had in filmmaking. Butler and I, in about two hours—this fellow's name was Jack Baron, he still has a place I believe in Chicago, he showed us how to use the Arriflex camera 16mm, how to load it, how to get focus on it, and then how to achieve synchronization with the Nagra tape recorder, which had just come into wide use. We had three hours on that, and that's the only lesson I've ever had in filmmaking.

We then set out to make this documentary about a fellow on death row. Now, I didn't know what a documentary was; "What the hell is a docu—what do you do? I mean, you show up, here's a guy, he's going to the electric chair. You know, there's the story, go get it somehow." And so the first thing I learned was you gotta get a lot of cooperation from a lot of people. I had to get the warden of the county jail behind this. And one of the things that you try to do when you want people to support what you're doing is you find out what their own needs are. You know, some cynical folk among us might call it the Achilles heel of the person that you're trying to deal with, but in my case I think it's really, you try to find out, "What are the needs of this other person?" and then you try in some way to show how your work can help them with their needs. I found out that the warden of the Cook County jail was seriously opposed to capital punishment, and yet he was the guy who had to push the button on executions, and he had had to execute three inmates in the time that he was there. In fact, I witnessed an execution of this fellow's cellmate, who was the last man to die in the chair in Chicago. And I found out the warden was more than happy to get somebody to try and make a movie to try and stop this fellow from dying in the chair. So, he cooperated with me in full.

And my own ideas about capital punishment at that time weren't really formed. I mean, it was a fact of life, you know, I was a teenager, they had capital punishment. That was it, I mean it seemed to work. You know, you committed a crime, like murder or something, you went to the chair. That was it. At those days, this was like the fifties, nobody really debated the problem, it was just de facto. But now I'm listening to this warden, who has actually killed people, and he's telling me, "It's awful, it's dreadful, it shouldn't happen. There's got to be another way."

And here's this fellow, whose name was Paul Crump, who's been rehabilitated. He's not the same guy that was convicted of this crime, and therefore he shouldn't die in the chair. So, now I'm making a film more about the rehabilitation of this man, and I found out that in order to make a documentary, especially about things that happened in the past, unless you wanted to fill this film up with a lot of dry facts, you had to create things, you had to make things happen that were sort of, well Harold Clurman's phrase "lies like truth," you had to create your own reality. So I basically went out with Bill Butler, and we improvised this movie around a guy who we wanted to save from the electric chair. There was no script, no story. We had to make stuff up. And not just his everyday life, or his relationship with other inmates, or the warden, or the chaplain, or other people, or his family, people in his life, but what I decided to do was not only recreate the circumstances of his crime for which he was convicted, but I showed the techniques that the Chicago police department used to extract a confession from him. And I knew a lot of policemen in Chicago, and they told me about some of the techniques that they would employ to beat a confession out of somebody, and then not show marks on them anywhere, not show the signs of the beatings.

And so I showed all of this in this movie, and there was really no precedent for it, I had never seen anything quite like that, where I'm recreating something in this guy's life to illustrate a point, and I decided very early on, that if I was going to continue making documentaries, they were going to all be biased. I'm not interested in doing something that gives equal time to both sides. I mean, I have strong opinions, and I decided, well, my opinion is going to be what's in this film, not a bunch of other people's opinions who go against mine. Now that is very frowned upon if you're trying to make documentaries. The documentary filmmaker says, "Well, I'm just in the middle. I'm not an advocate. Maybe I'm an advocate because I've chosen the subject, but I'm just showing things as I find them." That's not true. Every time you pick up a camera, you learn. And this was my first film, so I learned on the job. Whenever you pick up a camera, and decide to put it here, or here, or over there, or over there, or over here, or wherever you put it, it is a choice that you're making, and generally, that choice follows upon another, and another until the whole thing is choices that you've made.

So you happen on a scene, and you say, "I'm just going to show it as I see it," well "as you see it" is your point of view, and then how you put it together is even more a biased, one person's opinion. So I recognized that straight out; I could see that you could use documentary technique to sort of make the viewer think that they were watching something happening right now, and also that you could sort of create your own reality using documentary technique. And I kind of applied that in *Sorcerer* and *French Connection*, which is why I thought those would be two good films for you to see, because they contain the principles of applied documentary.

Now, style was one of the factors. The style of a documentary usually was you go somewhere, and you just pick up the camera and run around with it, and you didn't know where this guy was going to go, or that guy was going to go. You couldn't control it, you couldn't stage it. You got there to shoot something, an event that was taking place or whatever, and you got to be flexible enough to get the camera and the sound where it would best capture what was going on. Now, I decide to apply that to fictional technique, and one of the ways I did it was I wouldn't tell the cameraman where the actors were going to go. Like in *Sorcerer*, or in *French Connection*, I would go over to the actors and whatever, and I'd say, "You're going to come through this door, and you're going to talk to him over there, then the two of you are going to walk that way, go this way, do that," whatever. They knew what they were going to do, and the cameraman, I would just say, "Something's going to happen over here, and just follow this guy," or "Stay with that guy," and very often, I would shoot on the second camera, and I would induce even more of a sense of not knowing what was about to happen into the shot itself, because it seemed to me that one of the great principles that you could accomplish with a camera, the sense in a flat medium, a medium that is nothing but height and width, the screen, the illusion of depth can be created, and something even more than depth, but letting the camera free from its tripod to, let's say, start on an image here and then move around and see what's back here, what's back there where the camera used to be pointing from, and go this way, and then come back and go up there.

And it seemed to me that this was a kind of cinematic cubism that was possible with the camera. You're all familiar with the cubist painters that wanted to liberate painting and give the illusion of a three-dimensional image inside the flat canvas. Well I thought, so why not try to give the illusion of more than three dimension in a flat motion picture, give the illusion that there is a life back here that the audience never sees. You know, generally when you see a movie the camera is set up here and things happen in front of the camera. Very rarely does the camera start here and go over there, and then go down here, you know, and then go up there, or somewhere else. This propensity of the camera to do that was what really fascinated me, and what I discovered through documentary where we didn't light. What's one reason why they don't do that? Because the lights are over here. "You can't shoot back here, there's a bunch of lights over there," and technicians eating donuts, and all kinds of stuff that would be disastrous to show. But I thought "Hey, they never show what's back here. I want to show what's back there," and that was my impulse to take documentary, apply it to the feature film, and induce that sense of life, and as I say, the main way to do it is to create it. Create that reality. Don't tell the cameraman what's going to happen, and he's then got to fish around for it.

The sound I didn't worry about because I knew the sound you could always put in later, and I always do, by the way, put the sound in later. The dialogue as well as the effects, everything. I regard sound as a separate entity. I finish making the film, and then start thinking about the sound, and sometimes the sound will match the imagery, and very often it will be a counterpoint to the imagery. A great use of counterpoint in film is [Stanley] Kubrick. Ever see *Dr. Strangelove*? The counterpoint of what's on the track as opposed to what's on the screen is just mind-blowing. Anyway, that's sort of a longwinded answer to, yes, I started as a documentary filmmaker, and I've always tried to apply the principles of documentary to feature filmmaking. I guess that's what I'll do as long as I'm able to make a film.

Audience Member #1: Was your documentary about the convicted murderer the one called *The Thin Blue Line*, and did Errol Morris take the name of this movie?
WF: No, I made a movie called *The Thin Blue Line*, about twenty-five years ago or so, when I was working for David L. Wolper for the ABC network. We made a film called *The Thin Blue Line* which was about law enforcement in the United States, but the film I made about the guy going to the chair was called *The People vs. Paul Crump*, and it eventually did save him from the electric chair. The Illinois Parole and Pardon Board, there were three people, they voted two to one to send him to the chair, and they gave that recommendation to the man who was then governor of Illinois, and I showed my film to the governor and he pardoned Crump from the chair.

AM #2: Several years ago, I saw you at a show, an interview, and you said the approach to film you use, it harkens back to something you learned at Wolper, where you are showing something but never telling what you are showing them.
WF: Right.

AM #2: Could you elaborate?
WF: Yeah, I learned that at Wolper. I mean, a lot of filmmaking then and now is, to me, show and tell. You get a scene where generally two people are talking, and this fellow says to that fellow, in this scene, "Well, I'll meet you at the restaurant in an hour," and the next scene is at the restaurant in an hour, you know? It's all set up, and the element of surprise is gone from the process, from the storytelling mode. For the most part, the scripts I read and a lot of what I see, in American films—it's not true so much of European film—is they telegraph where the next scene is going to come from. And this was a principle that Dave Wolper drummed into our heads, which was "no show and tell." Don't put something on there that says, "Now we're going to look at this!" and then we cut to "this," you know? Let's have something happen. The great sort of phrase was, Diaghilev the ballet master of the Russian ballet, who said to this principal dancer, [Vaslav] Nijinsky, one day when Nijinsky was staging a ballet, and Diaghilev gave him a one-word direction, which is—well, I guess it's two words in French, and in English too, that is the best direction I've ever heard and that is, he said to him, "Etonnez moi," which means "surprise me," and that is the best direction that a director can give to an actor, that a director can give to a writer, or on anyone on the crew, and to the audience. "Surprise me."

Audiences go to movies because they want to be surprised. I do. Well, I guess today they go to see the same old thing a lot. You know, I mean, I guess that's true, but even then you gotta have some—but they constantly want to be surprised, and we're not surprised. I find, most often, like if you watch television, you're way ahead. You know where the next shot's going to come. You know what they're going to say when they cut to the guy. You know what she's going to say to him; you know where it's going. Why are you watching it? You know, what the hell are you—you know what's going to happen! You know this guy's never going to die. So, in a few films that I made, I said, "Well, I'm going to kill the hero," you know. "Fuck this, the hero's gonna die." You know why, because that's life; people die. You know, important, big people, small people die. People die. Not in the movies. They almost never die anymore. You know, you gotta have a hero. Well who wants to watch that? Not me. I feel a little out of touch with what people are watching today because it's so formulaic. It's such a formula.

I must tell you, you know, I think the last time I gave a seminar like this, it was at the old building and David Lynch was out there, and Martin Breast, and a number of other guys who work like that. And I felt then, I didn't know how good these guys were gonna do, you know, I saw their films, they were fantastic, but I didn't know how well they'd do. But I felt there was an opportunity for them to do well, given their particular talents, and their quirks, and their unique vision of the world. I thought, "Well, yeah, there's still some films, like what these guys are doing, that get made." Now I don't feel that. I don't feel that anymore. I look out there and I wonder which one of you people is gonna write *Robocop 18*? You know, or when you get out of here are you going to work on *Exorcist 7*, or some damned thing? I don't see that opportunity for iconoclasm as I did, let's say, twenty years ago. But, in any case, I persist, not reluctantly, but I persevere in my belief that you must try to surprise the audience in every way, given the limitations of your own abilities.

AM #3: What element of *Sorcerer* makes it your favorite?

WF: Oh, it's my favorite film by far. You know, for many reasons. I think it's because, first of all, it was so hard to do; it was so difficult to make the film. It took forever to make. It was extremely difficult. It was very intense. It was, in my view, at that time, because I had had a lot of success at that time; I had won an Academy Award and my films had done very well. And now I'm making a film that was really out of the mainstream. It was—you know where everybody gets killed in it, and there's no happy ending; it's totally unrelieved. You know, there's no humor in it; it's like a dark vision.

Now, at the time, I didn't know I was so dark. I now realize that my attitude then was so bleak about human nature. The theme of the film that attracted me— the notion of four strangers who don't particularly like each other who have to cooperate to survive, and are riding a load of dynamite—seemed to me to be a metaphor, a universal metaphor for the world, you know? The world is in just such a situation today; it always has been. A bunch of foreigners to each other. People who don't particularly like each other, who may be in conflict with each other, but who are locked together in a potential catastrophic, cataclysmic event.

So that seemed to me to be a very important theme. And then I felt, having made the film, and gotten over the tremendous problems of making it—half the crew wiped out, you know, with malaria, gangrene. I myself got malaria as a result of where we were; I was a wreck. And then the film came out and it didn't do well. It came out and it just didn't do well at all; and so it becomes like your black sheep of the family, so called, the child that goes out into the world that doesn't do as well as one or more of the other children; maybe that's it with me? I don't have a favorite anything. I don't have a favorite jacket, or shoe, you know, but that film has a particular meaning for me, because it, more than anything I did, expressed how I felt, uncompromisingly. Even though that wasn't the greatest kind of a message to give to the world, it was my message, you know, just as [Franz] Kafka's message is not "good news," you know, but it's Kafka. What he sees. Bam! Oscar Wilde, you know, *De Profundis*. It's not good news. Or T. S. Eliot. But you are convinced that the person creating this believed it. And for the most part, the films I see, and many that I've made, I didn't believe it. I was just hired to do a job, and I did it. I guess some of me got into it, but only by accident, by osmosis.

But here was a film that I set out to do, that was more than I realized at the time expressing my own cynicism, my own dark side, and I felt that it was pretty good. And now I haven't seen it for thirteen years, but I just recently made the video of it. Took me a month to make a video; it's never come out on video. And the video will be out in October now, and a LaserDisc in December, and I worked with it for a month, painting the frames, and I achieved an absolutely beautiful tape of this film now. And I sort of liked it; I thought "Hey, that's not bad. The guy's really depressed who made this picture."

AM #4: Given the spontaneity that you're going for, your style, I'm wondering how you work with your writers?
WF: Spontaneously. Same way. No, I mean, Wally (Walon) Green, who worked with me on *The Brink's Job*, and on *Sorcerer*, and worked with me at Wolper, wonderful. You know, the best collaboration with a writer, two people are on the same groove, you just talk about something that's maybe tangential to the work, and you agree on an approach to it, and then it somehow gets into the script. If as a writer, or as a director, you are not in total sync with each other, nothing too good is going to happen. You don't have to agree on what's going into the movie. I mean the writer can bring his or her approach, and you as a director must bring yours, but you gotta have an outlook on life that's pretty close, you know?

I've worked with Harold Pinter, and he's a terrific, one of the greatest writers in the English language, and I learned a lot from him, but it was basically his thing, and that's fine too, because I was happy to interpret it. I've had some relationships with writers that have not been as good, but wavelength is everything. One of the things you're gonna have to do, like I told you, a very important thing is if you're going to go out and con people to either give you money to make a movie, or let you use their building, or their parking lot, or something to shoot your film on, you gotta find out what their needs are. That's a very important thing I've just said to you, more important than anything else. More important maybe than anything you'll hear all this semester. No, really, you gotta be able to deal with people, and make them happy about what you're doing.

The other thing you want to do is put that vibe out there for your collaborators. David Lynch and Frederick Elmes, you know. I mean, here are guys—I don't know if Frederick Elmes totally supports everything in David Lynch's attitude, but they have an artistic aesthetic which crosses, and out of which is produced this incredibly individual work. That's because of a vibe. Now, Lynch's films might not be as good if they weren't done by Elmes. The scripts of people like Billy Wilder and Charles Brackett. Orson Welles and Herman Mankiewicz, you know? That synthesis, that vibe. These two guys were able to find common ground, an attitude that they could share and get behind, and that's what's on the screen. That vibe! That's how I work successfully with writers, when I've been able to find writers who I can get on their vibe, or they get on mine, or we found, miraculously, we're on the same vibe. It has happened to me where I've worked with writers where we weren't, and then because you're the director, you're sort of dictating, and it just doesn't work as well.

As a director you'll get scripts a couple of ways: you'll either initiate them yourself, or someone will give you a script to work on, and then you may want certain changes in them, but if you find that the changes run counter to what the writer wants to do with the project, and the writer has created the work, I generally would say, "Run. Don't do it." And if you're the writer, and the director's saying to you, "What I think is that this story about this nun and this priest should have a lot of nudity in it, and rampant sexuality," I would say, "Well, you know, get another director" even if it's Kubrick, you know, because it ain't gonna be your script. You'll know that right away. This happens a lot; you write a script, you go to a filmmaker that you really admire, he says, "Yeah, great." He or she says, "Yeah, I'd like to make this film; however, I want to take the guts out of it," you know, "I also want to bring an elephant into the second act, and I think we need a car chase upfront." Don't do it. You won't be happy, and a good reason to make films is to be happy. Why not try and be happy, you're like chosen people. Most people work for a living. There's not a soul in this room, that if you go into filmmaking, will ever work another day in your life. Really. I swear to you man, it's just fun, you know? The hours are basically what you make them. It's a good living. You know, it isn't all Gucci shoes and autographs—there's a lot of sunglasses involved too. [Audience laughter] It's a great life! I'm sure most of you've done the other thing—punched in, driven a cab, sold papers. I sold pop at Wrigley Field as a kid, oh man, that's work.

Host: Let me ask you something here before we go on, because you talked about how you work with writers; you laid out your visual principals. That must have profound consequences in how you cast your movie, and how you work with actors. **WF:** Casting is generally a compromise, in almost every case. Every case that I've been involved in, it's been a total compromise. And in the films *The French Connection* and *The Exorcist*, I had sort of the angel that watches over movies. Would you like to hear a couple of stories on how that film was cast? I'll tell you, *The French Connection*, which won Gene Hackman an Academy Award, he was my last choice. I remember saying to the producer of the film the weekend before we had to start shooting, everybody we wanted didn't want to do the picture or the studio wouldn't go with some of the other people that I wanted, and there was only this other guy Gene Hackman, who bored the shit outta me. I thought he was just boring. I met with him in New York, I had lunch with him. I was falling asleep at the lunch. It was a hot day, and the producer was with me and he said, "Well, what do you think?" I said, "I tell you something, if I ever choose to do the Gene Hackman story, I will not use this guy!" [Audience laughter] So now, guess what? There's nobody else. So boom, we go and make the picture, and every day on the set, he and I fought, every single day. And it was not a pleasant experience.

Even the French guy, the guy with the little goatee. The way we used to cast—this fellow produced this film, Phil D'Antoni, we were friends, you know, we would just—"Who do you want to use in that part?" This is how our conversations went: "What about that guy who was in *Belle de Jour* that does all of those Luis Buñuel films?" He'd say, "Oh that guy's great!" We'd say to the casting director we didn't know his name. We'd say to the casting director, "Hey, the guy that was in *Belle de Jour*, works for Buñuel all the time. Let's see if we can get him. Okay." Now we'd go do something else. The casting director goes out, he comes back, he says, "Okay, we got the guy. His name is Fernando Rey. He's available. He's gonna cost this. He's all set." "Terrific! Hire him." So now I go out to the airport to meet the guy. He's coming in on a plane; he lives in Spain. I'm meeting him at the airport, and I'm going to take him to his hotel. I get to the airport to meet this guy; I'm looking around, and I don't see the guy. So now I get paged, right? "Paging Mr. Friedkin," I go up to the booth, and there's this guy standing there. It's Fernando Rey, but he's not the guy that I was talking about. [Audience laughter]

The guy I was talking about, turns out it was Francisco Rabal, who was in *Sorcerer*, the guy who plays the hitman in *Sorcerer*, who's in the truck with [Roy] Scheider. That's the guy that was in *Belle de Jour*. Not the other guy, the other guy was in another Luis Buñuel film, he was in twenty Buñuel films. He's Buñuel's favorite actor, Fernando Rey, but he ain't the guy I wanted. He's a slick-looking dude, you know, he looks like a duke, he's got this little goatee. Now I'm driving him to his hotel, and I'm thinking, "I know this guy, but who the hell is it? Holy shit!"

Because the guy I had in mind for that part was the guy you saw in *Sorcerer*. So now I'm saying, "This guy, the character's more rough, you know and maybe you gotta shave." He says, "Oh, I can't shave my goatee. I can't shave. You don't want me to shave because I have scars all over my chin, it was very—looked terrible." So now he's got to play the movie in his goatee, right? So I thought, "This is ridiculous." He says, "Oh, another thing," he says. "There's a lot of this dialogue in French," he says. "You know, I don't speak French. I'm Spanish." I said, "Yeah, but some of those films . . ." He says, "Yeah, well, Buñuel made films in France, but I spoke Spanish; I don't speak French." Oh my god.

So now I get him to his hotel, and I run over to the hotel phone, and I call up the producer. I say, "Phil! We got the wrong guy here. This ain't the guy." He says, "What are you talking about?" I said, "Get over here! This is a whole other guy. This ain't gonna work. We gotta get out of this thing." So, Phil comes over. We go up to have a drink with the guy, and Phil's looking at him. He realized it's like apples and oranges to who we wanted to cast. So, we say, "Thank you," we go out of the room, we go back to our office, and we get the casting director by the throat. He hired Fernando Rey, we wanted Francisco Rabal. The connection with Buñuel the both of them had had. So, he finds out the guy we wanted was Francisco Rabal, so we now call Rabal's agent, we're gonna fire this guy, get Rabal, and it turns out that a) Rabal does not speak a word of English either, and b) he was unavailable. So we had to make the film with that guy, with Fernando Rey. And look at the result, I mean the guy's terrific. But I didn't want Hackman and I didn't want Rey.

In the case of *The Exorcist*, the studio did not want Jason Miller, they didn't want Ellen Burstyn, they didn't want anybody. Sometimes the God of casting, you know, watches over you, he did me certainly. In *Sorcerer*, I wrote *Sorcerer*, Wally Green and I wrote it for Steve McQueen, and Steve McQueen, who I thought was the best film actor of his time—we wrote *Sorcerer* for Steve McQueen, and we sent it to Steve, and Steve said, "Yeah, okay great." At that time he was just getting married to Ali MacGraw, and he said, "Well, I'm just getting married, so you gotta put a part in there for my wife" in this picture. And also, "Well, she's got to be associate producer" or something "because I want her around all the time, and you've got to shoot the picture somewhere in America." And I was pretty cocky, and pretty successful at that time, and I said, "To hell with that! I'm not gonna do it. The hell with Steve McQueen. Pass!" You know, today, I would have done it, all of it. Today I would have met every one of his conditions, because what I didn't know then what I do know now, so sadly but wiser, that the closeup is more important than the wide shot. The guy whose face is up there is more important than the greatest scenery you could possibly put in front of the camera. Now if you can get both, that's terrific. But there was no face on screen like Steve McQueen's at that time, maybe even now. I haven't seen anybody who could bring off that kind of—who could act silently, without words. You want to see a great movie in here; run *Bullitt*. *Bullitt* is a classic. Forget the car chase; it's good, but Steve McQueen, that's it, that's the end for me. Film acting right there, where it's all in his face, everything. And his attitude, the way he moves. And today, given the same problem, if there was such a Steve McQueen, I would make that compromise. I'd shoot it here, write in a part for his wife, and make her associate producer. You know, go ahead, call me a whore, whatever.

AM #7: How did you come upon the script for *The French Connection*?

WF: Phil D'Antoni was a guy I knew around New York, he produced *Bullitt* by the way, and he and I had met. He said, "I got this story about this guy named Eddie Egan and this other cop named Sonny Grosso. You gotta meet these guys," and I met them in a steakhouse in New York, and just their names turned me on: "Eddie Egan & Sonny Grosso." It seemed to me, right in there, there was a kind of a conflict at work. Something that was, you know, a black Irishman, and a sort of real downhome Italian guy, and they're partners. And now here's this "French Connection" case that there was about seventy-five people involved in, not just those two guys. The case spread out over three years; it was unmanageable. But I met these two guys, they turned me on, and now I'm starting to go out and see what they do out in the street, all this stuff you see in the movie. They're going into all black bars and kicking ass like that, you know, and getting away with it, and living, and cleaning up, you know, and all this shit's working against them. It just was interesting. There's a book out by Robin Moore called *The French Connection* that D'Antoni owned. It sold about eleven copies. I started to read the book; I couldn't read it, I couldn't finish it. It was boring. I threw it away. I've never read the book to this day. But I'm following them around, and they're telling me the story from their perspective.

So then Phil and I, we try to get a writer. We had a couple of people, two writers who took drafts at it. One was a very good writer, he's deceased now; his draft didn't make it. Then Phil found this guy Ernest Tidyman, who was a reporter for the *New York Times* covering the crime beat. And Ernest Tidyman had written a novel that we read in galleys called *Shaft*, that we thought was pretty good. And he had never written a screenplay, and Phil payed him $5,000. He gave us a draft; he worked on it for about three weeks. It was not really anything we could use. Then we get an order to go make the picture; somebody had said okay. The picture had been turned down everywhere, by every studio, at least twice.

And one day Dick Zanuck called Phil, he was the head of Fox, he said, "I'm going to get fired over here in a couple of months, I always liked that crazy story you guys had." He said, "I've got a million and a half dollars hidden away in a drawer over here. If you can make the film for that, go ahead." And we made it, and we had to get started because he was going to get fired, and he did before the picture came out. So we had to start the movie; we didn't have a script, but what we did have was months of research, and we basically improvised the picture. The film was basically improvised on the set, and I sent Hackman and Scheider out with Egan and Grosso; they'd come back with stories, dialogue, scenes, and we'd shoot 'em.

The whole first scene where they're chasing down this black guy and they sort of whack him around and talk to him, that was almost verbatim from an Egan/ Grosso interrogation. The first day of shooting that I shot that scene, I decided to have the scene staged in a car, which is where I saw it. They would grab a guy like that, and they would sit him between them in a police car, and then they would throw all this surreal shit at him, like "Did you ever pick your feet . . ." and all that stuff, and it was very [Harold] Pinter-esque, you know, to screw the guy's head up. And I sort of laid the scene out, I wrote the scene, and I had them play it, and the guy was sitting in a car, and they were doing the scene nine times, ten times. The first day of shooting was no good, and Gene had to slap this actor, Alan Weeks, who's a terrific actor; he couldn't do it. He could not hit the actor, and Alan Weeks, after like thirty takes, and Alan Weeks saying, "Come on man, just hit me! It's okay. Just let's do it and let's get out of here." You know, "Hit me! Come on!" Couldn't do it, couldn't say the lines; and I realized after we shot it that a part of the problem was my staging. I had seen the scene done that way by these two cops in a police car, but my actors weren't free; I had my actors just sitting there doing lines.

So, it was a policy at the time: no retakes at 20th Century Fox without special permission of some guy, I don't know, who's dead now, and get his permission. At the end of the movie I said, "This scene's no good. It's the first scene of the picture." We couldn't get no permission for nothing, but I just reshot the scene. And what I did, I said, "Okay, you guys know what happens now; go out and improvise it." I'll tell you what, and here again was this documentary thing. I put two cameras on it; I said, "Go over against that wall. Just go anywhere you want. Walk anywhere and say anything. Just wail the way they do it. You remember what they said; now make it up, and go out there and do it, and you're free to move anywhere. You want to turn around and go like this? Or you want to come back at the guy? Or pick up something and hit him? Do whatever you want to do; you're free." Now when you tell actors they're "free," something happens. That's one take, they did that scene [claps hands], boom, that's in the picture. They made up all the words; they overlap, so its rhythms are like life. There was real fear in Alan Weeks, because he didn't know what they were gonna do, and they didn't know what they were gonna do, and I didn't know what they were gonna do, and that's heaven on a set. When you see it fucking happen! Jesus, look at this!

AM #8: This is just a "nuts and bolts" question, but in *Sorcerer*, visually how did you accomplish the huge truck on the precarious bridge, tilting around?

WF: There's no miniatures in that at all, and we dumped a few. I dumped out of that truck three times, but what is was, we built the bridge. It's a hydraulic bridge; it looks like a rickety old wooden bridge, but it's actually made out of metal and steel that's just painted to look like wood, and it's controllable. I could make [it] sway, and what I did was I hooked the truck, the truck is bound to the bridge, it's locked to the bridge with like arms underneath it that are holding the truck fast to the bridge, so it couldn't possibly dump, which it did. I mean, and dump, and dump, and go over on its side many times. But we held it fast for the most part, and we had control of the movement of the bridge, and the actors are walking on pretty solid pieces, and you know, the sound is what makes it. You hear rickety sound and you think, "Jeez, this is an old wooden bridge. It's going to fall apart any minute."

AM #9: Would you speak just a little bit about the process of—*The Exorcist*'s stairs, for example, left a lasting impression. What do you do when you're looking for locations?

WF: Oh, when you look for locations? You look for something that nails you, like those stairs. What do people remember? I had a guy tell me at lunch today, "You know, the thing I remember about *The Exorcist* is Jason Miller's face and a head turning." A lot of movies that I remember, what do I remember about the movie? Marilyn Monroe's ass. You know, or Gary Cooper's walk. People see movies in a different way, I'm convinced. They don't see the story, they take things off the screen. They're like scrambled icons. People will take things off the screen and will remake their own movie, and that's why they like it. They don't necessarily like what's going on, but they like this actor, or this location. So, when I'm looking for locations, I'm looking for something that'll be memorable and it'll grab me like that. You know, "Hey, those stairs," well once you see those stairs there's no other, or "this house" or "that bar," no other bar will do, and then it comes down to "that face." Now when I've made mistakes on certain films I didn't get "that face," you know, I got the wrong face let's say. But you're always looking for the icons that will impress you. Sometimes a location will speak to you and sometimes it won't. When it speaks to you, that's the one you want. The same is true of an actor.

AM #9: I have a question about a sequence in the *Sorcerer*, in the village when they're riding after the charred bodies are brought back, and whether you were able to maintain some kind of control there?

WF: You mean that riot?

AM #9: Yeah, the riot.

WF: Yeah, that was totally controlled. But we went to a village in Latin America where that situation was true, and again, I shot it like a documentary. I would tell people what was happening, and how they were supposed to react, then I left the rest up to them, because people in a third-world country know very well that sort of privation and suffering and victimization. If you can tap into that, what they know, you'll get something like that scene, which I think really rings true. You know, it was true; it was what they had seen and experienced.

AM #10: I see in most of—all of—I was very happy to see that most of the people, all of the actors were so . . . alive. Most of the people you see nowadays, they're so controlled, or they're told "no, less, less, less," and everywhere you speak now is "Just do it. Go ahead and be big, do whatever you want," and I'm so used to being told, "No, lower."

WF: No man, let your voice be heard. I mean, my philosophy of filmmaking is the exact opposite of Nancy Reagan's philosophy, you know, I say, "Just say yes."

You know, just do it! Let it happen, and take a chance and surprise me. It won't always be good, but everything's so safe, you're right, everything is within narrow parameters. If you guys can go out and either write or photograph, or edit, or produce, or direct pictures that come up, you'll revitalize the art. It's pretty dead, as far as I'm concerned. It's all—it's dead. I don't look forward to going to a movie today like I did in the sixties when you had the French New Wave and the Italian New Wave, you had—for the first we're seeing films by [Federico] Fellini, I don't even know if these names mean anything to you anymore, and [Jean-Luc] Godard, you know, and [Michelangelo] Antonioni who has knocked me—Have you guys ever seen an Antonioni film? Jesus Christ, I mean, like *L'Avventura*, *La Notte*, and *L'Eclisse*, these movies, they moved. *Blow Up* is great. They moved differently; they move like laterally. One reason they move laterally is because Antonioni almost never repeats a shot. And that's what I learned from Antonioni; don't ever repeat a set up. Most films are shot, you know, over here, boom, over there, boom, over there, boom, and they gotta keep repeating these three set ups. That's why you know what's going to happen. You're watching TV, you know, even by the way they're going to cut the thing you know what the next shot is, so then you figure out—you're so bored figuring out what the next shot is you start figuring out what the words are going to be, because they're boring too. But now, a guy's making films and he's not repeating any shots. He's saying, "This scene will be shot from over here," okay, "and the next scene will be shot from over there," and then maybe he'll cut in here, but he's not going to do a matching cut. Jeez, now I'm paying attention, because he's broken with that standard bullshit thing about complimentary angles and complimentary sizes.

That's one of the things that killed the movies. Killed it. The other thing that killed it was young executives from television who took over the movie companies, and agents who don't know anything but the bottom line. But try not to repeat set-ups. When you look at a novel, you know, it has its own rhythm, but the story keeps going, you start over here and it's going out there; boom, it goes off the page somewhere. But if they kept repeating the same shit you'd say, "I'm bored with this novel." But like a book that turns you on, or a story where the writer is constantly vying for your attention, that's what grabs you. It could be fiction. This guy Robert Caro who writes wonderful nonfiction books, he wrote *The Path to Power*, the Lyndon Johnson book, read that, that's great. Filmmaking, boom, this guy's doing it in a novel, and one of the things he's doing is constantly surprising you, not simply with revelations, but with sentence structure, and other things. So I would try to break out of that if I were you, even if it's taught here.

AM #11: I was listening to your comment about letting the actors be free, and just say go, and do what you feel like doing. I've had a tendency, or a problem, and I want to ask how you address this. When you know, or had some little bit more experience or reputation as a director, people listen to you and sort of do what you say. Either I'm in a position when I'm making everybody furious, so I can't get that freedom and get them to feel open, to keep control on the set, or I lose control. I was wondering, does that just come with reputation or are there some psychological tricks you can use?

WF: That's a great question. That is really a great question, and it really applies. Well, you start out by realizing the difference between actors and directors. Why does someone become an actor, and someone want to become a director? An actor wants to be controlled; the director wants to control. It's that simple. There are many variations and of course background and experience all factor in, but you boil it down to the simple basics. Actors, even though if they make it, they're famous and successful, and give a lot of autographs, they basically don't want to control anything, with rare exception. They want to be controlled. If you're working with a real actor, you will find that the actor, I don't care if it's Audrey Hepburn or Marlon Brando, they want the director to have a point of view. They want the director to know what he or she wants from them. They don't want the director to say, "Well, jeez, I don't know, maybe." "Maybe" is the worst word you could use. If you say "maybe" to an actor, it frightens the shit out of him or her. "'Maybe'? You mean there's nothing finite about this?" When an actor is dealing with his or her own insecurities constantly—most actors are terribly insecure, and one of the reasons they're acting is to compensate for these insecurities. So you want to obviously, as in human nature, you don't want to come in and give orders because that's counter-productive. You want to try and make the actor feel that it's his or her idea, but that you know what the right way is. You know, and you want to do it in the form of suggestions to the actors. You want to make suggestions.

When I go on a set with actors, whoever they are, even if they've never done anything and I've made a couple of pictures, I don't have any reputation. It's totally one-on-one. To make this thing effective I've got to communicate effectively with this person. In the case of like, Linda Blair, it was a twelve-year-old in *The Exorcist*, never acted. I couldn't come out and say, "Do this! Do what I tell you!" She's a kid, she's gonna freeze. You must, on the set, create an atmosphere of play. Which is what it is. In other words, this movie's not the end of the world, you know, this thing we're making, it's a lot of fun. I love what I'm doing. I know you love what you're doing. Let's find out together how we can have more fun. Now let's talk about your part in this thing. You want him to come in the door—come in the door and then come over here and say a few words then sit down. The guy says, "Jeez, I don't want to come in the door. I want to be found laying here on the floor. I think that's better." You say, "Okay, great. Let's do it that way." Alright, so you shoot the guy the way he wanted to do it. He's laying on the floor. You say, "Yeah, you know it's pretty boring though, you're just laying on the floor over there. Now, if you come in the door I can move my camera and I can pick this other person up over here," so you bring them into it, and then pretty soon he's doing it your way, but you make him think it's his or her way. "Hey, that was great when you came in the door, the way you looked around over there, that's beautiful." Compliment, compliment the actor, because they are children, really! I don't care if it's Robert Redford. If you direct Robert Redford, you can't think that he doesn't want you to tell him what to do. He's scared to death of you or Sidney Pollack, that you won't know how to use him best. And if he thinks that you will know how to use him best, because you have your shit together, so you must come on the set with an aura, as I think you probably have just in an instant of knowing who you are, and what you're about, and what your limitations may be, and with a consciousness to want to overcome them. If you know that that's what you have to do and you say to this actor, "I would like you to do this, and here's why, okay," it's gonna fly.

Now, often you'll find the actor has a better way; be open to that. Be open, because you have a plan, but remember what I first said? You can put the camera anywhere. You know, you gotta make a choice, and some of your choices may be suggestions of other people. Some of the best ideas in my films come from people on the crew who are just standing there, who are not afraid to say, "Hey Billy." Everyone calls me Billy. Not Mr. Friedkin, or sir, or any of that. It's "Billy, what about this?" "That's pretty good," or I'll say, "Naw, that's terrible," or "Hey, I kinda like that. Let's do it that way." You must be open, but while I'm open, I have figured out the whole movie in my head. Don't go to the set unless you got the whole movie in your head. If you have the whole movie in your head, then you'll be able to improvise. When I told you about the scene in [The] *French Connection*, where I knew what was wrong with these guys, I had staged it badly. That was my fault. They couldn't play it the way I wanted, because I had locked them in to a staging that didn't work. So, you gotta be open to see that. So now I'm thinking, well, "Why? Why? Why did this scene not work? Oh, boom! I gotta free 'em up. The only way you can free 'em up is if you know what you want. I knew what I wanted in that situation. I wasn't getting it, so I had to relate why I wasn't getting it to what I wanted, and then go out and figure out a way to get it. Do you follow that? You know what I mean? You gotta have that movie in your head. If you do, then you're open to all sorts of other ideas. And filmmaking is collaboration. That's what it is, it's collaboration. An artist faces an empty canvas. A musician faces a music sheet and a piano, or whatever. A writer faces a blank page. A director has a one-ton pencil that he carries around with him all the time. And you gotta move all this crew, all this support, all this equipment, all these people, and guess what? For the most part, they're all there to help you, and they will. If you know that, you'll come out with some good pictures. If they make ideas you don't like, don't use 'em, but be open to what you like.

AM #12: Was Roy Scheider [a] compromise in *Sorcerer*?
WF: Yeah. I like his work in it, and more and more as I see it, I appreciate even more what he did. But yeah, it was written for Steve McQueen.

AM #13: Since there was comparatively [little] dialogue in *Sorcerer*, I'm wondering what the script looked like?
WF: It's a terrific script. What it looked like, and perhaps I should get a copy over here, it's a great script because Wally Green describes everything. Everything you see on the screen is in Wally's script. And film script doesn't just have to have a lot of people with their jaws moving. One of the other great scripts I've ever seen is *Shane*, the script for *Shane*. It's fantastic, and it's not a lot of dialogue in that either, but everything you see in the movie *Shane*, and everything you hear on the soundtrack is in that script. It's a masterpiece. And a lot of scripts don't have a lot of dialogue. I wanted, in *Sorcerer*, I was trying to get toward a kind of "pure" filmmaking, not rely on words. I used words only where I had to, and very often I let the words play in a foreign language. Because what I found out from some of my earlier films was when you run a film, and many parts of the world today, for example Thailand—if you run a film in Thailand, they generally can't afford a version dubbed into Thai, so they'll get a version that's either French language or English, or whatever, German. They run that, and every so often a guy standing by the screen stops the movie, and they explain to the audience what's just happened for the last ten minutes. "This guy did that, and this guy did this. Right. Boom,"

and then they go on with the movie. I wanted to make a picture that would play in Thailand without words. Where the guy would never have to stop the screen. Where you could just look at the thing and know what was happening. Know the attitudes of people towards one another, see the events take place, a kind of "pure" filmmaking, as pure as I could get it.

AM #14: Talking about style, kinda a director's personality in film, and just watching [The] French Connection on the screen for the first time, and in Sorcerer for the first time ever, I was really just overwhelmed by the personality behind it. And you're talking about films today, and really, they're just kind of faceless, and you can almost insert one director in place for another, just a lot of repetition. So, another thing that I've been thinking about a lot lately, what separates a director who's in there and a director who's not? You talked about your documentary background, but is that it, or is it just something unconscious which you're not even aware of?

WF: For the most part when you get going as a filmmaker, you do operate on automatic pilot. And one of the things that I'm conscious of is, well, almost everything I do is going to be compared to stuff that I've done, like [The] French Connection or [The] Exorcist. So, knowing that I try to maybe not do something as close to what I've done. But then I wind up doing it, and it does get compared, and it's found wanting, but today I don't believe that they're looking for people to express themselves on film, as it was when I came up. Today they're looking for people who can clone out big hits that are like comic books. That's what's called for now. Now you have to realize that that might change. On the other hand, it's been the case for about thirteen years. I mean, since Star Wars came out, that kind of film, or a variation of it, the "commercial cinema" is all about. Not just in America, but everywhere in the world. Those films are popular.

So, you don't need a personality, you need a technician. You need a good technician. So one of the things I say to you, "Become the best technician that you can." Depends on what you want out of life. I must tell you that I wouldn't want to be the guy who made Exorcist 3, okay? I don't care how much money in the world. $100 million; I wouldn't do it. Why? Because I'm a schmuck? Maybe. But basically, I gotta live with myself, and I didn't get into the film business for money. I mean, I like the money, I think it's great. But that's not why I'm making films. And I couldn't live with that. I've made some bad pictures; I've made films that didn't work. I mean they are just no good, and they don't work, but I didn't set out to do that. I failed, but I didn't say, "Well, I'm going to do this piece of shit because they're paying me a fortune." No, but that's me, and there's nothing wrong with going the other way either, but for me, I couldn't do it. I couldn't watch it. It's tough enough today to watch some of the stuff I've done. One of the few films I can watch is *Sorcerer*. One of the few. I can keep going back and looking at it, even though it's depressing. You know, there's an intensity there that says something to me, and I was able to communicate ideas that I had, that I stated to you ladies and gentlemen. I was able to in some way convey it using the metaphor of film, and so I'm pleased about that. It's not a totally successful film. It's not *Citizen Kane* in my book, you know, but it did represent how I felt at the time, and I want to go out that way. When I go out, I don't want to go out, "Oh, he cloned himself out six times," you know, It's just not in my personality to be able to do that.

But you know, to just complete the answer, there's nothing wrong with these great technicians that are out there doing it, like [Paul] Verhoeven, you know, really good technicians. Today, that is much more valuable than the guy with a—I mean Verhoeven is a guy who has subverted his personality to becoming a technician, because that's what they want. This guy made very dark and brilliant films. Some of them satiric in Holland; now he's come over here and he's making *Total Recall*. Does it very well, because they don't want *Soldier of Orange* at Carolco [Pictures Inc.], they want *Total Recall*. So, you gotta think about that.

AM #15: Hi, I understand that *Sorcerer* [was] cut [by] thirty minutes.
WF: No, in Europe. Not in America. At that time, I had contractually, I had final cut in America. It never occurred to me, or to my lawyers, to put in final cut anywhere else. And so, what happened was a lot to do with—a great deal of chicanery occurred, and a bunch of guys got together and decided that they could put *Sorcerer* out in Europe better than I could put it out.

AM #15: So, you had nothing to do with the cuts that were made.
WF: No. I've never seen those versions. However, in a couple of countries there's a thing called the *droits morale*. The *droits morale* is a French phrase meaning "the moral law," and what it means in, like, Sweden and France and Germany in particular, they recognize as a matter of law that the director, or the creator, of the film is the owner of the film. Not the studio that put up the money. There have been very few cases where anyone has sued the studio on the *droits morale*, and when I found out that's what they did, I sued Universal and Paramount in Sweden, under the *droits morale* and I won, and they had to restore the versions. I become very unpopular for having done that. Even to the point where today, almost every standard director's contract in America mentions the *droits morale*, and they constantly come to you when they're trying to get you to make a picture, when you're negotiating your contract they ask you to waive the *droits morale*. "Waive the *droits morale*!" And I always say to them, "Waive this!" Because I had occasion to sue on the *droits morale* and win. I had a guy who ran a studio, he was a friend of mine. He says, "I'm your friend, I'll never fuck ya." Hey, you know, if you

wouldn't fuck me just leave the *droits morale* in there. And I didn't do the picture, didn't make the film because he wouldn't leave it in.

AM #16: You spoke earlier about giving your actors specific direction and then kind of letting them go, and then pointing the camera to point in that direction and seeing what happens. I want to deal with, or I would like you to deal with the DP in pointing them in that direction, and have you found that prior to reputation and what have you, that it's hard to deal with DPs, and how you get their respect, or some psychological tips on dealing with them, because I've heard some can break a director.

WF: Oh, I've had great experiences and bad. I'll tell you a couple of both, and I'll give you some advice. The first thing I ever did in Hollywood, outside of documentaries, was I did the very last *Alfred Hitchcock Hour*, when they were making them in black and white, and Hitchcock was alive. It was a thing called *[Off] Season*. The cameraman on it, who was the regular DP on *Hitchcock Hour*, he was there every week, and I'm a kid coming in who had never done anything, and this guy had won the Academy Award for a film he shot called *The Country*, beautifully shot, his name was Jack Warren, and he was a great old guy but he was a bullshit artist like most old-timers in the business—totally full of shit and full of themselves. And this guy, he used to call me "Chief," right? He'd say, "Well, Chief, what are we gonna do today?" This guy's made five hundred movies, you know, worked with Grace Kelly, and I'm coming in, I'm a schmuck. He's saying, "Well, Chief, what are we . . ." Now the guy who produced the *Hitchcock Hour* said to me, "No matter what you do, make sure that the first shot is the easiest shot you could make, and you get it in one take, okay? Get it in one take. Because the crew has to have confidence that you know what you're doing. So if you're out there banging away at take seventeen, your first time out, you're going to be history before lunch."

So, now, I'm listening to this, and guess what, when I hear things like that it goes right against my—you know, I'm just sort of ornery. So I set up as my first shot, a shot that started here, and then came back there, and then went over there, and flew over here, and did everything over there, you know, what they don't do on television, where they go bang, bang, you know, even on the *Hitchcock Hour*, they [*Imitates gun noise*], like shooting ducks in a pond. So I set up this complicated shot and Jack Warren freaks out, he's "Holy Christ, it'll take me four hours to light. What the fuck? I don't know what's going on," you know, "Oh, Jesus Christ!" and I say, "That's the shot. That's what we're gonna do. We're gonna do the shot like that," and I walk away. Never argue. Never get into a debate. I said, "That's the shot. Okay, Jack? You got the shot? I'll see you later, I'll be in my dressing room," boom. It was totally a front on my part. So now he goes out and lights the shot, takes forever, we make the shot, and I managed to do about three or four pages in this one shot, and there in television, page count is the most important thing. It's like body count in the Vietnam War. All they were interested in was body count; we don't care whose body, any bodies. You know, in television it's page count. "We don't care how it looks or what's in it, but how many pages did you shoot today?" So, I knocked off a lot of pages but without all this bullshit. Bang bang. Now Jack was saying, "Oh shit, these guys aren't going to like it," you know "These guys are not going to fucking like this, they're gonna— Where's the coverage?" and all this shit. Anyway, the rushes come out, the executives saw them first, and the next morning the producer of the show, a man named Norman Lloyd, very sweet man, he's still around, he's acting. He's a wonderful man.

Host: I'm so glad you said something nice about him.
WF: He was the producer of the *Hitchcock Hour*. He was, like, running the shows, and all he had seen of mine was that documentary about the black guy going to the electric chair in Chicago, and he said that that film had more suspense in the first five minutes than any *Hitchcock Hour* that he had shot all year. So, he said, "I'll give this kid a chance to make a *Hitchcock Hour*," and he was the producer. So now he's standing on the set the next morning, guys in black suits in the shadows, you know, you're working up here in the light and out there behind you are cats with dark glasses and black suits. And the suits were just standing there, and now Norman Lloyd was one of the suits, and he comes up, and Jack Warren was standing right behind be, about three feet behind me, and Norman Lloyd came up to him, and I had sort of peripheral hearing, right? I have "peripheral hearing," and I'm standing there rehearsing a scene with the actors, and I hear Norman say to Jack, he said, "Jack, that first shot, it's incredible. It was beautiful," and Warren said to him, "Did you like that shot?" And he said, "It's fantastic, we've never had anything like that on the show." Warren says, "It was my idea." I knew then that—and that has been my experience with the so called "pros" of Hollywood. The old-timers that have been around, know the shit, with rare exceptions, they have one way of working. If you break that, you're in trouble with them. To a great extent they will do things simple because they want to go home. They want to, for the most part, get the hell outta there. And they don't want to take too much time to change things because you have something you want to express.

So, you want to try and, on the one hand, if you find yourself with someone like that, who's experienced and has it down technically but is set in their ways, you've got to work on igniting them. You've got to somehow work on them like you would with an actor. You gotta turn this person on. You gotta show this person that if he lights the shot this way, he's liable to win an Academy Award, or he's gonna get recognized. Also, you gotta show a way that, "Hey we'll get a lot of pages done," you know, and you gotta make it his. You gotta motivate him to want to do it if you work with him, because basically he ain't gonna want to do it your way; there's no other way around it. He will never think of you, as a first-time professional filmmaker, as an equal. He can't, and he shouldn't. So, you have to—if you have another idea first of all it better not be stupid. If you have stupid ideas that don't work, then just get out of the business, and save him trouble, and you, and him, and everybody else. But if your ideas aren't stupid, but they're different, then persist in them, but try to get the other guy to do it because he can see how he will get recognized for doing it. Once that producer, who I knew—see, I was making the shot for the producer not the cameraman, and I knew that he had appreciated what I had done in my *Paul Crump* documentary. Once I knew that he would like this shot, and tell the cameraman that, then I owned the cameraman for the rest of the show, okay?

Okay, that's one phase of it. The other phase is: Try not to ever work with those guys. Here's what I did. When I went to do *The French Connection*, I went back to New York and there's a friend of mine who runs General Camera in New York where they rent equipment, and I've known this guy for years. I went back there, his name is Dick DiBona, I said, "Dick, you know a good young cameraman around? I don't care what he's done. I don't give a shit. I don't want to work with any of these warhorses. I want to work with a young guy who's just up for everything." He said, "Yeah there is a guy. He's thirty years old, he's never done a feature, he's done some commercials, his name is Owen Roizman. You'd like to meet him?" I said, "Sure." He said, "Well I got a reel of his commercials that he's shot, want to see it?" I said, "No, let me meet the guy." I had not seen a frame of film that this guy shot. Not a frame, and I hired him to shoot *The French Connection*, and he was nominated for an Academy Award. And I hired him to do the *[The] Exorcist*, and he was nominated for an Academy Award. A great career, but I never saw a frame of film the guy shot.

I cannot put too much emphasis on "vibes." Vibes in everything. In love, in hate, in politics. You feel it; follow it, because guess what, that's what you're going to be left with at the end. The choices that you have made is what you are going to be left with. If you fucked up and put a jerk in the thing, and the film doesn't work, it doesn't matter what your reasoning was at the time, if you messed up. So, you know, if you wear the name, play the game; and that is, trust your instinct. The only thing you have is stock and trade as an editor, as a cameraman, as a writer, as a director, is your abilities. What you do, which is what you are. So be what you are, don't be like what the other guy is. And even all this advice I'm giving you, if there's anything in it that you can use, great, take it, discard the rest as hyperbole. You've got to follow your own vibe, that's the most important thing. I started by telling you I never spent a day learning film, I spent two hours in an equipment rental house, I followed my vibe. I wanted to make a film about that particular man who's going to the chair, you know, I didn't know that it would launch my career as a filmmaker or save his life, but I felt it was a story worth telling. I said to myself, "I would want to see this if it was done"; start with that. Now, after that, these experienced guys that you're talking about, they'll give you a lot of headaches because they know more than you; they've been there. So, what I would do is try to work with somebody else who hasn't done anything. Not that I could control, but who I thought had talent, and something of his or hers [they] want to express, and was open enough to express it. That was what my vibe was with Roizman. I felt the guy was honest; I looked in his eyes and I said, "This is an honest man. This guy's not bullshitting me. He doesn't need a job, he's making commercials. He really wants to do this thing, and he's gonna try. He's got to prove his reputation. So I've worked with both, and my best experience has been working with the young dude who had a lot to prove and was gonna be honest with me, and because I was giving him his break, you know.

Host: Thank you.
WF: It's a pleasure.

William Friedkin: Auteur of the Dark

Alex Simon / 1997

From *Venice Magazine*, August 1997. Reprinted by permission of Alex Simon.

Venice Magazine: Did you come from an artistic family?
William Friedkin: Not at all. No one in my family had anything to do with or any interest in the so-called "arts." Perhaps they did in the old country, which was Russia. But by the time they got to America, they were too busy trying to make a living. Both my mother and my father came from very large families. Eleven brothers and sisters on each side. They both came from the same town, Kiev, in the Ukraine.

VM: What did your father do?
WF: My father did a lot of things. He made cigars. He played semi-professional softball. He worked in a men's clothing store. He had a great number of jobs. Sometimes with his brothers. They had a men's clothing store in Chicago.

VM: What was it that initially drew you to film and filmmaking?
WF: Well, I was in television before I ever got into film. I was in live TV in the 1950s. I answered an ad in the newspaper and went to work in the mailroom of a local TV station right out of high school. I graduated high school when I was sixteen. Of course, television was such a new medium in those days. I remember as a young boy seeing an image of an Indian that was the test pattern they used in the morning. I know that millions of people were staring at this test pattern, not believing that this image was coming into their homes, including me. I was mesmerized by the profile of this Indian. And that's not that long ago, that's the fifties. And the early television shows, which today we'd probably consider to be pretty lame, were all live and they just fascinated me. There was even a live western out of Philadelphia we used to see called *Action in the Afternoon*. I remember racing home from school to watch this western on CBS. So, I answered this ad in the paper when I was sixteen and by the time I was eighteen I was directing live TV. In those

days there were no schools where you could learn this stuff. You could learn some of the technical things . . . but in those days most of the directors worked their way out of the mailroom or were ushers . . . but I never really got interested in film per se, until one afternoon when I saw *Citizen Kane* while I was working in television.

VM: How old were you then?

WF: Probably eighteen or nineteen. And someone said, "Hey, you ought to see this movie. It's really great." Before that I had always regarded film as pure entertainment, nothing to get too concerned about. I had mostly just gone to the movies with my friends on a Saturday afternoon to see cartoons, a western, a short subject . . . but I never viewed it as an art form until *Citizen Kane*. It was a revelation to me, as it was to a lot of people. All of a sudden here was this massive, complex, involving story that left the screen with you. It didn't stay on the screen and lay back there like certain kinds of food that you eat and then five minutes later you're hungry again. It really stayed with me and I saw it again and again, five or six times. It's kind of a quarry for filmmakers, like Joyce's *Ulysses* is a quarry for writers. It seemed to me, on reflection, to synthesize all of the art forms: photography, lighting, acting, music, editing, writing. And I realized, soon after, that film could really transcend the other arts and synthesize them, but this was only through *Citizen Kane* and this led me to seek out other ambitious films and, now we're in the sixties, and I really became hooked on the films which came from Europe and some from Japan.

VM: Who were some of those?

WF: Fellini, Godard, Truffaut, Kurosawa, H. G. Cluzot, especially. I remembered being especially moved by films like *8 ½* and the Antonioni trilogy of *L'Avventura*, *La Notte*, and *L'Eclisse*. Going to films then was an adventure and an education. Here were all these extraordinary visions from all over the world. The American film industry, for the most part, was pretty lame at that time. The promise of *Citizen Kane* really hadn't been realized in this country. I remember seeing a film called *Ordet* by Carl Theodor Dreyer, a Danish filmmaker, and it was a very simple, beautiful black and white film about literal resurrection. And I'm sure that it implanted in me the approach I took to *The Exorcist*, which was simple and straightforward. Not a kind of traditional horror film.

VM: That's what made that film so scary to me. You almost shot it like a documentary.

WF: Right, it was very straight, without any zooms, or pumping it up with weird angles. I just shot it like it was going on. And that I'm sure stems in part from that film *Ordet*. Because if you're interested in filmmaking or writing or anything creative, you sort of store away all of these references. Unconsciously at first, and then consciously. Not that you mean to copy them or imitate them, but they do provide little beacons on how to approach them. And nobody, unless you're a genius, comes into this world with a full knowledge or storehouse of equipment as to how to do anything.

VM: The thing I notice with all your films starting with *The French Connection* is that you avoid dialogue whenever possible and rely on visuals to move the story along.
WF: I had heard a long time ago that when a film is run in Thailand or any foreign country where they can't afford a dubbed or subtitled version, the way they run the film is, they'll run about five or six minutes of it, stop it, then a guy stands up next to the screen and explains to the audience what they've just seen. Every five or ten minutes. It occurred to me then that the only way to make films would be to make them so you'd never have to stop them in Thailand. People could just look at the screen anywhere in the world and understand what was going on.

VM: That was Chaplin's theory.
WF: Was it? Today I think it's a great theory that's gone too far. Today movies are as visual as they've ever been, but they don't make any sense! They've got no heart, very little story. The dialogue is very often a little bit above a grunt . . . now, for the most part, people just stare at the screen for two hours and it's like opium for the eyes and you're not moved at all . . . it's an escape from reality. So, there it is. This vision that I had has been fulfilled, and I can't stand to look at most of it.

VM: How much collaboration do you do with your cinematographer before you shoot?
WF: Well, we're very collaborative. I listen to suggestions from everyone, but I always have a vision of what I want. A guy can talk me out of it if I think it's a better idea he has. But I'll discuss with the (cinematographer) what the mood of the scene is, where the light's coming from, how the characters should look.
    I usually come to every set with a shooting plan.

VM: Let's talk about *The French Connection*. How did you come to be involved?
WF: I knew the guy who produced the film, Phil D'Antoni. We used to play racquetball together. We had the same sensibilities and he'd seen my documentaries and wanted to make a film with me. One day he called me up and said, "I've got this story, *The French Connection* about two cops in New York. It's right up your alley, documentary style. . . . There's a book by Robin Moore, who wrote *The Green Berets* about the case." So, he sent me the book and I started to read the book and I couldn't. I've never read the book. So, I went to New York and met with the two

cops that it's about, Eddie Egan and Sonny Grosso . . . and I was fascinated by them. First of all by the alliteration of their names, Egan and Grosso. And then when the names were filled in by these two guys, I could see wonderful contrasts. A big, bluff Irishman and a short, sort of paranoid Italian guy. They seemed to represent a wonderful sort of Mutt and Jeff. And I went out with them for several weeks while they were out busting dealers . . . and all the dialogue and scenes in the movie were things they actually said and did, like busting up that bar, and so on. So, Phil and I then set out to get a script done. We had four or five writers. No one could crack it. We took some of these scripts around to the various studios for over two years. All the studios turned it down, most of them twice. Finally, Phil gave me the galleys of a book that was about to come out. It was called *Shaft* written by a guy who was a crime reporter for the *New York Times* named Ernest Tidyman. We thought it had very smart, New York street dialogue. We met with Tidyman, paid him $5,000 to write the script, which he did, and later won the Academy Award for it. The script was by no means good enough. His position with that script was like my coming off my documentaries to make *Minsky's*; it was over his head. Again, we took this around, no interest whatsoever.

Finally, it had been almost three years. Dick Zanuck, who was head of Fox, called us in and said, "Look, there's something in this screwy idea you guys have. . . . I have a million and a half dollars hidden away in a drawer and if you guys can make it for that, go ahead. I'm getting fired in a few months anyway, and I probably won't be around to see it, but I'm fascinated by it." We had a budget at the time of $2.8 million, and we wanted to get Paul Newman, or somebody like that, for the lead, and half a million of that was for Newman. Zanuck said, "Newman's not going to want to do this. Who else do you want?" I said my real idea of this guy is Jackie Gleason: a big, heavyset black Irishman waddling down the street trying to catch some junkie for a nickel bag. I talked with Gleason about it, and I just loved the guy. Zanuck says, "We just made a film with Gleason called *Gigot* . . . that tanked. We don't want Gleason. We don't need stars in this picture. Get anybody! Make the film for a million and half and be a man!" I knew a journalist from my New York days named Jimmy Breslin, a big, fat, heavyset, drunken Irishman. Used to write bad things about the cops. They hated him. I asked Zanuck about him, he said, "Fine. Hire him." So, I got this guy named Bob Wiener, who wrote for the *Village Voice* and knew every actor in New York to be my casting director. He got us guys like Tony Lo Bianco from *The Honeymoon Killers* and Roy Scheider, who'd never done anything, except for this film that hadn't come out yet called *Klute*. . . . At the time Roy was working off-Broadway in a Jean Genet play where he was playing a cigar-smoking nun [laughs]. Roy came in, talked for a half hour. I said, "You're the guy. You've got the part." Meanwhile, I'd go out with Breslin and Scheider and some other characters I knew, not actors, and we'd improvise scenes on the street based on the scenario I had. One day we were out rehearsing on some pier in Harlem and we had a scene of Scheider and Breslin beating the shit out of this black guy, and all of the sudden three guys in white sheets and white hats come running at us with white broomsticks. They were thinking, "Here's a couple white boys beating the shit out of a brother." And the black guy got up and said, "No brother, it's okay! It's only a movie!"

Then one day Egan and Grosso drop by unannounced, and they see Breslin, who the cops hated! And Egan thought Robert Redford should play him. Redford or Rod Taylor, thought Rod Taylor looked just like him . . . he had a casting list on the board at his precinct where all the cops could write in their casting choices for his part . . . his choices being Redford and Taylor. Newman was "okay" with him, too. Now he sees us running around with this big, fat, drunken left-wing slob who hates the cops! He says, "What's going on?! This is bullshit! Let me fuckin' do it if you're gonna go with this asshole! Audition me!" And I did, and he was terrible. And I said, "Eddie, your vision of yourself and mine is at odds." So, I kept working with Breslin. One day he'd be brilliant. Another day, he'd show up not knowing what he was doing. The third day he'd be completely drunk. The fourth day he might not show up . . . and I realized this was going nowhere. Then one day he says to me, "I hear you guys are gonna put a chase in this movie. I gotta tell ya, when my mother died, I promised her I'd never drive a car again." And that nailed it for me! So, I called Zanuck, told him my great idea wasn't gonna work. Then (agent) Sue Mengers, who represented Gene Hackman, suggested Gene, and we met with him, who'd never really starred in a picture . . . and we frankly had no other choice, that was it. The way that film was cast, it was like the Movie God took care of it.

VM: It seems like every great film in history had a hard time getting set up.
WF: Yeah, and even after we made it, we had problems. Fox was afraid of it, wanted to change the title. They had done some stupid survey in supermarkets, and when you mentioned the title *The French Connection* to a bunch of women in a supermarket, it either meant a foreign movie, a dirty movie, or a condom! [laughs] So we were about to give in and said, "Okay, we'll call it *Popeye*." But of course we couldn't call it that. Then they wanted to call it *Doyle*. They had a whole bunch of posters made up with *Doyle* on them. This is about a month before the film opened. So we went to them and said, "You can't call this movie *Doyle*. If you do, we'll go public and denounce it!" At that time, Dick Zanuck did indeed get fired and there were this whole group of dissident stockholders trying to take Fox over, led by David Merrick. And we called David and told him our problem. And David was looking for anything he could find to throw shit on the present management of the studio, and he used that, and we stopped them that way. Then they tried to tell Phil and I once we backed them down, "You've just dug a grave for your own picture (with the title *The French Connection*)."

VM: Were there anymore trials and tribulations?

WF: A guy named Elmo Williams was running the studio then. He'd been Darryl F. Zanuck's film editor his whole career. And he was put in charge until the dissidents took over, the week *The French Connection* came out. And Williams saw the film in his cutting room with the guy who was then his editor, who fell asleep at the screening. Williams sat through the whole thing, whispering notes to his assistant. And before the screening, I thought this guy was a brilliant editor. He had edited *High Noon*. He told us stories that he had saved *High Noon*, that (director) Fred Zinnemann didn't know what he was doing, that he was in love with Grace Kelly and shot most of the movie on her . . . and Elmo cut all that out and went with the Cooper story. Elmo told us he got the guy to record the theme song that became so famous, that he went out and shot the clock ticking and made all those montages that are really what you remember about *High Noon*. So, I thought, "What the fuck, we're gonna learn something here." So, Elmo comes in with dozens of pages of notes, but they were things like, "That scene when the guys go in the bar, take four frames off the beginning of that shot. Add nine frames to this. Take thirteen frames off that." Then he wanted narration over the whole picture, because he didn't understand it! And I'm listening to this shit. We thought we had a good cut! He was then going away for a week . . . and wanted to see all these changes when he returned. So Phil says to me, "What do we do?" I said to Phil, "This guy is full of shit. He's a bullshit artist. All that stuff about *High Noon* is horseshit, and this is horseshit! He doesn't know what's in those frames. Maybe if I add one or two frames, the boom mike drops in! Not all those cuts are made for style, but most cutting is done because you cut away when something stops working for you, either for an emotional, or a technical reason."

So Elmo comes back, we tell him his ideas were marvelous, tell him what a genius he is, how he saved our asses. We run the same picture in front of him. After it's over he says, "Well, it's a lot improved, isn't it?" [laughs] "But what about the narration?" he says. "Let's get Hackman to narrate it." I told Elmo that was a great idea, then rushed out to call Gene. I said, "Gene, you're gonna be out of town for a while, okay? This is what's happening." He says, "fine." I go back to Elmo, tell him Hackman's out of town, in Europe. I said, "Gee, Elmo, you want me to fly over and record Gene?" The movie cost $1.8 million. They didn't want to spend the extra money because I was already $300,000 over and they wanted to kill me. So Elmo says, "Well, I guess we'll have to put it out the way it is." We put it out, and it's an instant hit, much to everyone's surprise, including mine. The film's out for about a week or ten days, then the new management comes in. Dennis Stanful and Gordon Stulburg, who'd headed up CBS films, for whom I'd made *Boys in the Band*. We had a great relationship. So Elmo's out of there, but he's still hanging around. The sound mixer calls me one day after the films been out for ten days, tells me that Elmo's ordered a new sound mix for *The French Connection*. So I call Gordon. The money from the film is just rolling in . . . I tell him the whole Elmo story from page one. He says, "Let me handle this." While I'm sitting there he calls Elmo. Says, "Elmo, I hear you want to go in and remix *The French Connection*." Elmo says, "Yeah, well we hear the mix is too loud and that some people can't hear some of the dialogue. . . ." Gordon says, "Well, that's fine Elmo. Will you send me an estimate of what it's going to cost?" Elmo says, "Well, when Darryl was running the company, we just did it if it was right. We never bothered to figure out what it cost." "Elmo," Gordon says, "just figure out what it's going to cost to recall those hundreds of prints and remix and then put them back out again." Elmo comes back later with a figure of $150,000. So Gordon shows him the box office figures, which were all through the roof, and all the incredible reviews, and he says, "You know what, Elmo, I think I'll use that $150,000 for extra radio and TV spots to promote the picture!" [laughs] And he kicked his ass out of there and Elmo was gone soon after. That's typical of the kind of moronic behavior I've run across since day one. It's a constant struggle.

VM: It sounds like you have to be a real chess player to survive as a filmmaker.

WF: The toughest problem any filmmaker has is with the studios. And it's a classic encounter. They're not always right, you're not always right. But for the most part, you have people making decisions who don't know what the fuck they're talking about! People who've never really been involved in the making of a film at any level! They've been lawyers, agents, stockbrokers . . . and they're making the big decisions! It's very seldom that a guy who's never been in the trenches winds up running a studio. And unless you've been there, you don't know the problems.

VM: Tell me about the genesis of *The Exorcist*.

WF: Well, I knew (author) Bill Blatty. I used to see him at the races. Periodically he'd send me one of his novels or a script that he wrote. I thought they were always nice stories . . . light stuff. I liked him. Nice man. One day I'm on tour with *The French Connection*. Bill calls me up, says he has this book he's written that he wants me to read, that Warner Bros. wants to make it into a film. So, Bill sends me the galleys, it reaches me on the road. I put it off for a while, until Bill called me and asked if I'd read it yet. I said "no." So, feeling obligated, one night at dinner I opened it up and started reading this book called *The Exorcist*. And I couldn't stop. It was like, unbelievable. Another dimension. It was as good or better than anything I'd ever read by Edgar Allan Poe. Just brilliant. So, I called him up and told him how much I loved it. He tells me he had started writing it as an undergraduate at Georgetown. Took him fifteen years to complete it. He had seen the files at Georgetown University of this actual case that occurred in 1949. "You want to do a film of this?" he asks. "Absolutely." So, he goes to Warners, and Bill had director approval on this, and they say they're making a deal with Mark Rydell to direct it. Mark Rydell had just directed *The Cowboys* with John Wayne.

Warners thought it was their best movie ever and told Blatty that he had to see it. Blatty, who was very Machiavellian, had [told] all sorts of people in the executive office at Warners what was going on. Turns out Warners had originally given it to a guy named Paul Monash to do. Monash was going to rewrite it, set it in Salem, Massachusetts, change everything. Blatty hauled out his contract and backs them off. So Blatty goes down to see *The Cowboys* to humor them, walks out after the first reel. Frank Wells, may he rest in peace, calls Blatty to see what he thought, and Blatty tells him that he wants me to direct it. I understand they had to pay off Rydell since they had a deal with him. Mark's a very good director. I really like his work and I like him. But Bill felt he could communicate with me. So, I got that picture because of Blatty.

VM: Your next film was *Sorcerer*, one of my favorite films. You really brought your own voice and sensibility to it, rather than "remaking" *The Wages of Fear* directly. I also remember it was really overlooked by the public when it came out. Why is that?
WF: I have no idea. It's usually not a huge hit because the audience didn't like it. It's never the fault of the distributor in my opinion, or a bad campaign or anything else. It just didn't work enough for the audience enough to make it a hit.

VM: A lot of people now view it as an overlooked masterpiece.
WF: I had seen *The Wages of Fear* and I thought it was a great film. It was really a theme about brotherhood. You had four guys, total strangers to each other, hated each other, and had to cooperate with one another or die. Make a last stand together or die. And I thought that this was really a metaphor for the world, for all the various nations of people who hated each other, yet had to find a way to live together, or perish. This theme should be continuously revived and presented to an audience. So I didn't want to remake *Wages*, I wanted to take that theme and do a new version with my own kind of spin on it that was based on the Georges Arnaud novel. I just thought it was another interpretation of a great classic. At one time I had Steve McQueen, who wanted to do it. He read the script, by Walon Green and I, loved it, thought it was one of the best scripts he'd ever read. He asked where were we gonna shoot it. I said, "I don't know. Mexico, the Dominican Republic. . . ." He didn't want to leave the country, thought we should shoot it here. He was just starting his relationship with Ali MacGraw and didn't want to be away from her, so he said, "Why don't you write something for her." I said, "You just told me it was one of the best scripts you ever read, now you want me to put a whole new character in there for her?" "Well, make her associate producer or something." I said, "Ah Steve, fuck off!" One of the biggest mistakes I've ever made. I wasn't thinking of the importance of the close-up versus the wide shot. The most beautiful location in the world doesn't mean shit next to Steve McQueen's face. I didn't know that then,

but I certainly do now and I just let it slide with Steve. And Roy Scheider is terrific in the film, just wonderful, but Steve . . . just had the whole baggage he brought with it. And there were other actors I had who would've done it with Steve, like Lino Ventura and Marcello Mastroianni would've done the film with him. That's the cast I had if I could've gotten Steve. I said, "I don't need stars, I'll just make it with four good actors." And I did.

VM: *Cruising* is your most controversial film. Did the public outcry surrounding that surprise you?

WF: It did to a great extent. Really the gay community was split. There were people who did not want shown anything that would present the gay community in anything but a good light, because the struggle for gay rights was in its very early stages then (1980). And I could see where the leaders of a certain element of the community would find this abhorrent because it wasn't showing the image of gays that they were promoting. On the other hand, there were a great many gays who saw the film who knew and understood that world and felt it was honest to that. A few years ago it was rereleased in San Francisco at the Roxy Theater in a brand new print, and the same outlets who'd ripped the shit out of it fifteen years earlier, like *The Chronicle*, gave it four stars. It got glowing write-ups in the gay press and guys were saying, "This is how some of us were." I never made the film to have anything to do with the gay community other than as a background for a murder mystery. It was not meant to be pro or con, gay rights, or gay anything. It was an exotic background that people, I knew, hadn't seen in a mainstream film. That's what intrigued me about it. I had never seen it, but heard about it and decided to go around to the various (gay) clubs and saw what was going on, said that this was incredible. And I decided to write the story based on what I'd seen and on a story that one of the [*The*] *French Connection* cops told me, Randy Jurgensen, that he'd experienced when he was sent out as a decoy in the gay world to catch a killer who was targeting gays. And Randy was hung out to dry in that situation and it really screwed him up. It made him start to question his sexuality. And I made the film, which I think leaves a lot to be desired as a film. It was severely cut, some of the best stuff was cut out of it. It was compromised severely then. It should've gone out as an 'X' picture, but they couldn't.

VM: One thing I've noticed in a lot of your films is that you have morally ambiguous protagonists, many of whom are unsympathetic initially, but you wind up caring about them, even if they're scumbags. What do you think it is that draws you to darker subject matter and characters?

WF: My belief that that's really closer to the way the world is. I can only deal with characters that I know and understand and I've found that most of the people I know and have met are a combination of a great many things. They're not all good and not all evil. There's evil in good men and good in evil men. Hitler was beloved of his inner circle, and of Eva Braun and of his dog, Blondie. There's photographs of Hitler with little German children, him just beaming at these beautiful little kids, and them looking up at him like he's this benevolent granddaddy. And it's Hitler! Even though the foundation of American films is based on good guys and bad guys, that's not my experience in life. Or in self-analysis. There are times when I know my own motives are low, base, self-serving, and there's other times when I'm able to do things that are quite selfless and kind and helpful to others and warm. I have and we all have these forces, good and evil, constantly at war within us. And sometimes the war is lost badly for the forces of good. Like Jeffrey Dahmer, or (Andrew Cunanan) for the Versace murder. I don't believe that he was born evil. But there was a mother that loved him at one time when he was a little child. And I tend to see these things. I don't want to make the guy a hero, by any means, but my initial impulse when I hear someone has crossed the line and committed a violent act is sadness. Sadness at the loss to all of humanity. And I feel that same sadness when I lose that battle within myself. Why make a film about someone, unless you're going to reveal something about their humanity?

VM: What prompted you to remake *12 Angry Men*?

WF: A couple years ago my son and a few of his friends were around the house talking about "What is a jury?" and "What is reasonable doubt?" in the Simpson case. I had a video of *12 Angry Men* and I showed it to them. And while it really wasn't their kind of film, they were fascinated by it because it did sort of answer those questions. While I was watching it with them, I said, "This is great! This is a classic!" I had been reading a whole bunch of lame scripts that had been sent to me where I couldn't get past page ten, and now all of the sudden, here's this great piece of material. And I started to think that they just don't write them like this anymore and why aren't we making films like this and wouldn't it be great to do this with a superb cast today, and with every generation because it tells us a lot about ourselves as well as the American justice system. . . . It was actually revived in London on stage last year, directed by Harold Pinter!

VM: You assembled an amazing cast. What was it like working with actors of such varying ages and styles?

WF: Everyone has their own style and way of working and some of it was a surprise to me. For example, I expected that the real veterans would come in knowing their lines from the get-go, having it all down, which is usually how the old-timers of that period worked. Jack Lemmon comes in like a contemporary actor. He's read the script, but doesn't have a clue what he's going to do until the rehearsal. You find it together. A man like Hume Cronyn comes in with the whole thing and he's got it and the work there is to keep him from being so set, and helping him to discover it more. It was twelve guys with twelve different approaches to acting. And they brought with them total dedication because they saw what I saw in the material: that they don't write them like that anymore.

VM: How much was changed from the original text?

WF: Not that much. We wanted to keep it pretty timeless. Originally, I thought about having some women in it, but it's really not written for women. It's about men. About testosterone. In the same way that *Little Women* is about women. But I did know that I wanted to have some minority actors in this version instead of the all-white cast like in the original. Besides that we added a few modern references to the dialogue, but . . . the clothes, the room where it's set, we all tried to keep very timeless. But it's an all-male jury because that's the title! The attitude towards it now is very different from when Reginald Rose wrote it in the fifties as a very liberal statement coming out of the McCarthy era, saying that even though some people appear to be guilty of something they may not be, and we have to examine that and not be quick to label people.

VM: How long do you rehearse before you shoot?

WF: Generally, I don't rehearse at all. I rehearsed *12 Angry Men* for eight days. But generally, I don't believe in rehearsal. I believe in talking with the actor, working out what you're going to do, then putting it in front of the cameras to get spontaneity. The biggest concern I have with any film I make is that it seems too set where all the words are spoken perfectly, and all the camera moves are perfect. I don't like films like that. I want my films to seem like real life, like it's really happening. The best films for me are the ones where you're not conscious of a writer or director or photography or anything and there it is. That there's just these people and they seem to be just who they are. I rehearsed *The Exorcist* for a month and the best performances I ever saw of it were left in the rehearsal room. When we finally got to the shooting, it wasn't as fresh.

VM: How do you maintain tension on the set during a tense scene?

WF: By keeping the set tense. By getting in actors' faces. By getting them shook up. Very often I would fire a gun to get people's nerves completely frayed, then shoot. I have gunshots being fired all over the set.

VM: Are studios today making the sort of pictures that attracted you to filmmaking in the beginning?

WF: No. If I were a young kid today, I wouldn't want to go into film. I remember years ago when I met (the directors) Billy Wilder and Richard Brooks. And some of the films we've talked about I talked to them about. And I would hear them constantly bemoaning the state of American film, realizing that the shit that we were making was not impressing them. They thought it was better when they were doing it. And I remember thinking then, that if I ever get that way, I gotta hang it up. Because I loved the films of that period (the sixties) because they spoke to me. And I realized that they had made great films in another era, but that's past and changed. And that's my attitude about it. I frankly don't like most of what I see. I think it's imitative and derivative and usually done without anything coming from inside. Most of the films are manufactured like a product rather than being born of the need to communicate some idea onto film. But I recognize that they're not making these films in a void. Audiences today are responding to them. So, you can sit back and say, "That's a load of shit," or you can go out and make your own film that you hope an audience will respond to in whatever terms you can live with. It's like that old joke Mort Sahl used to tell about Werner von Braun, father of the rocket (who developed explosive rockets for Germany during WWII). He said, "Werner von Braun's autobiography is called *I Aim at the Stars*. What it should really be called is *I Aim at the Stars, but Sometimes Hit London*." I very often aim at the stars as a filmmaker, but sometimes I hit London [laughs].

Harold Lloyd Master Seminars with William Friedkin

American Film Institute / 2003

From AFI's Harold Lloyd Master Seminars, March 12, 2003 © 2003, courtesy of American Film Institute.

Host: This seminar is called the Harold Lloyd Master Seminar and I just want to underline the word "master" in this context. I don't think that we have ever had a guest who was more appropriately called a master than Billy Friedkin. His work is staggering. I mean, you've saw the works. Nobody makes films the same way after *[The] French Connection*, or *The Exorcist*, or *To Live and Die in L.A.*, all those films just profoundly altered the cinema landscape. It's such a privilege to have him here with us. Please help me welcome Billy Friedkin. Where should we start, Billy? I mean, I think it would be nice to visit your auteur. How Billy Friedkin creates. And, of course, everything starts with the choice of the material. What do you do? You must have received a lot of offers, a lot of opportunities. How do you make your selections?

William Friedkin: Okay. Well usually I have to say that the project finds me. I don't find the project, it somehow finds me, and that continues into the process of making it. I have no idea what the final shape of a film is going to be until I make it and then get it into the editing room. There was an interview with Stravinsky, the great Russian composer, [who] had written amongst other things probably the most significant piece of music of the twentieth century which was *The Rite of Spring*. When it was first performed in 1913, it was outrageous. How many of you have ever heard that? Quite a few of you. It was, at the time an outrageous, almost an assault on the senses. And Stravinsky was asked how did he come to write *The Rite of Spring*, how did he think this up. And he said, "I am the vessel through which *The Rite of Spring* passed. And this is true, I think, for filmmakers. The composer, before he can write down the music, notate it, he has to hear it. In order to hear it, you have to be open to it; you have to listen for it. I mean, you have to really concentrate to listen to the music before you can write it. As a filmmaker, the film is always talking to you. It is telling you on the set, and in the cutting room, "I am not this; I am that," "This is what I want to be," "I can't carry the weight of that, but I can carry this much weight"; and you listen for that. You open yourself to what the film is telling you, about its rhythms, about its subject matter, about where the cuts should come, and it really is a process where, if you can attach yourself to it, the film speaks to you. I had no idea about many elements in *The Hunted*, or in any of my films, how they would finally evolve, and we can get into more specifics, how they would evolve until I heard the film in the cutting room, and so a lot of things were changed, including the beginning and the end was never scripted. It was almost a completely different movie that I set out to do. But the movie, it has a way of speaking to the filmmakers, and then it's a question of "Are you willing to listen to it?"

Host: We watched, the last couple of days, *The French Connection*, *To Live and Die in L.A.*, and this film, of course. I couldn't help noticing themes which reoccur in these films. For instance, when I saw this I was, "Okay, here's a film which is instead of the urban grit, which is the two previous films, and has an incredible kinetic energy, with all the grittiness, and chase, and aggressiveness, and here it is a bucolic nature. And how do you transfer this, transform this into something which allows you to have the same cinematic energy with the hunting, with the chase, with the movement forward, I mean that's something must have occurred to you.

WF: The style of the picture is, believe it or not, mostly dictated by the locations. I will get an idea of no more than "Gee, I think I'd like to shoot a film in the Pacific Northwest," and I knew Seattle somewhat, but I didn't know Portland that well, and that set off an alarm. I haven't seen Portland used a lot in films. I know there were a couple of early Gus Van Sant films made in Portland, but it hadn't really been used, so that idea attracted me. It could have been shot anywhere, but you know, you've seen a lot of L.A., and New York, and Chicago, and even Boston now. So I went up to Portland and I found that the city was very unique and interesting, but what was more interesting was the area around it. The Silver Falls area and Mount Hood, and that's what attracted me to make the film in that part of the world, and so then the locations, you know, "what's happening at this waterfall," or that bridge in the city. I will let the locations, I open myself to how the locations dictate how I might do a sequence there, and we don't have anything written; there was nothing written for the bridge in Portland until we got there and said, "Well that looks interesting, let's use that." "Well how?" And the same thing happened to me with [*The*] *French Connection*. The chase wasn't written, I just walked for fifty-five blocks one day in New York with my producer. We needed to come up with a chase, and we just started throwing ideas out, while the subway was rumbling underneath our feet. A couple of years before, the film *Bullitt* had come out, which had a really celebrated car chase, and I wanted to do something different, and so just listening, you know, I heard the subway, and then, "Well, how can I use this subway? Do the whole thing on the subway? No, maybe a car chasing the subway train." Then I had to go and figure out if that was possible. I had no idea how fast a subway train could go at top speed. When I found out it was only fifty miles an hour, I knew I could do a chase with a car that had started way behind the elevated train in this case. I start with the theme of the film, and the theme of, I think of almost all of the films I made, is the thin line between the policeman and the criminal, the thin line between good and evil; that's what attracts me. If something comes along, and it's unconscious, even though I know this and I can verbalize this to you, that that's my theme, I'm not conscious of it when choosing the story, or not conscious of it as a body of work, unless in a situation like this, I'm forced to examine it. But that is the theme that attracts me—my belief that there's good and evil within all of us. I don't make films about heroes and villains. Each person, with rare exception, has both things going on at all times.

Host: That actually categorizes your endings, which are never euphoric. There's always a certain amount of resignation, that things cannot be resolved.
WF: I don't think they can, you know? Just look at the world, look at life. There's so little resolution to anything. Ultimately, we have no idea where this life will lead us, or if it will lead us anywhere, other than belief. You must have a strong belief, and that's what carries you through everything. But that's the theme I see myself coming back to, and it's echoed in all of the films I made. I try to not resolve the endings, because I like to have a lot of stuff go out into the audience, and let the audience decide what this is about, and very often people will come to different conclusions, and that's fine.

Host: Back to your methodology of how you construct your story and respond to locations and environments; how much do you credit your documentary background? All your films are very astutely aware of what can be done: locations, gestures, objects. There is a texture or quality which is quite unique.
WF: Yeah, thank you. Well, I made documentary films before I did feature films, and before I made documentaries I did live television. I learned only one thing from live television, and that was that the whole process is about communication. Communication between a filmmaker and his crew, or his cast, or the writer, or the cinematographer, and in the case of live television you don't even have those titles, you know, "cinematographer," the cameraman. But in order to fulfil whatever notion you have, you've got to be able to communicate it through other people. You know, it's the one art form which is totally based on collaboration. Unlike writing, which is a very solo business. You can sit alone with a blank sheet

of paper. Painting with a blank canvas. You don't need to work with anybody; you go inward. Film has been called the one-ton pencil; you need a ton of equipment, and you need to communicate. So, the only thing that I learned from live TV was you must communicate, and ultimately communicate with an audience. That's what you're doing, is trying to communicate with an audience.

From documentary, I learned a bit more. I learned that, for example, when you go out to film a documentary, you have no idea what's going to happen, unless you're doing something about the past. If you're doing something about the present, things are happening and you're trying to capture it; you don't know what people are going to say or do, and so the camera has a little bit of nervousness about it, and you have to move around to follow people, or to follow a car, or so follow some—a group, whatever, soldiers in the Vietnam war, or whatever it is, you can't control it until you get in the cutting room. And I learned that you could take that notion of being unable to control the picture and induce that into the style of telling the story in pictures, and that's what I do; that's really all that I do. I induce a documentary style. For example, the camera is always handheld. Every shot. Even a still shot of two people. The camera's always handheld so there's a little bit of nervousness around the edges, giving the audience the sense that anything might happen in this moment. Yeah, two people are just stationary someplace, but somebody may move, or say something, or do something, and the camera's ready.

The other thing that I try to do is stage a scene like what I describe what happens in a documentary, and that is people move around and you have to follow them. This opens up the fourth wall. As you all know a film is nothing more than height and width; it's the illusion of depth, but there is no real depth, and when the camera just stays concentrated on one scene, and then cuts here, or cuts there, you're still utilizing the fourth wall that is used in a stage, you know, when you're sitting out at a play and you're seeing only what's happening on that stage. What I like to do is stage a scene and follow actors or actresses from over here, over to here, maybe back this way, maybe then back that way, and do 360 degrees and break the fourth wall. I will always attempt to do that. There's one shot that comes to mind in *The French Connection*, when you see Gene Hackman running down the stairs from an elevated platform, and the camera follows him down the stairs over to a view of a street this way, where he tries to hail a car down, and he can't, they pass him by, so he runs over here, tries to do the same thing, and then comes back this way where he finally does succeed, he gets into a car and goes around that way. And so that breaks the fourth wall, and makes a scene like that, which is almost—you know, it's certainly fictional, it's very hard to do that in real life, but I'm showing it to you to try and "convince you" with quotes around it, that it's actually happening. And you can do that by the induced documentary style. Bust the fourth wall whenever possible.

Host: The camera is always just a tiny bit behind, therefore giving us the illusion that the camera discovers what is happening right there.
WF: Absolutely.

Host: "I didn't stage it, I discovered it."
WF: That's exactly right. And then in the editing style, the only principal I take with me is from another filmmaker called Michelangelo Antonioni, whose work is completely different from mine. Totally different in every way. I admire his work tremendously. But what I perceived from him is the sense of not repeating a shot. You can look at an Antonioni film and there'll be maybe ninety or a hundred cuts without a repeat, as opposed to what people are used to, who are mostly conditioned by television, where you'll see, if [HOST] and I are standing here, there's a camera here over my shoulder to him, camera over his shoulder to me, then a closeup of each of us, and as an audience you can sit out there and go like this. You know what the next shot's going to be. You know the minute they go to his close up they're gonna follow with mine, then drop wide, and it's a predictable pattern that the audience can sense; they're way ahead of all the filmmakers, but Antonioni would do a scene and then never intercut within the scene, he would then go to the next scene. If there was a cut, if he shot over my shoulder to [HOST], the next shot would not be a close up of [HOST], but a shot from over there, followed by another shot that wasn't used before maybe from down here or whatever, but there's no repeated pattern of cutting, and that's what I try to do.

Host: Enormous courage in his cutting, from extreme long shots to extreme closeups; it jolts you. I recall the first and the second shot I think, in *To Live and Die in L.A.*, there's a very long shot and then you cut to the flag of the car moving, and it's like "Wow, where is that coming from?" and then you open up later to actually discover it. That is something that Antonioni did quite a lot.
WF: And a great master of that in American film was George Stevens. Look at the editing in the fight scene in *Shane* between Van Heflin and Alan Ladd, where there's enormous wide shots of two guys fighting. You can't even hear them, you can barely see them, there's some horses in the foreground, and then there'll be a tight closeup of a horse's flank from a big wide shot . . . dynamic. Stevens was a director I urge you guys to study because he had a great sense of the possibility of dynamic cutting in film, and always to surprise the audience. The greatest piece of direction that I've ever heard about was Diaghilev's advice to Nijinsky. Serge Diaghilev was the great ballet master of the Ballet Russes de Monte Carlo, and Nijinsky was his principal dancer. He was considered one of the greatest dancers who ever lived, and one day before a performance, Diaghilev said to Nijinsky—because they were mostly appearing in France or Monte Carlo he spoke French to him—he said,

"Etonnez-moi," which means "Astonish me," and to me I think that's the greatest thing a director can say to an actor. You know he said it in such a way that he really infused him with the ambition to astonish, and that's what you're trying to do with your actors and whoever's working with you. But you're not going to go up to a cameraman who's from New Jersey or Brooklyn and say, "Etonnez-moi," you know, they're gonna look at you like you're crazed or something, but that's what you're trying to do. You're trying to inspire the people you're working with to do better.

Host: Talking about acting, it's also different again—you talk about the spontaneity, the documentary background is something, but if I recall, Gene Hackman, my god—*The French Connection*, the reality of the looseness, the spontaneity of the performances are extraordinary, and that's running throughout the film you made. How do you rehearse, or do you rehearse with them? Or do you select actors simply who can give it to you? What gives that?

WF: Ninety to ninety-five percent of it is the casting. If the person is cast right, the director doesn't have to say a lot, but you never know if you've cast it right 'til after the fact. But I don't rehearse at all, not at all. I rehearsed *The Exorcist* for a month, in a room above a restaurant in New York, before we shot it, and what I finally saw in the rehearsal I could take and put on a stage. It was so locked. The actors were so into their parts, and then after, like, the second week, they started to repeat stuff, and they started to fix in on what we had rehearsed, and I don't want that. I want the performance to look like it's living. So, I then had to change the whole blocking, and everything else before I took *The Exorcist* to the cameras, because they were fixed, they could've played it on stage the same way every night for a year, and since then, and that was about 1973, I don't rehearse. I'll just talk to the actors, you know, we just talk, and I'll tell them basically what the shot's about, what I'm going to do.

I worked slightly differently, for example, with Tommy Lee Jones and Benicio Del Toro. I've worked before with Tommy Lee, he is the most intelligent actor I've ever met, and that's what you're looking for more than anything else in an actor, is intelligence; without that, forget it. By "intelligence" I mean, how deep do they get it, and Tommy Lee gets it very deeply. And he's been around a long time, so you don't waste time with him. The way I work with him is I'll say, "Alright, you come in that door, you walk over here, come up this, you stand over here, you talk to the gentleman over here, and then you go over there and you sit down, stand up, look around, speak from down there, then you go back out the door that way." And he'll say, "Let me see if I've got this right," and he'll repeat it to me, and he'll say, "Okay, would you put a mark on the floor there, put a mark here, put a mark there. Fine, I'm okay." And then we go out and shoot it, and he invests it with his incredible humanity and understanding of what the camera's doing. We never talk about the meaning of a scene anymore, or anything relating to trying to push something out there. With Benicio Del Toro, he wants to talk about, you know, stuff that isn't even on the page, stuff that isn't in the script. "What happened to this guy twenty years ago?"; "Why has he come to this moment?"; "What are the options that he has?"; "If I don't do what you just asked me to do, what else can I do?"; you know, and he will study and research his character. I mean, he talked to endless numbers of guys on the special forces before he came to do this. So, he works very hard to absorb the reality of a roll that he's undertaking, and Tommy Lee instinctively gets it, goes out, and does it. So, they arrive at the same destination, but they take different paths.

Host: How would you block with Benicio though? I mean, would that be so precisely directorial? You say, "This, and this, and this, and that, and go," or would that be a more spontaneous interaction because of his methodology?

WF: What you do is—and because both those actors, for example, respected each other, and respected each other's process. You know, Tommy Lee would let me spend a little more time with Benicio, and I'd let him try and find his way into the scene a little more, and if I saw, what often happens if you tell an actor, "Okay, just don't worry about the camera or anything, go over and do what you feel," you know, "Do what you want to do, and then let's work the scene through that way." Nine out of ten times the actor will turn and face the wall over here and go somewhere where you can't even shoot them. This happens inevitably. Or he'll want to—not Benicio—if you just say to an actor, "Do what you feel like," they're gonna hide instinctively. So, I'll let the actors who work that way go through that process, and then I might just say, "Well, if you do that, if you go over there and turn your back on me I won't be able to have a shot of you"; "Oh, okay." It's not extreme, I mean it literally works out that way, so you'll suggest a staging, let the actor try something else, and then let him realize the adjustments, and very often you as the director have to make adjustments because they could come up, and often do come up with a better staging than you've given them. And the camera always has to be flexible to catch whatever. On *The French Connection* and on [*The Hunted*] I would often say to the camera operator, because so much of it was shot outside, "Guy's going to be coming along over here," and then the operator would have to find him; no rehearsal, no focus marks, you know, and so everyone is on edge to perform to the best of their abilities, but there's no rehearsal of it, and that is why you said earlier there seems to be an improvisational air to a lot of these films. There is, because it is. It's improvised, but we've done a lot of talking beforehand. I've talked to the actors, I've pointed them in a direction that I think they can take, and in the case of Benicio he goes out and studies it, Hackman and Scheider went out with the New York City cops and experienced what it was like to go in and bust a bar or put a frisk on somebody, you know, put your life out there every time you go out. So the two actors, they had that feeling before I asked them to do it in front of a camera.

I like the fact that an actor will research his role, go out, get a sense of it. Then what I do is I will always cast other people in the scene with them who are really doing that job. Like every FBI guy in this picture is a real FBI guy, either from Portland or L.A. Every time I have a doctor in a scene, I'm not talking about major roles, but a doctor, or a nurse, or whatever. A policewoman, or an FBI woman like Connie Nielsen. She did that scene where she briefs the FBI in front of thirty real FBI people. And I'll very often use bad guys to be in a scene where there's supposed to be bad guys around. This gives a sense to the stars of the picture, a sense of reality that you cannot infuse. First of all, they get confidence if they're doing well. If somebody's playing a cop, and another cop or two is in a scene with them, and the cop goes like this after a take [gives the "okay" sign], the actor, "Oh, I must be doing the right thing." Or sometimes the cop will say, "You know, we wouldn't stand like that," or "If you're gonna frisk the guy you gotta do it this way," and I let that happen, because it gives the actors tremendous confidence being in a scene with people who are really doing that work. It also affords me the opportunity— there are people who do certain things that you cannot get a day player to do. You know, you cannot teach a day player, someone who comes in for one day on the film, to behave like a real, for example, FBI person, or a member of a SWAT team, or whatever. The guy who does that job knows it better than you could ever get out of an actor who's not a principal.

Host: Let's talk a little bit about your collaboration with your cinematographer, production designer. . . . I mean they may get the misconception that you are totally spontaneous. I'm pretty sure there is a lot of planning that's going on, which allows you the spontaneity.
WF: Yeah, with the cameraman, with the director of photography, the first thing is you tell them the way you want to do it, and he listens and he comes up with suggestions that make it possible. You know, he's contributing as much as I am.

Host: In the blocking process?
WF: Oh yeah, you know I'll say very often, I work with Caleb Deschanel, who's world class, on this film, AFI graduate, but I don't hold that against him, because I never studied film as you can probably see. I had one lesson that lasted a half hour, along with Bill Butler, who was my first DP. But I'll very often say to Caleb, once he's infused with the idea of shooting the film in this way, I'll say, "So maybe we should be over here and let him go this way," and he'll say, "I've got a better angle from up there." "Let's take a look. You're right . . . let's do it." It's a total collaboration, in which the cinematographer, for example, is improvising as well.

My production designer and art director are on the set, and you know, here's this set, it's real, but then we'll say, "Geez, it'd be great if there were some trees in the foreground here, you know—boom, they come up and make it happen. I don't work from designs; I work from just talking with the people I'm gonna work with. I don't storyboard. I don't recommend that, but I can see a film in my head. It's not the film I wind up with, but I see some film in my head, and I set out to make that, and as I'm doing it I realize how misconceived it is because I need that chaotic edge, and I have to get back on the surfboard before I collapse. And so, I need that edge. I can't go out there with storyboards and a plotted schedule of shots, and stuff that's predetermined. I've tried that, and I just don't get interested enough, or energized enough to go forward. I like to make the set experience one of tension and everybody working on the edge.

Host: Discovery. A process of discovery.
WF: Yeah. Now if I was making a comedy or something that was totally reliant on timing of jokes and stuff like that, you can't do that for the most part. You can't do that. Or a musical. Like, I direct operas as well now, and that's a marvelous process, and you're working with a score. Very often a score that's over a hundred years old or more. And it's set; you can't change a note. That's the score. And the guy who wrote the score, like the next opera I'm doing, was Richard Wagner. He did the libretto too and you ain't gonna change that either, not a word of it. But that's a great discipline for me, to work with a finely structured piece of work, where I stage the singers like I would a play, but I can't change anything.

Host: But can you find yourself in it though? I mean, can you feel that this is something that you're part of it, despite the fact that you can't change it?
WF: I only will do an opera that I feel a kinship with. And so yes, what the director of an opera is doing is staging it, thinking up the concept of how it's going to look, how it's going to be lit, what kind of sets, whether the sets will be real, or three dimensional, or projections, or what. And then the other wonderful thing about that—and I urge any of you who are trying to direct to do things other than make film—it is a necessity, collaboration in an opera. You're collaborating as a director with the conductor, and he has as much to say about how this thing is being presented as you do. You know, the tempo and the levels, and everything else, are dictated by the conductor. And if I want to stage a singer in a certain way that the conductor doesn't feel he has enough eye contact with him, I have to adjust the staging. That's why you often see an opera that's little more than a concert, where the singers come down and sing and look at the conductor. So, I'm trying not to do that, but I still have to maintain that contact, so what I do is put monitors all over the place, you know, in the wings, wherever, down here, back there, so that

the singers can look away from the conductor and still see him conducting off in the wings. But it's collaboration, and that's what filmmaking is. Whether you do it in an unorthodox way, as I do, or by the numbers, you've got to collaborate with the people you're working with.

Host: I really didn't tell Billy to emphasize this, but this is our main theme in this conservatory.
WF: Collaboration?

Host: Absolutely.
WF: Well that's it. I mean, communication, that's what directors do. I mean, look, the worst guy I ever met in terms of communicating on a personal level, was Alfred Hitchcock. He was extremely uncomfortable in public. He was uncomfortable with applause, or if people would tell him they liked this or that; he was extremely shy. Now you wouldn't think of that seeing his movies. But then, I directed the very last *Alfred Hitchcock Hour* that was made, but I also observed him, and I saw him when I was a kid growing up in Chicago. And he had come to Chicago to do some location shots for *North by Northwest*, and there was a shot of Cary Grant coming out of the Tribune Tower and walking over into a car or hailing a cab or something, but I remember he came out of Tribune Tower, and it was a night shot, and I used to work at Tribune Tower, and I watched Hitchcock direct this scene. Hitchcock never got out of his car. The assistant directors would run back and forth to Hitchcock's car, and Cary Grant must've walked out of that building thirty times. Now, I couldn't tell what the difference was, you know, I'm standing on the street with a bunch of other people going, "Oh, he's doing the same thing again. What's different?" Nothing we could see, but Hitchcock could see it. And he didn't have to go out and talk to the actor. He didn't want to. That was too close for comfort. That was like dialogue with somebody. But he had the film in his head. I've had assistant directors and cinematographers who worked with him tell me he communicated to them everything that he wanted, and it was all drawn out, so he never had to say a word, and didn't.

Host: Robert Boyle is in our faculty.
WF: Robert Boyle! Great production designer.

Host: Every scene which was produced as it was written, is given to the production designer.
WF: And he doesn't say much to the cast or to anyone else. They knew; they had a sense of it. I mean it helps also to be working for Hitchcock, where you've seen, I don't know, forty great movies done in a certain way, so a cinematographer

working with him will have an instinct of what he wants to do, or an actor will get it without Hitchcock having to say, "Do it this way, or that way." That comes only out of reputation, and a body of work that's extraordinary. I met the guy. I met him once, or twice actually, and I was very young, directing this *Hitchcock Hour* at Universal. And at that time a guy named Norman Lloyd produced the *Hitchcock Hour*, Hitchcock didn't. He would occasionally direct one, but he mostly came in and just, he read his introductions, those marvelous introductions he did, off of what we called an "idiot card" next to the camera. And he'd come in, and say his stuff, and then leave. And one day I happened to be shooting a scene at the Bates Motel on the Universal lot with John Gavin, who's in *Psycho*, and Hitchcock was walking around the lot, and they brought him over to introduce him to me, and I was like twenty-six or twenty-seven or something. And Hitchcock, oh my god, he had a phalanx of about twenty guys in dark suits, sort of floating with him, and he came over to me and Norman Lloyd introduced him to me, and he said, "Mr. Hitchcock, this is Bill Friedkin." And I said, "I'm really honored to meet you. This is an incredible honor." And Hitchcock put his hand out like this, I thought I was supposed to kiss it, it was like a wet fish. And I said, "It's really an honor to meet you," and he said, "Mr. Friedkin." "Yes sir." He said, "Usually our directors wear ties," and I thought he was putting me on, because he had a great sense of humor. But I said, "No, well, I guess I forgot my tie . . ." and he just turned and waked away. That's the only thing he ever said to me, about that show that I did, or anything. You know I carried this with me for a long time, and I saw the streak of cruelty that ran through those films, and five years later, was the night of the Directors Guild Awards. It was a the Beverly Hilton or some hotel where there were tables, and I had just won the Directors Guild Award for *The French Connection*, and sitting right down there was Hitchcock with a table, and I don't know if he was being honored that night or just showed up, I don't remember that. But there he was and I saw him down there, and so I accepted this award and made a little speech, and then I walked right down to where he was sitting, and I had on one of those clip-on bowties, because I don't know how to tie it, and I sprung my tie at him and said, "How do you like the tie Hitch?" And he just stared at me. He had no idea, but I did. I carried that with me. Five friggin' years. "Usually our directors wear ties" . . . but he's the greatest, I mean look, nobody better in filmmaking. That's it. Stops and starts right there basically. He encompasses all the vocabulary.

Host: You're the product of the sixties, which celebrated cinema. And of course, if you think about what Scorsese, Spielberg, Coppola are doing, I mean the image-making process is a supremely important part of what filmmaking is, and that this ethos that's coming in the sixties when cinema was cinema.

WF: In the seventies when most of the people you mentioned were making films, and I was, our influences were the classic American films and current foreign films. People who were making films then, like Godard, and Antonioni, and Fellini, Truffaut, Kurosawa. Foreign film, we were glued to it. And a foreign film used to come into your town, or wherever, stay in a theater for weeks if not months, one or two theaters, and now I believe that most of the people who make films, and the audiences that watch them, are mostly influenced by television. Because television had no influence on us in those days. And by the way, television was pretty good back then. It was really good; it wasn't formula. You know, there were shows like *Playhouse 90*, with directors like John Frankenheimer, and Sidney Lumet, and Franklin Schaffner; some of the people who became the best American filmmakers did live television shows, and they were exciting and astonishing. But television today, to me, is worse than pornography, in my opinion. I mean, they have a laugh track that tells you when to laugh. Imagine Harold Lloyd with a laugh track on his picture, to tell the audience when it was funny. But that's what they do, you know, you'll see some stupid comedy, two people sitting in a kitchen, he's talkin', she's talkin', she sits down and talks, he stops eating his krispies and talks, they're saying a bunch of jive, and you hear this [exaggerated laughter], "Martha, I told you that wasn't right" [exaggerated laughter], it's terrible, and you know, this conditions people to what's funny today. It's like the television producers feel they have to prod the audience and get them over the hump for everything. And a lot of young filmmakers are influenced by television. They can't help but be. It's not that easy to see a foreign film anymore. I personally don't think there are enough great foreign films as there were. There's no Fellini, there's no Antonioni, Kurosawa, not on that level, no. Or the classic American directors, going back to the silent era, and beyond, up until about the sixties. That to me is the golden era of filmmaking in this country, and those films were worth studying. Films beget film. You learn to make films primarily by watching them, and then thinking about them, and then analyzing them, hopefully with someone who understands.

Cruising with Billy

Alex Simon / 2007

From *Venice Magazine*, September 2007. Reprinted by permission of Alex Simon.

Director William Friedkin restores his controversial classic for a new audience—and a new age.

Released in February of 1980, William Friedkin's (*The French Connection, The Exorcist*) murder mystery *Cruising* had a seemingly simple premise: a cop (Al Pacino) goes undercover in New York's gay S&M leather bar scene to catch a serial killer who is preying on the young men who frequent them. Having made his bones as a documentary filmmaker, Friedkin shot the film neorealist style, using many nonactors, and shooting at the actual clubs and locations that made up the city's homosexual underground. Excoriated by critics, the public, and gay rights advocates alike on the cusp of the Reagan era, *Cruising* proved to be a box office disappointment, and Friedkin didn't make another film for three years.

Nearly thirty years later, time has been kind to *Cruising* and, like several of Friedkin's films (*Sorcerer* and *To Live and Die in L.A.* to name two) that were met with tepid receptions upon their release, it has been re-evaluated by many critics and scholars who have begun to hail it as an overlooked, and much misunderstood, classic, never more evident than after a screening at this year's Cannes Film Festival, where it was featured as part of the Director's Fortnight program, and received two standing ovations from a filmgoing crowd renowned for not suffering fools, or bad movies, gladly.

Long unavailable on home video (and never on DVD), *Cruising* has undergone a painstaking restoration of its audio and video, supervised by Friedkin and editor Bud Smith, with the final result looking like it was shot last week, and feeling like a very contemporary look at a very different time

William Friedkin sat down with *Venice* to speak about *Cruising*, and other cinematic ruminations.

Venice Magazine: Your screenplay for *Cruising* was actually inspired by several different sources, correct?

William Friedkin: I was offered the book *Cruising* by Gerald Walker to direct as a film, by Phil D'Antoni, who had produced *The French Connection*. I read the book and didn't think much of it. It was sort of interesting, but I wasn't compelled to make it into a film at that time. Then Phil went out and got Steven Spielberg interested in making the film. And the two of them tried to get it set up for quite some time and weren't able to. And D'Antoni is a great producer, really tenacious. We were turned down on *The French Connection* by every studio twice until Fox made it. But they finally gave up on *Cruising*. Three or four years later, Jerry Weintraub brought it to me, and said, "I heard you were interested in this, which is why I bought it. I want to do it with you." I said, "Jerry, I wasn't interested in it. In fact, I turned it down with Phil." He said, "Read it again. I think it would be a hell of a film." Jerry's a very persuasive guy, but I still wasn't interested. Then several things happened: there were a series of unsolved killings in New York in the leather bars on the Lower West Side. The mysterious deaths that were taking place in the gay community, that later turned out to be AIDS, but really didn't have a name then. And the fact that my friend Randy Jurgensen, of the New York police department, had been assigned to go undercover into some of the bars, because he resembled some of the victims. Then, the Arthur Bell articles about the unsolved killings. He wrote them for the *Village Voice* as sort of cautionary tales. It was great reportage. Then, there was a fellow who had a bit part in *The Exorcist*, in the NYU medical center during the arteriogram sequence, which was performed by an actual doctor and his assistant in the film. The assistant was later accused of a couple of the murders in the bars. I saw his picture in the papers and I got in touch with his lawyer, who arranged for me to meet with him at Rikers Island Penitentiary. I asked him what happened, and he told me. He also told me the police had offered him a better deal if he confessed to eight or nine of the murders, whether he'd done them or not. And I put that line in the film, because I found it so horrifying. I found out that he got out of prison three years ago, which means he got twenty-five years for what I took to be multiple murders. All of these things came together for what I took to be a kind of perfect storm, and I called Jerry back and said, "I think I know what to do with *Cruising*."

VM: How you came to shoot in the actual bars is also an interesting story.

WF: Most of the real estate where the bars were located was owned by the mafia at that time. I knew one of the guys who ran everything from 42nd Street to the Lower West Side. So, I went to him, and he referred me to the guys who were running them. I met the managers, the bartenders, and a great many people who frequented the bars. I went back a number of times. They knew I was doing research for the film, and they're the ones you see in those scenes. There are no screen extras guild members. These guys were paid as extras, but they were just there, doing their thing.

VM: So, there was no hesitation from any of these guys to being put on film engaging in these very graphic sexual acts?

WF: No. If there were a few guys who were uncomfortable being put on film, they just didn't show up when we were filming. They never protested it.

VM: When I was watching the film, I was thinking that 90 percent of the guys in those scenes must be gone now.

WF: Oh yeah, and a number of the members of my crew died of AIDS later, as well.

VM: Let's talk about Pacino's work in the film. One thing that's really palpable is the obvious discomfort he had being in those leather bars. His unease in those scenes seems to come from a very real place.

WF: Yeah, since all those people and situations in the bar scenes were real, I just put Pacino inside them. But Randy Jurgensen who was the police officer who was assigned to those bars years earlier, it was his discomfort as he would tell me about his experiences and the way he processed those experiences that allowed me to believe that Pacino's reactions were on the money. He was a stranger in a strange land, but that's what the film's about: the crisis of identity. Al was very uncomfortable in those scenes, but he wanted to do the film desperately, although I don't think he had any idea how I was going to go about doing it.

VM: I notice it's the one film he never seems to talk about. During some of the retrospectives of his career recently, it never comes up.

WF: Well, that's a good thing. I don't think that he's the best spokesman for any of the work that he's done. There are some people who can eloquently discuss their work, and others who can't, that just do the work. There's the work, and it speaks for itself. And I think that's him. With many actors, you don't want to hear this stuff anyway, because it robs the audience of the magic that screen acting is all about. And there are many actors who have been in films that don't completely comprehend what it is they're doing, and that's true of Pacino in *Cruising*. And even today, it would be difficult to get an excerpt of *Cruising* on primetime television.

VM: I think one reason the film works so much better now than it did in 1980 is that there's a distance from it now: New York isn't the same city now that it was then, and that gay underground scene really doesn't have to exist anymore because homosexuals are much more accepted by mainstream society today.

WF: Yes, they can look at it as a film, and not put it in a political context, which I never intended it to be. It never occurred to me that the film would be interpreted in a political context.

VM: But you knew it would be controversial?

WF: I knew that not everyone in so-called straight society accepted the gay lifestyle. I also knew there was a split in the gay lifestyle: of people who wanted to stay in the closet and people who didn't give a damn about the closet anymore. And those people who wanted to keep their sexuality private are the ones who objected to the film, and the leaders of the gay community who felt that it wasn't the ideal way to present gay lifestyle in a major studio movie.

VM: I remember sneaking into see *Cruising* when it was first released, when I was twelve.

WF: You owe me three dollars!

VM: You owe me thousands of dollars for the years of therapy I had to undergo after seeing that movie at age twelve!

WF: (laughs) Fair enough. I'll drop my claim if you will.

VM: Done. But what I remember was, it was the toughest time I ever had sneaking into an R-rated movie. In fact, in Phoenix, where I grew up, they had a special rating created for it: an R/X.

WF: Just like the prescription symbol.

VM: Exactly. People were really unsettled and scared of this movie.

WF: I didn't understand their fear then, and I still don't. To me, it's just a murder mystery, with the gay leather scene as a backdrop. On another level it's about identity: do any of us really know who it is sitting next to us, or looking back at us in the mirror? But the vitriol that the film was greeted with still confounds me.

VM: Did you resubmit the film this year to the ratings board?

WF: Yes.

VM: And it still got an R and not an NC-17?

WF: Yes, because the ratings board is different today. It's much more liberal.

VM: How did it get an R then?

WF: I had to cut forty minutes from it, but none of those forty minutes would have affected the story or the characterizations at all. It was just more footage, for the most part, in the clubs. Everything you see now in the clubs in part, you saw in full in my first cut. The sexuality was actual. It was not simulated. I took the film back to the ratings board fifty times before they would give it an R. I know because it cost us $50,000—a thousand dollars a day—to work with the consultant from the ratings board whom we'd worked with in the past when we were faced with other films that had to be resubmitted for a mainstream rating.

VM: I assume that footage is now gone.

WF: We tried to find it, and Warners was happy to put it all back in, either integrated back into the story as it is, or to run it as "extra footage," but we couldn't find anything. United Artists, and all the studios in those days, destroyed everything: outtakes, negatives. They weren't interested in their legacy whatsoever. I felt that if we could find any of it, I wouldn't have put it in as extra footage, because that would have just been playing to prurient interests, because it really was pornography. It was justified that they took it out to give it an R rating, which is what we had to have. But when I was in the clubs, I couldn't give the people boundaries. They were doing what they were doing, and I was filming it.

VM: Tell us about the process of restoring the film that you and your editor, Bud Smith, went through.

WF: When we got the negative from Warners, it was almost totally out of synch. There were soundtracks missing, the picture was out of synch with the sound. The negative looked like they'd held the six-day bike races on it, and it was awful. But because of the digital process, we were able to go in and time every single frame again from the start and sonically clean the picture, so it had no scratches, no splices, no anything. Then we remixed the soundtrack into a 5.1 mix. The sound is now perfect. If there's anything about the film that now achieves perfection, it's the soundtrack. It took months to do it.

VM: I have to admit, the first couple times I saw *Cruising*, I really hated it, both because much of it was over my head, and also the ambiguity of the story and the structure really threw me, much the same reaction as I had to *To Live and Die in L.A.* upon my first viewing. Nearly all of your films, going back to *The French Connection*, are both morally and structurally ambiguous. Why do you like to tell stories that way?

WF: Because that's the way life is. Most of the murders that occur are unsolved, for various reasons. It's hard to convict someone due to the constitutional rights people have and the rules of evidence, that's one thing. The other thing I'd say is that a lot of the guys who investigated these crimes are not the brightest pennies you'll find at the bank. But I'm attracted to unsolved murders as a subject, and it started with my interest in the Jack the Ripper case. There were five murders, four of them right out in the streets of the East End of London. They took place in 1888, and it's unsolved to this day. It's an open file at Scotland Yard. There are so many suspects and rumors about this, and other killings throughout history, I've always been intrigued by it, and I'm not sure why. I've got interests in police matters anyway because of the thin line between good and evil that's in everyone.

VM: I remember you telling me that when you were growing up, in a tough part of Chicago, you ran with a gang and ran afoul of the law a few times yourself.

WF: No question. I didn't know right from wrong when I was a teenager. I had no particular education to speak of. I loved my mother and father and it was finally the fact that I was getting so much on their nerves, I just quit cold turkey and tried to be a human. This happened after I saw my mother crying when I'd been picked up for robbery at Goldblatt's department store as a teenager. But then I developed this fascination that stems from the notion that we all battle good and evil every day of our lives, and it's a struggle for our better angels to triumph over the evil that exists in all of us. So that's what led me to get interested in the world of *Cruising*.

VM: And obviously the gay subculture has interested you for some time. While you're not gay, you directed the screen adaptation of Mart Crowley's landmark play about gay men, *The Boys in the Band*, in 1970.

WF: I've always had many gay friends who were as close friends to me as people who weren't gay. They were just people to me, human beings who I knew and cared about. Society is filled with prejudices and I've spent most of my life trying to rid myself of mine. I take people at face value, and I don't believe that people are defined by their sexuality. It's a small part of what makes up a human being. I don't look at somebody as "a gay," let alone as "a fag," or a black person as "a nigger." I just don't see them that way, and I don't understand that way of thinking, other than my understanding of the fact that human nature has a great many dark passages and impenetrable subterranean basements.

VM: I think it makes people more comfortable to assign labels to things they don't understand.

WF: Absolutely. If you can degrade this other person because of qualities they may possess that are different from yours or, even more frighteningly, that you possess these qualities yourself but can't face them, this often brings about the sort of people who go out and murder blacks, or Jews, or women, or gay people, or any minority out of a self-loathing, or self-hatred. I think the young man who opened fire at Virginia Tech, what drove him was self-loathing, pure and simple. I'm sure he had nothing against most of those people that he fired on.

VM: And that's something you've always touched on in your films, that almost nonexistent line between good and evil. In *To Live and Die in L.A.* I thought Willem

Dafoe's villain was in many ways more admirable than William Petersen's "good guy," because he was very straightforward about who he was.

WF: And the Charnier character in *The French Connection* is a much more admirable human being than Popeye Doyle. That's the thin line between the policeman and the criminal, and between good and evil.

VM: Many of your films have achieved greatness status long after they originally premiered, which is what is happening with *Cruising* now. Do you get a sense of redemption when that happens?

WF: Well it's a good feeling, sure. But it's the same film, and I'm basically the same guy and I often think about the people who are really artists, and I don't place myself in that category, but someone like Vincent van Gogh, who painted for ten years, and made over thirty-five hundred works—oils, drawings, watercolors—and he couldn't sell any. They were hated. No one was interested. Then a few years after he died, because his sister-in-law had managed to preserve his unsold work, his work was recognized and thus she gave van Gogh to history. But you say, "What happened?" A few years after his death, this groundswell started, and there was a complete re-evaluation. Why? Same paintings. Same artist. It's one of life's mysteries that will also most likely remain unsolved.

Exorcising the Past: A Retrospective with William Friedkin

Ian Johnston / 2012

From *The Quietus*, June 22, 2012. Reprinted by permission of Ian Johnston.

When I spoke to William Friedkin back in May 1998, he was promoting the UK rerelease of his 1973 horror landmark *The Exorcist*, though we also conversed freely about other seminal films from his illustrious multidecade career, such as *The French Connection* (1971), *Cruising* (1980), and *To Live and Die in L.A.* (1985).

Next week the seventy-six-year-old director returns to cinema screens in style with *Killer Joe*, starring Matthew McConaughey, Emile Hirsch, Gina Gershon, and Juno Temple.

Adapted from Tracy Letts' play, this ultranoir comedy thriller is an alluringly disagreeable sliver of hardcore Texas intemperance. McConaughey is in particularly fine derisive form as the titular Joe, a West Dallas detective who operates a profitable secondary occupation as a hired assassin.

Ian Johnston: I saw *The Exorcist* again the other day and it was just as chilling as it was the first time I saw it.
William Friedkin: Snuck in the first time 'round?

IJ: Yeah.
WF: I agree with you that it has lost none of its power. It's just an extraordinary story that continues to hold.

IJ: I was wondering what do you think, personally, is the key to the public's continuing fascination with the film?
WF: First of all, it deals with something that is never out of our minds—the whole concept of good and evil. Is there a palpable force of evil in the world? Does it manifest itself in individuals, and if so, is there a force for good out there as well?

So, that's a universal subject that has occupied writers and painters and people of various artistic disciplines and religious disciplines since time immemorial. *The Exorcist* brings it right down into modern times. This is not a film set in biblical times, or in the ancient days, or eighteenth-century New England where they burned witches at the stake. It's set in the contemporary world. It's very realistic and yet it is about inexplicable things, that we all think about and affect us all the time. I think *The Exorcist*, even though it's been ripped off by a lot of very second-rate ideas over the years, it continues to make its presence felt because it takes those things seriously.

IJ: *The Exorcist* makes the practices of modern medicine look really archaic. Was that a point you wanted to make?

WF: Well, it says that modern medicine and modern science—which have supplanted religion in terms of, shall we say, a cure for what ails us—still have their limitations when it comes to certain inexplicable things. You can seek out modern medicine for what is tangible, but what is intangible and tragic are not answered by modern medicine. There is no answer.

IJ: Looking at the picture today, it's refreshing that the pacing is so measured.

WF: It's like that with a lot of films of the seventies, Ian. *The Godfather*, of course, being an example of a film that moves slowly but inexorably. That wouldn't be allowed to be made today. What they are calling "the great films" of Hollywood in the seventies, I don't think they would have anywhere near the same effect today. Audiences have been conditioned by MTV. The kind of action films that everyone seems to want to see, to get it fast. An exception to that is *Titanic*, but it's the exception that proves the rule.

IJ: Things aren't made immediately obvious in *The Exorcist*. The audience has to do some work.

WF: Yes, that's something I think is very important about the film. All of the answers aren't there. I've found over the years, I've said this before, what people bring to the film is what they take from it. If you think of the world as a dark and evil place, unrelieved by anything else, that's what you take from the film. If you think, on the other hand, that there is hope, and that hope and salvation are to be found, you take that from the film.

IJ: Are you a religious man?

WF: Very definitely. Not in a secular way. I don't think that any one religion has the answer in preference to the others. I think there is a lot of good inherent in all of them. I just don't think one has the answer exclusive of any other.

IJ: Is it true that you fired a gun on set to get a reaction from certain actors?

WF: Never with bullets, just blanks. That is something that has been done by film directors for years, before I came on the scene. I remember reading about it when I was just starting out. There was an article in *Life* magazine about George Stevens doing it on the set of *The Diary of Ann Frank*, to get a reaction from people in this house that there was a Nazi occupation. It is very difficult to ask actors in film technique to go from a dead start and to create surprise or fear or shock. It's very difficult. Most often it looks corny or unbelievable or like overacting. So as a film director you will utilize certain techniques to simulate the actions . . . that are real. It was overstated in the documentary [Mark Kermode's 1998 TV doc *The Fear of God: 25 Years of The Exorcist*]. They make much too much of it, naturally, because it sticks out like a sore thumb, so a lot of people ask me about it.

IJ: What do you think of Mark Kermode's theory, in his pretty exhaustive guide to the movie, that *The Exorcist* was mirroring the breakdown of the nuclear family and the struggles within America during that period?

WF: All of that is after the fact. None of it was intended, I can tell you. All we intended to do was to tell the story. What implications that may or may not have had, I for one was oblivious to.

IJ: The sound is fantastic on the print that I saw recently. What was the process you went through to produce that?

WF: There were a lot of different processes and a lot of trial and error. I was always of course influenced by radio drama. When I was growing up in Chicago, before television had any impact we still listened to radio. It would conjure up entire worlds just through the use of the human voice. So, I have always approached the soundtracks to my films as a separate entity and quite apart from, and unique from, the filming process itself. There were a lot of things that were trial and error on *The Exorcist* to produce that track. I didn't have it totally in mind at the outset, and I had a lot of inspiration come to me during the making of the track that went into it.

IJ: Were there any unusual methods used?

WF: Are you talking about the stuff I did with Mercedes McCambridge [the voice of the demon]?

IJ: Yes.

WF: Well, yeah. I don't think that has ever been done before or since. I took her, tied her to a chair, put her through various painful things, including drinking alcohol and eating raw eggs and stuff like that, to produce this sound. But it was stuff that she [McCambridge] understood and wanted to deal with, because she knew that a lot of what she was doing had to be unconscious.

IJ: Do you think your classic 1985 film, *To Live and Die in L.A.*, will get a similar rerelease treatment to *The Exorcist*? Was it overlooked a little at the time of its original release?
WF: I don't recall. I know it got a lot of attention over here and in other countries. I know it won a lot of film festivals, film noir festivals and whatever. I think it's a damn good film.

IJ: The themes within that movie recur in a lot of your work. The highly ambiguous relationship between William Petersen's driven secret service agent and Willem Dafoe's counterfeiter villain . . .
WF: The most important theme in my films is the thin line between good and evil. The fact that, very often, there are equal parts of both in all the characters, which is what I encounter in life. I don't know anyone who is all good, or all evil.

IJ: Do you think that was an aspect of your work that was overlooked in *Cruising*?
WF: I don't know if it was the same in England, but it was a national scandal [in America]. But what's happened, curiously, is a lot of the gay organizations that at the time denounced the film, now praise it. And very often, gay publications that denounced it when it was released, give it a four-star review and say, "Well, you might not like it, but this is the way things were for a certain segment of the gay population." It may be the last time things were like that.

IJ: Would you make a film like that again?
WF: What do you mean "like that"?

IJ: Well, so confrontational and . . .
WF: It's a very unique picture, Ian. I was not trying to make a statement about gay life at all. I was just using a certain segment of gay society as a background for a murder mystery. It was an exotic background. It was the kind of scene that most people were unable or unwilling to look at. It was going on right in the underbelly of New York, as well as elsewhere, where there were a great many murders.

IJ: In that scene?
WF: Yes, in that environment. A friend of mine who was a cop, an undercover cop, who was involved with *The French Connection* case, had the same sort of situation that Pacino had [in the movie]. It was really his story. He told me about his encounters and his reactions to it, which I put into the film.

IJ: It must have been incredibly difficult to do that. He was straight, the cop?

WF: It was very disturbing for him, there was no question about it. It affected him in ways he was not really prepared for. It's affected him even to this day. I still see him. He's just recently retired from the department.

IJ: Could you tell me about *Rampage* [made in 1987 but unreleased in the US until 1992]? I don't think that was given a proper release in the UK at all.

WF: *Rampage* is probably the most realistic and most disturbing film I've ever made. It's kind of an examination of the death penalty, again using an actual case and the change of feelings within one of the major characters, who is a district attorney, about prosecuting the death penalty. I have a feeling that *Rampage* will be a revelation to a lot of people.

IJ: In a number of your films the police feature prominently. Where does your interest in that world come from?

WF: Well, my uncle was a cop. I used to hang around him and his cronies and I used to hear stories about what it was like to be a cop in Chicago in the 1930s. Guys like Capone were still around. My uncle dealt with these kinds of people. So I had an entrée to that world. I was, of course, fascinated by it and terrified to a great extent by it. So I maintained that interest. Most of my films, in one way or another, deal with the thin line between good and evil, the thin line between cop and the bad guy.

IJ: The Popeye character in *The French Connection* is a good example.

WF: Yeah, he is of course the guy with the badge, but in many ways he is just as bad as the dope smuggler.

IJ: He breaks nearly as many rules and laws.

WF: Yeah. The smuggler is a gentleman: he's well dressed, he's respectful to women, especially his wife. He's a gourmet, has fine tastes, and he's otherwise a decent guy. But he's a guy who is smuggling millions of dollars of heroin, with no conscience whatsoever. Whereas the cop—the guy with the badge—brutalizes women and brutalizes the public. He doesn't really care about the public's safety and he steps outside the law. Those characters are real. I didn't make them up.

IJ: Do you find that it's more difficult to make films that you really want to make today? Studios thinking that audiences have to be spoon-fed every detail of plots and so forth.

WF: To that extent, yes. I'm working on six different films now at the same time. And my approach is the same as it always has been, and of course it's very much against the grain today. It was with the grain in the seventies but, yes, audiences want to be spoon-fed today and I find it difficult to do that. I don't make films for the lowest common intelligence. I really respect the intelligence of audiences. I think, for the most part, they are ahead of every filmmaker working today. But there are some of us who keep on doing what we do because it's all we know.

IJ: Whatever happened after *Star Wars* obviously changed the face of cinema. The massive repercussions of that seem to be reverberating on and on.

WF: I think you're right. The reverberations from that are still going on. I think you put it very well: spoon-feeding the audience, giving them stuff that they are very familiar with and where everything is clear from the outset. I prefer films that are more ambiguous, where there is no ultimate answer and the audience has to think through the meaning of the film.

William Friedkin: Why *Sorcerer*'s Spell Refuses to Die

Alex Simon / 2013

From *TheHollywoodInterview.com*, April 2013. Reprinted by permission of Alex Simon.

In the mid-1970s, there were few American filmmakers riding as high as William Friedkin. *The French Connection* swept the 1971 Academy Awards, nabbing Friedkin a Best Director statuette. *The Exorcist*, released two years later, broke box office records to become one of the top-grossing films of all time. Boasting creative power that most directors could only dream about, Friedkin opted to film an updated version of French auteur Henri-Georges Cluzot's classic *The Wages of Fear* (1953).

The result, 1977's *Sorcerer*, became one of the most notorious box office bombs of the 1970s. Its dark, unrelenting tale of four desperate, disparate men (Roy Scheider, Bruno Cremer, Francisco Rabal, Amidou) who undertake a suicide mission by driving truckloads of nitroglycerine across the rugged South American jungle wasn't what the changing tide of audience tastes were buying then, compounded by the fact that *Sorcerer* was released the week before a little picture called *Star Wars*, which changed the Hollywood production (and marketing) landscape forever.

Nearly forty years later, *Sorcerer* is getting a second life. After spending nearly a year painstakingly restoring the film's picture and sound, William Friedkin is presenting its US premiere at the TCM Film Festival on Saturday night, April 12, at the iconic Chinese Theater in Hollywood. Now regarded as an unheralded classic by cinephiles and filmmakers alike (it's among Quentin Tarantino's top five favorite films), *Sorcerer* is also receiving a Blu-ray/DVD release from Warner Bros. Home Video on April 22.

William Friedkin sat down with us at his Los Angeles home recently to recall the birth, death, and resurrection of *Sorcerer*.

Alex Simon: I'm very excited to see the restored print of *Sorcerer* at The Chinese. I haven't seen it projected in over twenty years.

William Friedkin: This new [digital cinema package] of the film is just gorgeous. It looks as it looked when I saw it through the viewfinder. It's just perfect. I remixed the sound into 5.1 and it looks and sounds as I always hoped it would. In Denmark, Tangerine Dream is performing their score live, while I'm there. They're also recording it and doing an extra half hour of music that I didn't use in the film, that isn't on the soundtrack CD. So hopefully, there will be a new *Sorcerer* soundtrack album released soon.

AS: When they scored the film, they hadn't actually seen it, just read the script.
WF: That's right. I told them what it was about, then they sent me the music and I cherry-picked the pieces I liked best. Since they're basically an improvisational band, I said, "Just write your ideas based on what I've told you and what you see in the script."

AS: Let's talk about the restoration process.
WF: 35mm film deteriorates terribly over time, kind of like the old 78rpm records: they were great to have at the time, and were often the original recordings of the artists. But the technology was so flawed, eventually the 78 would get all scratched and you wouldn't have a perfect range of sound. Now we have high-definition sound, which is the way things should sound. I've never understood the purism of the original recording technique. I also don't buy this idea that film is the only pure cinematic form, as opposed to digital, which reproduces the image the way it was meant to be seen.

AS: Was the film in bad shape when you went back to it?
WF: No, it wasn't in bad shape, but neither were the colors true anymore. The prints had long since deteriorated and the negative, even though it had been stored well, the colors had started to fade. You couldn't make prints off it that would have decent color. But it wasn't a fucked-up negative like *The Godfather* was when they went to make a Blu-ray of that. Paramount spent over a million dollars restoring the negative of *The Godfather*.

AS: How long was the entire restoration process?
WF: About seven or eight months, doing color timing and remixing the sound. In the color timing I do, you have to go into each frame, so it's a lengthy process.

AS: Let's talk about why, after the one-two punch of *The French Connection* and *The Exorcist*, you joked you could have gotten a film of your nephew's bar mitzvah financed, you decided on a reimagining of Cluzot's *The Wages of Fear*.
WF: It just struck me as a very solid framework for a story about the mystery of fate. I had just made a film a few years before about the mystery of faith. Those

are the eternal mysteries to me, and Cluzot's film struck me as a great vehicle to deal with the idea of man's fate in the simplest of terms. I was never interested in characters that were all good or all evil. They were engaged, as the world still is, in a constant struggle to survive. That framework struck me as being timeless.

AS: You chose Walon Green, who'd written *The Wild Bunch* with Sam Peckinpah, as your collaborator.
WF: Yeah, Wally Green was a good friend and one of the best young writers around. We created new characters and new situations throughout and kept Cluzot's essential framework. I always thought of it as doing a new production of Hamlet, or one of the classics, as opposed to a remake.

AS: How carefully did you both study *Wages of Fear* before you wrote the script and then shot *Sorcerer*?
WF: We didn't, and neither of us read Georges Arnaud's book, because it was in French. Wally and I were both huge fans of *Wages of Fear* and remembered it well enough that we just worked from those memories. Remember, this was before DVD or even VHS and it wasn't a film that had been widely seen here in the States. There probably weren't a lot of subtitled prints around then, either.

AS: You've talked before about how not casting Steve McQueen in the lead, which would have secured you a cast of international superstars including Marcello Mastroianni and Lino Ventura in support, is the biggest professional regret of your life.
WF: It was a huge regret for years, but not anymore. I think the cast is terrific. I don't know that those three huge stars would have gone as far as the guys we cast, because what they did was life-threatening. McQueen was kind of a daredevil, but we did things that were really unsafe. You want to talk about a regret, that's something I regret. We were very lucky no one was seriously hurt or killed. Very lucky.

AS: I'm thinking of the rope bridge sequence in particular. This was before CGI existed, so everything we see on the screen is real.
WF: Exactly, and yes, the rope bridge was certainly dangerous and all the driving, which was sometimes done by the actors themselves, literally had them behind the wheel on the edge of a cliff.

AS: Let's talk about Roy Scheider. He was just coming off the success of *Jaws*, which I understand through multiple sources, changed him, and not for the better.
WF: He was a piece of cake on *The French Connection*. He was trying to make it then and I mean, Roy would have lay down in front of an L-train if I'd asked him

to. I'm not sure what happened after *Jaws*. I thought about it a bit while we were doing *Sorcerer* and then afterward. I could speculate. I think he was not in a good marriage. This may have had something to do with it. He subsequently got divorced from Cynthia, who I made an assistant editor on *Sorcerer*. I think his personal life was not entirely good, but then it comes down to choices. I don't know, for example, if some other actor than Matthew McConaughey had done *Dallas Buyers Club*, he would've won an Academy Award for that. If it was an actor who didn't have to lose forty pounds, who knows? But McConaughey was on a trajectory. It's a matter of timing and choices and the grace of God. Success in this business has a lot more to do with luck than anything else, being in the right place at the right time.

AS: We're back to the subject of fate again.

WF: It all comes down to fate. There's no real reason I ever should have become a film director. I never studied film, unlike the movie brats of my generation I never went to film school, or even to college. I was never that enamored of film. I saw movies, but I viewed them as entertainment. I was motivated to want to get into live TV, which was a new medium when I was of age, in the middle fifties. So, I took an entry-level job and it just grew from there. It's the equivalent of independent film today. But why did I get the breaks that I got? I couldn't tell you. That's the mystery of fate and to me, that's what *Sorcerer* is about.

AS: The story of how you were finally able to blow up that massive tree trunk in the jungle is a funny one.

WF: There was this guy whose nickname was "Marvin the Torch." He was a Jewish guy from Queens who was in the beauty supply business. He used to use these flammable beauty supplies to take out whole blocks for insurance purposes. I knew a lot of these guys. My special effects team were having a hell of a time getting this tree blown up, and it was a key moment in the film. We couldn't just leave it out. I finally called Marvin in New York, out of desperation. His wife answered and I said, "Hi Mrs. Torch, is Marvin there?" Looking back, that probably wasn't the best strategy on my part. She got very upset and started screaming, "He doesn't do that anymore! You leave us alone!" I convinced her the job I had was legit. Marvin flew out to the Dominican Republic with his case of beauty supplies and he was the one responsible for getting that amazing explosion to happen that you see in the film.

AS: And the robbery of the church was based on a crime committed by one of your cast members.

WF: Yes. His name was Gerry. In a former life Gerry had an . . . interesting occupation. He and his crew had robbed a church in Elizabeth, New Jersey, where we were filming, although not in the same church, where they divided up all the donations from other churches and split them up, according to need. Gerry and his friends found out about this when they were at a gas station and saw a Brinks truck pulling up to the church every week. So I told Wally Green about it and we included it in the script. Gerry was what was known as the lead-off man, the first guy who went through the door. He was a real tough guy and part of the Irish mob that was run by a guy named Hughie Mulligan, at the time. I used Gerry in a few films, including *The Brink's Job*, where he had a major part. We were good friends, but I haven't seen him in years. I think he's still alive.

AS: That wedding scene in the church is also famous for the bride who was sporting a major shiner.
WF: The actor playing the groom is named Frank Pesce, who was a good friend of Sylvester Stallone. The girl was someone he brought, I think, maybe his girlfriend at the time, but the black eye wasn't real. It was make-up. The thing is, while it looks really incongruous today, that sort of thing wasn't uncommon back in the mid-seventies. Today it would be called an "abusive relationship," but back then, there wasn't even a name for it. It's just what went on among many couples and was accepted.

AS: *Sorcerer*, like some of your other films, including *Cruising* and *To Live and Die in L.A.*, were financially unsuccessful and, in some camps, really excoriated upon their release. Now, all three films are viewed as classics.
WF: The same thing happened with *Citizen Kane*. It was a box office bomb and excoriated by most of the critics when it came out and now it's almost universally regarded as the greatest film ever made. I'm not comparing my films to *Citizen Kane*, but again, it all comes down to timing and luck.

AS: I think *Sorcerer* is your greatest film and I'm not alone in that. Do you feel somewhat vindicated now that it's finally getting its due?
WF: It'd be easy to say that, but I don't know how it's going to be received yet by a new generation. That's who's really going to be seeing it. It's being rereleased theatrically. It's being released on Blu-ray April 22 from Warner Bros. Then it's going to be on television, all over cable and video on demand, all over the world. So it'll have a new audience. Most of my films, when I see them again, I would do everything over again and in some cases, would just shitcan the entire thing. Not so with *Sorcerer*. I can still watch it with some enjoyment. I still get pleasure out of it.

Exorcist Director: It Worked Because "I Made That Film as a Believer"

Stephen Galloway / 2014

From *The Hollywood Reporter*, March 29, 2014. Reprinted by permission.

William Friedkin reveals the film's star was an atheist, discusses how his belief in God helped make the movie a hit, and says he risked lives shooting *The French Connection* chase scene.

1973's *The Exorcist*, the first horror film nominated for best picture, earned $441 million because its creator believed in God, said director William Friedkin.

"I made that film as a believer," he said March 26, speaking to students at Loyola Marymount University's School of Film and Television. "What [the sequels] attempt to do is to defrock the story and to send the thing up."

The filmmaker said he never contemplated making a sequel, nor any other horror film: "I would never go back and do another *Exorcist*. Or anything with demonic possession or exorcism in it. I did it. I couldn't do it any better than that."

The director, whose other films include *The French Connection*, *Sorcerer*, and *Killer Joe*—which helped usher in star Matthew McConaughey's career rebirth as more than a handsome devil—was taking part in *The Hollywood Masters* interview series, conducted by *The Hollywood Reporter*'s Stephen Galloway. Others in the series include directors David O. Russell, Alfonso Cuaron, John Singleton, Judd Apatow, former Paramount chief [and Friedkin's wife] Sherry Lansing, Disney Studios chairman Alan Horn, and *Hunger Games* writer-director Gary Ross.

—Tim Appelo

Stephen Galloway: Hi everyone. I'm Stephen Galloway and welcome again to *The Hollywood Masters* filmed on the campus of Loyola Marymount University. I'm really thrilled to have our guest, one of the great American film directors. I don't know if he agrees with that assessment, we'll see. I think of his work as defined by paranoia, darkness, and I think the very way he uses the camera is completely unique to him. All these things he may disagree with. He's done classic things that have become completely part of our culture. We all know *The Exorcist*, *The French Connection*, *Sorcerer*, *To Live and Die in L.A.*, recently some very dark films. He's also recently written his autobiography, *The Friedkin Connection*. I've now read it two and a half times. It's really terrific. He talks about his mistakes. He talks about having the chance to get a free [Jean-Michel] Basquiat painting and throwing it away; having the chance to produce *Star Wars* and saying no; having the chance to be an owner of the Boston Celtics and turning that down. Then he says this: "I've burned bridges and relationships to the point that I consider myself lucky to still be around. I never played by the rules, often to my own detriment. I've been rude, exercised bad judgment, squandered most of the gifts God gave me, and treated the love and friendship of others as I did Basquiat's art and Prince's music. When you are immune to the feelings of others, can you be a good father, a good husband, a good friend? Do I have regrets? You bet." I'm delighted to welcome William Friedkin.

William Friedkin: Thank you. Thanks a lot. I have to tell you that I have bronchitis tonight. So, if I go off on a coughing or a sneezing jag, I hope you'll understand. It's like an epidemic of it out there. I've had this now this is the fourth week. I have to tell you, I don't know if you're aware, but I gave a commencement speech here about ten years ago and I was given an honorary doctorate by Father Lawton, who was formerly the head of the school. So, you could call me Dr. Friedkin. [laughter]

SG: You say in your book you did not have success in your DNA.

WF: No, there was no art in my family, no music. My mother and father were immigrants from the Ukraine and they came over at the turn of the twentieth century during one of the many pogroms that took place there. And there was no literature, or art, or music in my family at all. By the time I came of age to see movies—you know, not films, movies—it was just pure entertainment to me, nothing to do with cinema or art or anything like that. Just pure entertainment. I'm not sure that's not the best way to view a film anyway—as simply entertainment.

SG: When did that change?

WF: When I saw *Citizen Kane*. I was somewhere under twenty, maybe seventeen or eighteen years old. Someone told me that there was this great revival of a real film called *Citizen Kane* playing at a revival theater in Chicago. I put off seeing it. Then I saw in the newspaper that it was going to close in a day or two. So, I went to see it at this little revival theater on the near north side. I was just stunned by the experience. It's, I'm sure, what happens to painters when they first stand in front of a Vermeer or a Rembrandt. I first experienced film as art. And I stayed in the theater for five or six showings that day. And I've since seen it hundreds of times. Because to me, it's still a quarry for filmmakers in that everything about it is as well done as can be done; I'm talking about the acting, writing, direction, cinematography, editing, the design, everything. It's a quarry for filmmakers in the way that James Joyce's *Ulysses* is a quarry for writers. Or, in my case, [Marcel] Proust's *À la recherche du temps perdu.* Which I read continuously. Proust's writing is extremely cinematic. You have to work at it. You know, it's not going to lay down in front of you. You've got to give yourself to it, which I think is the mark of a great film. To me a great film is one that makes me think about it afterwards. The first thing I get from great cinema is, I'll say to myself, "Self," as I often address myself. [laughter]

SG: Doctor Self?

WF: Doctor Self to you. I'll say, what in the hell have I just seen? That occurred to me with *Citizen Kane,* and then a film like *Blow Up,* and *Belle de Jour.* Have you ever seen *Belle de Jour?* When I first saw that and it ended, and the way it ended, I thought, what in the hell is this? But I couldn't get it out of my mind and I still haven't been able to after thirty or forty years. The same with [Michelangelo] Antonioni's *Blow Up.* And both films sort of blur the line between reality and illusion.

SG: Well, don't all films, to some degree?

WF: No. Most films are probably worthless in that regard. [laughter]

SG: Yours too?

WF: Oh, absolutely. Beyond a shadow of a doubt. [laughter]

SG: Well, I don't agree with that.

WF: No, but we're talking about works of art. We're not talking just about a movie that's playing this week somewhere.

SG: Even though you did say three minutes ago that entertainment was a good way of judging a film.

WF: It might as well be because . . .

SG: You shifted.

WF: But if you're going for anything else, other than entertainment today, the chances are you may be disappointed. And that's with the onset of digital cinematography and computer-generated imagery where they can now do anything. And that's part of the problem. We can do anything. And I think the very best films were made when they had very little money but great invention, and great powers of invention, and everything was not at hand.

SG: Have you changed your mind about a film?
WF: In what respect?

SG: That you hated then loved, or the other way around.
WF: Well, I don't see a lot of new films today, to be very honest with you.

SG: Ever?
WF: Seldom. Seldom—maybe I see six or seven a year. My wife was up here a few weeks ago, I guess—Sherry Lansing—is still a great fan of the movies. I used to be, but certainly not as much anymore. I've taken now to watching a lot of the shows that you can stream or binge view on television, the cable shows, or stuff on Netflix or stuff like that, I think is more interesting than most of the films.

SG: But don't you think that it's interesting that some great films, is that you come to them, maybe with rules and formulae that you have in mind, and what makes them great is that they break those rules? And I think of some of the films that have most marked me is the ones I didn't initially always like.
WF: Well, I may differ from you in the sense that I don't come to a film with any rules. I just want to be swept away. I simply want to be overwhelmed by the ideas, by the performance, by everything else in combination. Because film is the most collaborative art form there is. And you know why? You want to be a painter, all you've got to do is fill a blank canvas yourself. If you want to be a writer, all you needed was a blank sheet of paper and a typewriter. Now you don't even need the paper if you have a computer. But you create this work of art, you the painter or the writer. But in film we call it "The Five Ton Pencil." You're working with literally hundreds of people; people who have great skills and who contribute so much to every film that's ever been made—

SG: And yet a great filmmaker puts his stamp on the film. How?
WF: Not necessarily. Look, it's possible, I suppose for a student of film, a film historian, to look at a piece of film and say Orson Welles directed that. Or possibly Federico Fellini. But Joseph Mankiewicz? That would be a lot different. Or even [Luis] Buñuel's film of *Belle de Jour*, which to me is a masterpiece, a great, great work of cinematic art. And yet it's filmed so simply. But behind it, behind the simplicity and the lack of style, the lack of technique, is the sensibility of Buñuel, one of the creators of surrealism. There's no more surrealistic film imaginable than *Belle de Jour* or if you really get into it, more disturbing than that. It's way out on the edge. It's about human desire. And it's about the difficulty of achieving a sexual relationship between a husband and a wife and the extent to which they both go

to make that work. And, boy, it's graphic without being upsetting. Although there are parts of it that could upset people.

SG: It's not very graphic. One of the things that makes it so great is Buñuel, who takes what would, in somebody else's hands, be a tawdry subject—
WF: Yeah.

SG: —and strips it of those elements. When he made that film his friends said, are you out of your mind? This is pulp fiction. Not that *Pulp Fiction*. A different pulp fiction. Why are you doing this? And what he did, he takes a story of the woman of the bourgeoisie who works on the side as a call girl and he took all sexuality out of that.
WF: You know what's happening though. You know what's going on with her at all times.

SG: But he does it in such a way, that the very thing that subject is about is not what you feel in the film and that's what gives it this disconnect that makes it a great film.
WF: Well, I won't dispute that. But I still do not believe that it is so profoundly stylistic that you could look at that, even having seen Buñuel's other films and said, this is definitely a Buñuel film. Whereas you can with *Citizen Kane*, *The Magnificent Ambersons*, even films that Orson Welles didn't direct but just appeared in you can see his touch, in *The Third Man*, which he was an actor in for a brief period of time. But the whole film reeks of Orson Welles, even when he's not on screen. So, there are great stylists.

SG: Did you ever meet Orson Welles?
WF: No, I never met Orson Welles. And I'm glad I didn't.

SG: Why?
WF: Because I heard he was a miserable son-of-a-bitch. [laughter] It wouldn't be too good for two such people to meet over a meal.

SG: Are there people going around saying the same about William Friedkin?
WF: Probably. Undoubtedly. You might, perhaps, after this evening. [laughter]

SG: I want to go back to what you said about rules.
WF: I don't have any rules. I want to be . . . I don't want answers. I don't want a film to give me answers, only questions. And the films I just named, like *Blow Up*—*Blow Up* is like a murder mystery with no solution. There is no solution and after you've seen the film—how many of you have seen it? Let me see your hands

if you've seen it. Yeah. After you've seen the film, you don't know what the hell to make of this, except you've been totally involved if you've given yourself to it. The same with *Belle de Jour*. When it's over, the last shot, what the hell have I just seen? That's what I'm looking for. And I don't get it a lot today. You get other things, certainly.

SG: When have you had it recently?
WF: What's a film that really captured . . . ? I love the film *Prisoners* [dir. Denis Villeneuve]. I thought that's the film last year that moved me the most in all respects: performance, direction, cinematography, the story which ends on an ambiguous note, it's filled with surprises. It's very involving and very disturbing. And that's what I look for. I no longer expect to find the kind of comedies that I once loved, like the Marx Brothers, or even *The Three Stooges*, or early Woody Allen. Those are comedies. But you don't go to Woody Allen anymore for comedy. He's basically not doing the kind of slapstick satires that he once did. He's doing more serious films.

SG: Does it bother you when you read about Woody Allen and his personal life? Does that impact how you view his films?
WF: I don't read about Woody Allen's personal life. I've known Woody Allen for fifty years. And I think I know about as much about him as there is to be known. I'm not talking about specific incidents in his life. I don't know anything about that. I know what you're alluding to. But that seems to me to be, I don't know, a he-said she-said kind of situation.

SG: But is there a point where morality gets in the way? Leni Riefenstahl: great director or not?
WF: She made at least one great film, *Triumph of the Will*, which is Nazi propaganda. But it's a great film as a piece of filmmaking. Do I agree with what she's propounding? Absolutely not. Nevertheless, it's a very powerful film. In its day in the early 1930s it influenced a great many people, millions of people, to follow this little madman into hell.

SG: You made a doc. You're a young man, you're coming out of high school, you're not going anywhere, you get a job for a television station and you hear about a guy on death row and you decide to make a documentary about him, *The People vs. Paul Crump*. At the time you believed he was innocent. But you admit in your book that it benefitted you to believe that.
WF: You could put it that way. I put it differently in my book as I will put it to you now, Stephen. I believed, because this man as a result of my film—he was going to

the electric chair—and when I met him, he had been at least seven years, maybe nine years on death row. And when I met him, I did believe in his innocence, but more importantly, I believed that his life was worth saving. As did the warden of the Cook County Jail in Chicago where he was. The warden had executed two people before Paul Crump and he didn't want to execute a third. So, he allowed me to make this documentary on death row. As a result of the documentary, the governor of Illinois—who later went to prison himself on criminal charges, his name was Otto Kerner, he was a big figure in the Democratic Party and on a short list to be a presidential candidate—he was the governor of Illinois and he pardoned Paul Crump to life imprisonment without possibility of parole as a result of seeing my film. And sent me a note to that effect. He told me that his parole and pardon board had voted two-to-one to let this guy go to the electric chair. So then Crump stayed in prison for, I don't remember how many years, at least twenty more, maybe more. Finally, another governor, another parole and pardon board that had no memory of this incident, decided to let Paul Crump out of prison with the proviso that he confesses to having committed the murder. And he did. He confessed. So, the point in my book where I say, am I now absolutely certain of his innocence? No, I'm not. But that wouldn't matter to me. He was a life worth saving. I think it's incumbent upon us—I'm now convinced that he may have been guilty. He may have been guilty. So, what? His life was spared. That to me, is . . . I was an instrument of God in my view in saving his life.

SG: Do you believe in God?

WF: Absolutely. I believe in God. I don't belong to any particular religion, but I believe in the teachings of Jesus as they're set down in the New Testament. I don't feel close to God in either a synagogue or a church or a mosque. But I can't help but believe in the teachings of Jesus. I think they're almost impossible to live up to, but they are a wonderful ideal. I've always sort of inherently believed that, Stephen, without any evidence. But what my life is about, what The Exorcist film is about is the mystery of faith. That mystery and all of life has been a great mystery to me. I raise the possibility there forty-five or fifty years after I made that film, that this fella whose life I saved from the electric chair, may have been guilty. He confessed to the crime in order to get out of prison. I think I would have done the same thing. If I was in his shoes and I had done as he had, forty years in a maximum-security prison, I would have confessed to any damn thing to get out.

SG: I want to show a clip from The French Connection. You know the clip. This is the most extraordinary car chase. We're just going to watch part of it, then we're going to talk about it.

[clip from The French Connection]

SG: That's really, it's pure filmic experience. You couldn't do that in another medium. So, here's one of things that's interesting about this film. First of all, you'd done four films before that.
WF: Yeah.

SG: Some pretty good films too. And then, here you are, in your early thirties and you can't get a job, for what? Two years?
WF: Something like that.

SG: What did you think of your life at that point? Did you think, I'm never going to work again?
WF: No, you just keep going. You just keep plowing ahead. That's my advice to all of you, whatever your ambitions may be. The young woman who interviewed me for the *LMU Magazine* asked me, what would you say is the most important thing for a young filmmaker, what quality should they most have? And I said, endurance. And a belief in yourself. With that goes the ability to take a hit. 'Cause you're going to get it.

SG: But you lost that belief in yourself at some point.
WF: Not really. I knew that I had lost touch with the public, and by extension the critics. But I've never lost belief in myself to this extent. I have never not believed that I could visualize a film in my mind's eye and not go out and make it. If I ever reach that point where I didn't think I could realize the film that I have in my head, I would have to stop at that point. And I'm not ready to stop on my own. It's going to take that act of God to stop me. If that happens in the near future, you'll remember I said it here. [laughter]

SG: So, here's what's interesting beyond what you went through at that early age, not being able to work: all the things you wanted in this film, you didn't get. You wanted Jackie Gleason for the leading role.
WF: True.

SG: You wanted Francisco Rabal for the role that Fernando Rey made famous. You weren't interested in an unknown actor named Gene Hackman.
WF: True.

SG: Working with him, and you weren't getting the performance because he was uncomfortable. And yet that film is as good as anything made in the 1970s.
WF: It's weird, isn't it? It's pretty strange that it turned out that way. And that's all I can say as a spectator. Now, of course, these chase scenes that they do today

are far more elaborate than that. The only difference is, we had to do everything you see and they don't anymore. They can generate it on a computer. But it looks pretty great, I'd say—the chases I see now. But all the stuff on the street, I had no permission to do any of that. For most of those shots, we drove the car at ninety miles an hour for twenty-six blocks with no crowd control, no traffic control. The only thing we had on top of the car, which you couldn't see when we made the point-of-view shots, was we had a police gumball on top, a siren, and a flashing light. Other than that, we just blew through twenty-six blocks of traffic at ninety miles [per hour]. Could you imagine trying to get permission to do that? I couldn't.

SG: You couldn't get some of your crew to do it. You did it yourself.

WF: I made the over-the-shoulder shots because the director of photography and the camera operator were family men, they had kids, and I was single. And it was the stuntman who drove the over-the-shoulder shots, a guy named Bill Hickman. On the floor next to me was an on-duty New York City policeman named Randy Jurgensen. He's told the story many times himself. He was there, all padded up, as I was. He had a badge in case we got in trouble.

SG: But you could have killed somebody.

WF: Possibly, yes.

SG: Did you know that at the time?

WF: Yes.

SG: Was that the right thing to do?

WF: No, I wouldn't do it today.

SG: At what point did you cross a line where you say, I'm not going to do this anymore?

WF: I guess I became an adult. I sort of matured. [laughter]

SG: At what point did you become an adult?

WF: To the extent that you see me now, and no further. No, I didn't care. I have always valued human life and my honest feeling is that there is not one single shot in any movie ever made—and I'm not exaggerating when I say this—that is worth a squirrel getting a twisted ankle, and yet, what I had then to compensate for that was total belief that nothing was going to go wrong, that I could pull this thing off. And it was only that faith, that belief, and my belief in my colleagues that they could pull this off with me. That's all. Given that faith, which I may have even further, I would never do such a thing, anymore, no matter what.

SG: Let's go back to the squirrel and the twisted ankle. Do you really believe that?
WF: Yes. To have someone's life endangered? For a shot in a movie?

SG: So not to totally escape the squirrel with the twisted ankle. What is the price you're prepared to pay for great art? Because you've offended some people—
WF: Good. [laughter]

SG: —you've hurt some people's feelings.
WF: It's good for them. [laughter]

SG: You have slapped people in the face to get the right performance.
WF: I wouldn't go there. That's very unfair. [laughter] That's totally unfair. I would have to go into such a long rap, that you don't even—these guys would be falling asleep by the time I explained what you're getting at. Let me say this, I do believe that anything a director does to get a performance from an actor is fair as long as you don't hurt that actor or cause that actor anything like major discomfort or even minor discomfort. But I think that anything you might do to shock an actor into a certain type of performance is fair game. We are working in an unreal world, there's a camera on me from over here. In a film, if I was sitting here and talking to you over there, you might be sitting there but the place where we were supposed to be wouldn't be in front of me. It would be an empty soundstage usually. I'm looking at you, and I'm looking at a bunch of stagehands smoking cigarettes, drinking coffee, walking around, scratching their asses, whatever it may be. I'm not looking at where we're supposed to be. You as a director have to overcome the actor's disbelief in the moment. And there are many techniques that do that. When you say I have slapped an actor, I think on three occasions I did, and they all thanked me for it. [laughter]

And one of them was the Catholic priest in *The Exorcist* who was not an actor but had to give the last rites to his friend who died from the big fall from the house. And in the scene, Father Bill O'Malley—who was not an actor, he is still alive, I believe he's at Fordham now—I chose him to play that role. I had met him through Bill Blatty who wrote *The Exorcist*, and I thought he was the guy that Blatty had created in *The Exorcist*. He had never been an actor. It was his first and only film. He might have done some plays at school. He had to break down and cry at three o'clock or four o'clock in the morning on a freezing cold night when the crew had worked for sixteen hours that day and he had to give the last rites and, according to the script, burst into tears. He couldn't do it. He couldn't get there. There was nothing I could say to him that could get him there. He had no technique. So, I resorted to something that I read that many directors have done before me over the years. I told the crew to just hang on for a moment and be ready to film. I lifted him to his feet and I hugged him by the shoulders. I said, Bill, do you love me? He said, yes, you know I love you, Bill. And I said, do you trust me? He said, of course I trust you. And I said, okay, we're going to do the scene now. And I looked away, and as I looked away I cracked him full in the face. I gave the sign to the camera man and I pushed him to the ground. And I said "action." And he did it and burst into tears. [laughter]

SG: Wow. Was there talk at some point though, that you were going to do another *Exorcist*?
WF: No, I would never do go back and do another *Exorcist*. Or anything with demonic possession or exorcism in it.

SG: Why?
WF: I did it. [laughter] I couldn't do it any better than that.

SG: But interesting, your films have got darker and darker and darker and more demonic in a way.
WF: I don't feel *The Exorcist* is a dark film. The girl is saved—

SG: —It's not a comedy.
WF: You figured that out. [laughter] How many years have you been writing film criticism? Now, you've come to that conclusion. Okay, you're right it's not a comedy. I remember that the original advertisement for the film I directed called *The Boys in the Band*, which was about gay life in New York in the sixties, the original ad was "*The Boys in the Band* is not a Musical." And no, it was not a musical, that's true. And *The Exorcist* is not a comedy. But in the end, the girl is saved, no longer possessed.

SG: I wonder how much you thought at the time, maybe you didn't know it was going to be such a gigantic hit.
WF: No, of course I didn't.

SG: How old was Linda Blair when you cast her?
WF: Twelve.

SG: An enormously difficult part to cast. Did you wonder how this would impact her life?
WF: Yes. She was the only one of several hundred girls of roughly that age whose life I felt would not be impacted by it. And I thought, we reached a point where there were at least two thousand girls, either put on tape, across this country, or auditioned by various casting directors and not put on tape, photographed or whatever. We couldn't find anybody. It was a part written for a twelve-year-old. I

started to think maybe we could find a sixteen-year-old girl who looks younger, or a fifteen-year-old. And we started to try and look for a young girl like that. Nobody. One of the main reasons was, in my meetings with several hundred of them, which lasted moments sometimes, I felt their lives would be impacted. Then one day when I was in despair, in my office in New York where we filmed the interiors, and where we edited the film, it was at 666 Fifth Avenue. That was the address. They have since taken down that number, I guess someone figured out it had another meaning. But that's where we made *The Exorcist* at 666 Fifth Avenue. Which was the Warner Bros. headquarters then. [laughter]

Yes. I was sitting at my desk in a kind of deep despair. My secretary buzzed me and said there's a woman out here named Eleanor Blair and she doesn't have an appointment but she's brought her daughter with her who's twelve years old. Would you see her? Took me a split second to say of course. She walked in the door and I knew instantly she was the one. Before we said hello, she came in the room and it was—I knew she was the one. She sat down, the three of us sat together in my office. I came away from my desk and sat with the three in three chairs. I said, so Linda— she was very cute, smart, adorable. Not beautiful, but really very giving and open and just a lovely young girl. I said, Linda, do you know what *The Exorcist* is about? She said, yeah, I read the book. I said, you did? I said, what is it? She said, well, it's about a little girl who gets possessed by the devil and does a whole bunch of bad things. And I said, like what sort of things? She said, well, she hits her mother across the face and she pushes a man out of her bedroom window and she masturbates with a crucifix. And I looked at her mother who was smiling. So, I proceeded on. I said, do you know what that means? She said, what? I said, to masturbate? She said, it's like jerking off, isn't it? I said, have you ever done that? I looked at her mother who is still smiling. She said, sure, haven't you? And so I hired her. Because I knew that she could handle this material with a sense of humor. And every day on the set I made it like a game for her. She will tell you today that she never knew precisely the implications of what she was doing in the possession scenes. She would just follow what I told her to do. I would literally do something I never had done before. I gave her line readings. I told her how to read the lines and I assured her and her mother there would not be her voice in those scenes and it wasn't.

SG: Have you stayed in touch with her?
WF: Of course. She's now [fifty-five] years old. I haven't seen her for a little while now. I've been traveling a lot and busy.

SG: Did it impact her life?
WF: She's done more films than I have. She was one of the leads in the road company of *Grease*. Many other things on stage, I don't know how many films she made. She's now extremely active with PETA.

SG: Did you ever talk about how she felt as an adult looking back on that? And whether she was happy she did it or not?

WF: She's very happy she did it. You guys, you can read all that. You can Google everything she's ever said in hundreds of interviews about pretty much what I'm saying to you now. And of course, she realized as she got older, that she was part of an extraordinary motion picture, which I have no hesitation in saying it is.

SG: Did the subject matter torment you at all?

WF: No.

SG: You didn't have—

WF: Well, I read the files of the actual case. There were three cases only in the twentieth century in the United States that the Catholic Church in America authenticated. This was one of them. It took place in 1949 in Silver Spring, Maryland, and it was a fourteen-year-old boy. Later when Bill Blatty, who was a graduate at Georgetown at the time, heard about this case, he wanted to write about it as nonfiction, but he couldn't get any of the priests or anyone else who knew about what had happened there. By the way, the story of this case was on the front page of the *Washington Post* in 1949. It ran about three pages. You can Google it right now. You can Google it: "*Washington Post* 1949 Exorcism." Or just "1949 Exorcism" and that story will come up. It was written by a journalist called Bill Brinkley who later became a novelist. He wrote a novel, it was very popular, called *Don't Go Near the Water*. But he was a reporter for the *Washington Post*. He states frankly in this article that this young man whose name he doesn't reveal—nor have I ever—but we know who he is and where he is, that this young man was possessed. An exorcism took place. He was moved out of that district, out of the Washington Diocese to St. Louis, Missouri, to Alexian Brothers hospital in St. Louis. The exorcism was performed there and was successful. The young man later went on to have a very successful career. He's retired now and he's moved back to that area, with no memory of what happened to him in 1949.

SG: Now, do you believe that can happen? And if you do—

WF: I read it. I read the diaries.

SG: Do you believe in the devil?

WF: I believe that there is a force of evil in every single one of us. Just as there's a force for good. I believe that every human being from Mother Teresa to Nelson Mandela has both good and evil within them. As we all do. That's just a belief I had. And it's a constant struggle for our better angels—

SG: Do you still feel that your greatest film still lies ahead?

WF: I hope so. Do I think it does? Stephen, I have no way of knowing that. But it would be difficult for me to come to an event like this. I would just drop out if I didn't want to make more and better films. One of the quotes I use at the beginning of my book is from Samuel Beckett and it's a very brief little four lines where he says: *Fail again, fail better* next time.

SG: Do you think you've failed? Or when you look at your career, how do you feel about it now? Because the sense of failure runs through the book. Anyone here would be on cloud nine to achieve what you've achieved.

WF: Thank you. I think I've failed and succeeded in perhaps equal measure, perhaps not. I'd be the last to be able to judge that. I have made some films I know that have stood the test of time, for at least thirty or forty years, which is not the test of all time. Some of the greatest films ever made aren't shown anymore. Should be. Now with the new technology, can be. This audience can go out and see the great films of [Charlie] Chaplin and [Buster] Keaton. I couldn't when I was growing up. We didn't have this technology. We didn't have Blu-rays, DVDs, we didn't have VHS. Now you can see all the masterpieces.

SG: I am going to show a clip from *Killer Joe*. It's a pretty brutal clip from *Killer Joe*, so be prepared.

WF: And don't try it at home.

[clip from *Killer Joe*]

SG: So don't you agree with my basic point that there has been darkening of your point of view on the world?

WF: I think it's edgy. I think it's pretty edgy.

SG: Yes or no?

WF: What? Do I have a dark point of view?

SG: Darker is my question.

WF: Oh, darker than when I was much younger, sure. I've seen more, experienced more, experienced more pain myself, and humiliation. There's nothing that I've ever depicted that I haven't felt in some way or experienced. I don't mean literally but I mean I understand what that is and why.

SG: I completely know that's true. I don't think an artist can create emotion he hasn't felt.

WF: I don't know. But I can't. I couldn't tell an actor what to do if I didn't understand the motivation of that character.

Student [Chase Mohseni]: You make challenging films, more and more as your career has gone on. Do you still think there is a place for such challenging films in the film marketplace or is that mostly in television these days?

WF: Mostly in television, in things like Netflix and HBO, and others that are coming along. But I'm much more interested in the work that's being done in those formats than any average week of movies coming out in theaters. I was addicted to binge viewing *House of Cards*, and well I loved *24*, and of course *The Sopranos*. I don't think there's anything since *The Godfather* that you could compare to *The Sopranos*, for example—and many others that I could cite. Is there a place for this kind of thing in commercial cinema? No, not anymore. No place.

SG: And yet *Killer Joe* did very well in foreign markets.

WF: Yes, and it's still doing very well for what it cost and for . . . it wasn't released in anywhere near the number of theaters that *The Hunger Games* was. [laughter]

SG: It's interesting to me that you respond to television. I've never had that connection with television. If you look at your films for instance, where sound is used in such an original way. The opening of *The Exorcist*, I don't know if you remember that, just the sound, is as powerful as anything you see visually.

WF: I treat them separately; the soundtrack and the picture are completely separate entities to me. I do the soundtrack all afterwards—even the dialogue. I for the most part loop the dialogue to get a better sounding performance.

SG: I haven't seen anybody in television who would do one of your distinct things. For instance, in the opening of *Sorcerer* in Jerusalem, that long, long, long zoom in down, down onto these characters walking through the Damascus Gate through the city of Jerusalem. The very shot you use conveys a sense of paranoia and danger that there is menace in this world. I don't see that on television.

WF: I sort of do though, Stephen. *True Detective*, did any of you see that? That's pretty damn good, I thought. Did you? Did anybody hate *True Detective*? I thought it was really good solid drama, not just television, and *House of Cards*? Did you ever see the British *House of Cards*?

SG: No.

WF: It's amazing. It's a masterpiece, unbelievably great. I thought nothing could top it and I didn't want to watch this thing and I watched it and I thought it was brilliant. I can't say that about too many films I've seen; that I thought they were thought provoking and powerful and would stay with me and have reverberations in my life. That's mostly pay per view now and what they call streaming. And it's mostly on weird, not major networks, on channels like Starz and Showtime and HBO.

Student [Chris Martens]: You've made films over a number of decades. Are there certain ideas or themes that you find yourself going back to?

WF: Yeah: good and evil in everyone. In all the characters I've ever worked on, the constant struggle for your better angels to survive, even thrive. That would be my main theme. The whole idea that we have no control over our lives, no matter what. That we're really in this world, sort of like the woman in *Gravity* who is mostly cut off from her spaceship. That's mostly the condition of the world. We're all mostly in our separate worlds. We try to live together and get together, but it's difficult. Recently I went down to San Diego with Sherry and we had a private visit with the three pandas that are in the San Diego Zoo. It's very endearing, they're certainly amazing creatures. They're very singular, all pandas live alone, they want no part of any other panda—not their mother or their father. These three have to be kept apart—the mother, the father, and the baby who is less than two years old. As I thought about that, I thought, they're not faking it, they just don't like other pandas and they show it. The rest of us have to somehow get along with other people in order to survive. If you walk into the grocery store and call the grocer a bunch of names, he's not going to give you the apples. And yet I do think, most of the condition of humanity is sort of singular like that. In order to get along—it's what Harold Pinter once said to me and I believe he probably wrote it as well. He said, "It isn't that we don't communicate with one another; it's that we communicate too well." We all know, no matter what the other person is saying, we all have a sense of what they're really thinking. By ignoring it, we make that conflict go away. Sometimes we don't. Sometimes we pick up on the insult, or we pick up on the other person's reaction or attitude, no matter what they're saying or doing and a conflict arises. You know the old story—maybe it's happened to some of you—you look at somebody the wrong way in a bar, and suddenly, bang, violence occurs. And I think it's because there is such a singularity to human nature. As we now see more and more every day, it's difficult to put these differences behind us as a country. We don't understand really why the world isn't completely at peace, do we? This is an earthly paradise. Why should people have to starve? Why should they have to die miserably or be stricken with disease? We don't understand any of that. Given all that, it's hard to be funny. Woody Allen is the only guy in modern times who's managed it. The early Woody Allen films were all done in times of strife, struggle, war, and yet they're funny. Especially the early comedies, the satires, they're really funny. The farces, like *Sleeper*, and *Take the Money and Run* and

Bananas. These are very funny. Now he doesn't go there anymore. To me, Woody Allen is the best living American filmmaker, by far. Hands down.

SG: Living? Really? More than Scorsese?

WF: Yes, to me. I don't rate or judge Scorsese or anybody else. I'm just saying, I think that Woody Allen is the most important and the most profound. Profound. You take a film like *Crimes and Misdemeanors*; this is worthy of Dostoevsky. Which I think is its model, *Crime and Punishment*, but it's a masterpiece. How many of you have seen *Crimes and Misdemeanors*? Put that way up on your list if you haven't seen it. It is a very powerful film; very moving, very deep.

Student [Matt Klein]: You've done, we've even seen today, a great many different types of films. We saw horror, a very dark comedy, an action movie. Do you feel like genre colors your directing style? Do you consider yourself a genre filmmaker?

WF: No.

Student [Matt Klein]: Or do you just approach films as films?

WF: That's it. You've answered it. I don't know what is going to attract me, but all my films have found me and for various reasons. I didn't find them. They all found me and I had to see them all in my mind's eye before I could go out and film them. There are many projects that I started and abandoned because I couldn't see them in my imagination. Usually, when I direct a film I don't need the script. I know all the shots. I have some idea how they'll connect, although the editor contributes mightily to that. And films are made in the cutting room. To me all the shooting of a film is nothing more or less than raw material for the cutting room. Thank you.

Student [Terrence Johnson]: As somebody who has directed a wide variety of film like *The Boys in the Band*, *The Exorcist*, and *Killer Joe*, what advice do you have for directors who are starting their careers out in terms of picking movies and projects to work on?

WF: You have to follow your vision and you can do more than I could ever do at your age. We never had the ability to go out and buy a little camera, even one as hi-def as the GoPro Camera that's this big and you could balance it on a stick. You don't even need a steady cam mount and you could shoot a hi-def picture. You could go out and buy any number of DCP cameras and you could go out and make a film that you have conceived and you could take it home and edit it yourself on your computer. Once you finish it or think it's finished you could put it on YouTube and someone will see it, often many someones. Sometimes tens of thousands of people will see your work on one of the many websites that you could show your work. I could never do that when I was at your age and wanted to be a filmmaker.

We had to get a job. There weren't even film schools that I could go to. I worked my way up from the mailroom of a television station in Chicago to live television. My first film was the film about this African American guy who was on death row. And I made the film primarily to save his life, and only secondarily—but it was there—to become a filmmaker. So, I learned by doing it and that film shows it too. You can make a movie. I couldn't. I had to go out and somehow con people into letting me shoot something. And when I did *The Hitchcock Hour*, I didn't know what I was doing. You have at your fingertips, all of you guys, the grammar of cinema available to you. The best source of where it's going to come from is from you. Not from somebody else, from you. Maybe somebody else you're working with. You can make it and you can get it shown. That's something that my whole generation of people, that some of you may really admire, we couldn't do that. We had no way to do that. Thank you, Terrence, and good luck to you.

SG: One last question.

Student [Elizabeth Quinn]: You've done a lot of adaptations from novels and plays, and I was just curious about how you approach adapting from one medium to another, that process.

WF: I wouldn't have adapted these works if I didn't believe in them as a film. At the very beginning of cinema, where did most of the scenarios come from? They were all silent, there were no words? But who did they get to write the captions and the stories? Playwrights. People who had written plays. Or they became caption writers because they had an ability to write, even though there were no words to be spoken. Sometimes . . . let's say *Killer Joe* for example. The problems of that were solved by the playwright before I came to make the film. I only saw it as a vehicle for cinema as well. My first obligation was very much like what surgeons are taught. You know what the surgeons credo is? *First, do no harm*. And that to me is the credo of someone adapting a play or something else for cinema. Don't adapt it if you don't like it. If you want to change it, go do something else. But films come from many sources. Most of them come from either plays or novels, or true stories that have been written, or one's imagination. And sometimes it's a mixture of all of those and none are to be ruled out. I find *Killer Joe* very cinematic in that it's about action and character. The action is sometimes weird, you might think, and the characters are all bent. There's no question about that. These are flawed people, but that's where drama comes from—from *the crooked timber of humanity*. That's not my phrase, it's Isaiah Berlin's. But that's where all great drama comes from, *the crooked timber of humanity from which we all stem*.

SG: Good. Wonderful last line, Doctor Friedkin. Thank you so much.

WF: Good luck to you all. I really wish you all, I feel for all of you something akin to what you must be feeling. I hope that you feel it deeply enough so that you will follow this ambition that you have now. Don't give up. Unless you've managed to convince yourself that you really don't like it anymore or that you have no fucking talent. If you think you've got the talent, don't let anything stop you. When I started, we couldn't even think then about women directing something, or running a studio like my wife did on two occasions, or producing. When I started in the mailroom, it was literally a male room. Women could not apply and certainly minorities were not welcome. Today, believe me, everybody is welcome. And if you have some talent, it's going to get out there, but you need the following: ambition, luck, and the grace of God. You notice that I did not mention talent. There are many untalented people out there making a lot of money. There are guys out there who are holding $5 billion for their work on film and I'm trying to promote a bag of popcorn out there. So it's not about talent, but you need ambition, luck, and the grace of God. I wish that to all of you. I mean that as sincerely as I can. And I hope you guys will do some original work someday. I'll see it, hopefully, and like it. That's my fondest hope. God bless you all.

SG: Thank you.

A Discussion with William Friedkin: "I See a Diminishing of All Art Forms These Days"

Sven Mikulec / 2015

From *Cinephilia & Beyond*, December 2015. Reprinted by permission of Sven Mikulec.

It was *The Exorcist* and *The French Connection* that put William Friedkin on the cinematic top of the world, but the attention-worthy films in this filmmaker's dossier are too many to mention in this clumsy little introduction. Mr. Friedkin proved to be a very friendly and open, albeit busy person, who agreed to sit down with us for a while. With a desire to hear his thoughts on some of the landmark films he made over the years and the projects he currently has in store for film lovers around the world, we embarked on this adventure without daring to suspect the conversation would stretch enough to discuss subjects like the contemporary degradation of art, the importance of film criticism, and the position of women in the film industry.

Cinephila & Beyond: You stated a couple of times that, when you made *The Exorcist*, your intention was never to make a horror film. The fact that people consider it to be one of the best horror films ever made says quite a lot about how frightening exploring the nature of human beings really is.

William Friedkin: Well, by now, obviously I recognize that audiences for generations have considered it a horror film. I won't deny that, but when I set out to make it, the writer and I never had any concept of it as a horror film. We thought of it as a powerful, emotional, disturbing story. But we did not think of it in terms of a horror film, let alone a classic horror film, or a lot of the stuff that passes for horror films. We just both found this story, which was inspired by an actual case, you know, to be very powerful, and I thought would be cinematic. But I never thought in terms of horror films, like the ones that I appreciated, like *Psycho* and *Diabolique*, and *Onibaba* and a handful of others. They are clearly horror films, and

I didn't think of *The Exorcist* to be one of them when I made it. Now I understand that the public thinks of it that way, so I don't dispute it.

C&B: And what do you think scares the public the most?

WF: Well, why bad things happen to good people. An innocent twelve-year-old girl, who goes through extraordinary symptoms that clearly represent a disease that medical science is unable to deal with. That's extremely disturbing to people. Because most people either have a child, or have been a child or are a child. So, whenever your child goes through the sort of illnesses that are depicted in *The Exorcist*, it's of great concern to everyone. And I think the fact that I made the film in a realistic way is what ultimately gets to people. It's not done as though it takes place on a planet far, far away or something like that, or in an intangible world— it's set in the real world, with characters who are portrayed as humanly possible. So, I think that the fact the story is portrayed realistically is what disturbs people about the events in it. It was a very productive and exciting period to work with William Peter Blatty on his great creation.

C&B: The characters in *Sorcerer* are forced to cooperate to save their asses, without fully trusting each other. They are thrown together in one hell of a mess, and getting out of it requires trust, faith, and collaboration. Would you draw a parallel with the world today? Especially in the last couple of years?

WF: Yes, it's even more relevant today. But at the time I made the film, in 1977, I felt that way, the way you just described. That the world had come to a crossroads, where the major powers would all blow apart if we didn't pull together. And I thought *Sorcerer* was a metaphor for that idea. I think it's much, much more dangerous today. I think the world is on a precipice today. I don't see any strong leadership to counteract the terrorism that exists in the world, as well as various other problems. I think if the world does not pull together, it will blow apart. And it has now affected innocent people sitting at an outdoor café somewhere, who have no politics, you know, no particular philosophy that would be disturbing to someone else. There is just evil in the world, and that's what relates *Sorcerer* to *The Exorcist*. There is a force of evil in the world that causes all these problems. Life is actually a beautiful gift, but people regard it not as something that is vulnerable, but as something that they take for granted. The major powers in the world just keep threatening each other, attacking each other, and there's going to come a point where there's enough nuclear proliferation to destroy the world. So yes, that is the metaphor behind *Sorcerer*.

C&B: Back to a brighter topic, I was certainly glad to learn about your attitude towards contemporary streaming television like Netflix.

WF: Oh yeah, there are much more interesting things being done, unfortunately, in streaming and on cable television than there are on movie screens. In this country, anyway, but in many other countries also. The whole idea of the art film, or experimental films, receiving an audience in theaters has virtually disappeared from the United States and so many other countries, except in fringe areas. And when I was growing up it was a staple of cinema.

C&B: You said that everything that Hollywood produces these days is just *Star Wars*, that the film completely shaped what we considered the American movies since it [came] out. How heavy is *Star Wars'* responsibility for the current state of American filmmaking?

WF: Well, it was hugely successful, beyond anyone's wildest dreams. Including the filmmakers. There are occasionally films that present a complete change in the zeitgeist, and nothing more than *Star Wars*. It became the goal of every studio—to make another *Star Wars*, or a version of *Star Wars*. And then they started to analyze, well, what is *Star Wars*? Well, it's kind of a comic book. So now, the mass production of films from the Hollywood studios are comic books. *Batman*, *Superman*, stories like *The Hunger Games*, so many, *Iron Man* . . . I'm not saying this in a negative way, this is what audiences want to see. Everywhere. These are the most popular films, and they very often crowd out other kinds of films. I imagine that's true in Croatia, isn't it?

C&B: It's the same here, yes. But what makes television the suitable home of quality visual storytelling these days?

WF: Cable television and the streaming services have to come up with an alternative to what people want to see in the cinema. And what they turned to, fortunately, for the most part—not totally, is well-written stories, with believable characters in situations that are both tense and dramatic and believable. Now, this is not true of all television certainly. But the kind of television that resonates with me are shows like 24, and *Homeland*, and *X-Files*, and *The Sopranos*, and many, many more example of things that could not be produced for the cinema in this country. And there's great television that I've seen from other countries! Like Israel or Sweden, England, and France. A lot of these films come over here now, and they come as television series. That's why television represents an alternative to the basically mindless experience of going to a cinema today. With rare exceptions, though. There are exceptions—I can't say there are no good films being made. There are, but they are of a far fewer variety and number than they were made, let's say, over thirty years ago.

C&B: But there must be a good chance this superhero comic book assembly line will die out soon; the market must become saturated at some point.

WF: I don't see that. I don't think it will die out, I think that's the new zeitgeist. If it isn't these particular films, it will be copies of them. It will be something else, that is completely unbelievable, and supernatural, and whatever. Just these fantasy comic books. That, I'm afraid, is the future of cinema. Until I see some change at least. When you say you think it's going to die out—it doesn't look to me as if it's going to happen. This is what the audience has become conditioned to. And the audience in the United States is for superhero movies, which to me are almost completely mindless.

C&B: The small, independent movies today are the closest we can get to what used to be made in the seventies.

WF: Yes, but they are very marginal now. It was possible to get a much larger audience for serious cinema not only in the seventies, but long before that. I'm sorry it's that way, but that is what people want to see in a cinema today. Because largely the people who go to the cinema are in a much younger age group. The largest number of moviegoers here are between the ages of fifteen and twenty-five. That's what they want. Even college graduates, or serious people, want to see that.

C&B: But besides television, can you name a couple of films that you enjoyed over the last couple of years?

WF: Well, I can tell you I have not enjoyed many. But I recently saw *Creed*, which is another version of *Rocky*. And I thought it was terrific, I thought it was really good. Well-written, well-acted, great story. They reinvented that genre. I thought it was sensational. I'm trying to think of any other films that I've seen at the cinema that I really enjoyed to the extent that I enjoy films from the past, and I can't think of anything to compare to the films that I really love. But *Creed* was very good. And you probably know that I saw the little Australian horror film called *The Babadook*?

C&B: You wrote about it on Twitter, yes.

WF: Well, I like that picture! It took me completely by surprise. That's a little horror film, but I thought it was just beautifully made, very convincing and very disturbing.

C&B: What about other contemporary horror films?

WF: Nothing! Nothing. Zero.

C&B: The box office results tailor the careers of all filmmakers, and yours was no exception. But it must feel great to see *Sorcerer*, *Cruising*, and others get the recognition they deserved, even after all this time?

WF: Look, I'm very happy when films that I've made are still recognized by whomever, decades after they were made. Of course, I'm very happy about that. But for most part you make films for a contemporary audience. The reason I haven't made more films since then is simply that I haven't found anything that interests me enough. It's not that I haven't been looking, but I'm not just going to do any film that I have no real passion for simply to make a film, and then ask people to buy tickets to see it. If I don't want to see it myself, I have no interest in making it.

C&B: And what attracted you to Don Winslow's *The Winter of Frankie Machine*?
WF: I think it's a very interesting character, in an environment that I know and understand well. I like his writing. I like his work very much. I think he's much more than a thriller writer. I think there's a depth to his work and a kind of realism that comes from his own experiences in life. He was a private investigator at one time, you know? It's rooted in reality. It's a character I think that I understand. It will have to be very well-cast. The ideal actor would've been Paul Newman, but unfortunately, he's not available now. But when we get the script, you know, it's something that I would give to Matthew McConaughey.

C&B: One close-up of Steve McQueen is worth far more than the photograph of the most beautiful landscape in the world. Your quote. There are no studio stars today like it was in the past, but taking charisma, talent, and charm into consideration, who would you say could fill the shoes of actors like McQueen or Newman?
WF: Nobody. And not only those American actors, but also people like Lino Ventura, and Jean Gabin, and Marcello Mastroianni, and so many others. So many others from past generations who represented a kind of movie magic. And many women, as well. I don't think there are any women anywhere near as interesting as the female stars of the past. And certainly there's no Orson Welles around. God knows I could name so many actors, not just movie stars, but actors whose light doesn't exist anymore in the English-speaking world. You know, Alec Guinness, and Peter Sellers, you could go on and on, it would just be name recitation. But for example, everything I've seen that Humphrey Bogart did was interesting in and of itself. Actors like Peter Lorre when he worked in Germany, and did things like *M* for Fritz Lang. We don't have actors and actresses like that anymore. On occasion you see some obviously good performances. I watch basically the same films over and over again, like reading a novel again, or listening to a piece of music again. I never tire of listening to the Fifth Symphony of Beethoven conducted by Carlos Kleiber. It's a masterpiece from which I get something new, some new detail, every time I listen to it. Or the Ravel String Quartet in F. And God knows, if there was anywhere else that I wished to live, it would be in the Netherlands,

across the street from the Rijksmuseum, where I could walk in every day and see a Vermeer or a Rembrandt. And that's not easy to do where I live (in Los Angeles). If I lived in New York, I could walk into the Metropolitan Museum and see about five Vermeers and more than a dozen Rembrandts. But nobody paints like that either today! I see a diminishing of all the art forms. Are you gonna tell me that painting has moved upward since the times of Rembrandt and Vermeer, and the seventeenth century? Has painting advanced today in terms of craftsmanship and interest of the viewing public? I really don't think so. I just don't think so. And the same thing is with cinema, and the same thing is with music. Who writes music like Beethoven? Or Bartok? Who plays jazz like Miles Davis? Who is as good of a popular music singer as Frank Sinatra? And when I give you these honest answers about my feelings about art, I sound like somebody who's stuck in the past. But I'm really not, I am looking to be inspired by the work of today. I don't see it in a museum, I don't hear it in a concert hall, and I certainly don't see it in cinema.

C&B: So you're saying there's a tragic situation since with the rise of technology . . . art can be presented in the best possible way but there's a constant diminishing of the quality of artists?

WF: I think so, but that's just my opinion. Yes, the technology affords you the opportunity to create almost anything, and to create it in three dimensions, or in a widescreen. . . . There are certainly more ways to paint and ways to compose music than there ever were. And there's a larger audience available. You know, Beethoven basically composed music in the nineteenth century for Europeans. And yet these works live on. I don't know how many musical works are going to live on into the future, I certainly can't predict that, but there's not a lot that has caught my attention. And I'm not complaining! These are just facts. I'm always hoping and looking for something that will inspire me. Well, like the film *The Babadook*, which was completely unexpected, or this film *Creed*, which is a kind of reinvention of *Rocky*, which is now forty years old. It's a damn fine picture, very well-made, with wonderful acting. It's the best thing Stallone has done since he did the first *Rocky*.

C&B: I'm still waiting for the film to come to Croatia.

WF: I'm sure you'll get it, and boy, did it take me by surprise! Because I try to see a lot of things, I try to watch as much as I can. There are some things I'm not attracted to, but there are a lot of films I do want to see, and very often I'm just disappointed. But I listen to new music, and I look at new artwork, and I look at new plays. In America, there are a lot more interesting things happening on stage than there are in cinema. There are certainly not many works that are in the category of what was done by Arthur Miller, Tennessee Williams, William Inge, Clifford Odets, and others. But Tracy Letts, who wrote *Bug* and *Killer Joe*, is a playwright who I would put in that category, with someone like Edward Albee.

C&B: You said it's easy for you to work with Tracy Letts, since you share the same worldview.

WF: We have a vision and a view of people and society that is rather similar. Neither one of us is particularly political, which is an odd thing to say to someone from Croatia, where politics is vital. But right now in the United States of America I don't feel that politics is serious or vital. I don't think a lot of people are really paying attention or give a damn who gets elected to the highest or lowest offices in the land. And unfortunately, because of the press, the best and the brightest people don't want to run for political office, because the media would immediately pounce on them and find any number of things that suggest that they are unfit for office. There's not a lot of people that would want to go through that. This wasn't the case many long years ago, when you had some of the best people in society running for political office. Unlike your part of the world, we don't come from a place where there have been dictatorships. The progress, for example, that the United States made during the Civil War is amazing. Forget the Revolutionary War, when the US broke away from England. But the Civil War was run by a bunch of guys wearing big, heavy, woolen suits and military uniforms, they were smoking tobacco, smoking cigars in small, unairconditioned rooms, drinking whiskey straight from the bottle. And these guys were making decisions about things that reverberate to this day in our country, like civil rights, for example. And they fought and died for civil rights. 750,000 people died in the American Civil War during those five years. The guys who made this happen were almost backward in their knowledge and intelligence, but what they had was a passion and a fire, a belief and faith that I just don't see today. Today we've got a bunch of well-dressed guys in $2000 suits and beautiful ties eating off the finest china and drinking the best wines, and they are gentlemen, they sit around rooms and discuss things for which there is no solution.

C&B: Since you mention civil rights and how the society changed over time, I want to ask you about the position of women in the film industry. There has been a lot of talk about the inferior position of women filmmakers. What are your five cents?

WF: Well, I'll give you my thoughts on that. I've been in Hollywood for fifty years and I have never met an executive of a television or movie company, or a talent agency, that was prejudiced against people of different colors or against women. I've never met anyone. Now, why there are more men directing films than women, I can't answer that. But it's not because of prejudice. I think the very best director of action and other films is a woman named Kathryn Bigelow. She's a great filmmaker, period. It's a question like why there aren't more white basketball or football players in America. Most of them are black, or from another country. Why is that? The only answer to that is that they compete and that they're better! Wherever women can compete, they get the jobs. I don't know anyone who's prejudiced against African Americans or women, I've just never seen it. Why is that there are more black athletes? Because they're better. So, what should we do? Should we get some legislation or pass some rules that there have to be more white players? No, you can't do that! Why are the greatest painters that ever lived mostly white men? I don't know! Women are free to paint. But you cannot pass diversity laws in an art form. If you could choose to do an exhibition of Vincent van Gogh or a woman painter from the same period, what are you going to choose? Why is that, I don't know. I'm not a woman, or an African American, so I can't speak to that experience except to say that I know it's an open playing field. And today there are many, many women in the entertainment business here who are in charge of everything. You know, my wife was the head of a studio thirty years ago, and ten years ago she ran two studios. Why? Not because she was a woman, but because of merit. When somebody auditions for an open chair in a symphony orchestra, they audition behind a screen for the general manager of the orchestra or for the conductor. The manager or conductor don't know if they are a man or a woman, or what color they are—they just play behind the screen the pieces they've prepared, they don't talk. So today, for example, if you go to a concert by the Los Angeles Philharmonic, you see a great many Asian women in the orchestra. The growing number of people in a symphony orchestra around the world are women, and in fact they are Asian women. I can't explain why that is, but that is an open playing field, and I believe that cinema is too. I have never heard of a man running a studio, talent agency, or a network saying, oh, I don't want to hire a woman for that job. But women have to put themselves forward. I mean, just today, or yesterday, a law was passed in America saying that women will now be present in all areas of combat in the military. There will be women on the battlefield, if there is one, equal to men. So that, among many other things, means there has been progress for women.

All I can say is that I'm certain people have faced obstacles in trying to work in all the art forms or in sports. I was a pretty good basketball player when I was a kid in high school, but I could never play on a professional basketball team. There was no way anybody could pass a diversity law so that I could. I just wasn't good enough. And that's hard for people to face. If you're good enough, you're gonna work. All this other stuff to me is just smoke screen. The fellow who directed the movie *Creed* and was one of the writers is a young African American man. He's talented, he's made only two feature films, he's basically recently out of college. But he's got the talent, and nobody gives a flying fuck what color he is. I had people work on my films who are African American, who are women, and not because they are African American or women, but based on what I thought was their merit. I don't know anyone that wouldn't do that. Anyone who would do that, anyone who would deny a talented woman, or a talented member of a racial minority, a job, is just an asshole, and not fit to be in a position to hire. Are there assholes in every business in every industry, in every country? You bet. But that doesn't mean it's going to be cured by some kind of diversity rule.

C&B: What do you believe is the importance of film criticism today and how would you compare it to what was being written decades ago?

WF: Let me just say this. And let's just stick to film for the moment. There are many more good film critics today because of the internet. I've seen reviews or appreciation of films—a lot of them on your site! And many other sites. There's a proliferation of interesting writing about cinema that I've seen in recent years since the internet. I wish there were better films to warrant this growth of film criticism. And there are far more film critics who are knowledgeable today about cinema because of the dissemination of information about all kinds of cinema, including classic cinema. There are far more, and more interesting critics than I can recall when I started. There are also idiots writing about film, there are idiots making films. You know, it's the usual number. I think right now the mainstream critics in this country go out of their way to praise some of the films that are made and that don't compare at all with the classics of the past. But as a film critic, you're just exercising your opinion. There's nothing finite about it. A review from the *New York Times* is no more actually important in terms of its overall impact than a review from you name it. *Rotten Tomatoes* or *Cinephilia and Beyond*. They simply represent the opinion of the writers.

C&B: Do you read reviews of your films?

WF: Yes, I do. I mean, not all of them certainly. I generally read what gets sent to me or comes to my attention. Good or bad. And I've read a lot of negative reviews on occasion that I find interesting, if not insightful. And I've read a lot of positive reviews that are just, you know, not that helpful. But there are very good writers writing about cinema today. All over the world. I didn't realize you, for example, were in Croatia. So there you go. You're writing about cinema thousands of miles away. You write essays. You write long think pieces about films. And that, in essence, is a review. It's not likely, is it, that you would write a long piece about a film you hated? What is the point? Why waste your time or the characters on an iPad, or a computer, or an iPhone, or whatever the hell you're writing on. Why waste your time if you don't like the film?

Writing about films is as varied as making them. There are good films made, and there are bad films made. There are good pieces about films, and then there's unintelligent stuff. To me, the motivation and purpose of a reviewer should largely be to try to get people to see the film. There's a guy who writes in the *Wall Street Journal*, and some of his reviews are so negative and so personal that they are worthless to me. Whenever I see somebody write very personal attacks on the works of filmmakers, I just wonder what the purpose of that really is. And the conclusion I've come to is a kind of, well, jealousy, of somebody who wishes they were doing it themselves. And aren't, because they can't. But then there are other reviews that you would have to say make you want to participate in cinema. If I was writing a film review, I would only review those films that I felt had merit. For me, the purpose of film criticism is to interest people in the art of cinema. What good is it to criticize a film that you absolutely don't relate to, that you hate and that you want to attack? Very often those films are beyond the reach of the critic. I mean, somebody can write the worst imaginable crap about *Star Wars*, and it's not going to affect the audience at all.

C&B: So, writing horrible reviews is a waste of space and time that could have been used to turn the spotlight on a film that deserves attention?

WF: My point exactly. Why waste the space? Why would I have to sit and read a piece about a film that the reviewer loathes? No, that I don't do, that is a complete waste of time. The reviewer's time and my own.

C&B: *To Live and Die in L.A.* is coming to TV soon. At what phase is the project?

WF: We've just finished the first script. The script is written by a guy called Bobby Moresco, who wrote the movie *Crash*, won the Academy Award, and he wrote *Million Dollar Baby*.

C&B: Are you happy with the script?

WF: Oh, very much. I love the script. My opinion is that it's one of the best scripts I've ever read.

C&B: You'll be directing the episodes?

WF: I plan to, but I've already asked a couple of friends of mine to direct a few of the episodes, like Walter Hill. I'm gonna ask Nic Refn to do one, maybe a couple of other guys. Not that I don't want to do them all, but these are friends of mine whose work I respect and I'd love to see what they would do with this material. There will be ten one-hour episodes.

C&B: But regarding the stuff you think is good from your filmography, you explained you were never bother[ed] by box office results, but that you valued your films according to how close they came to your original vision of them. Based on this criterion, which of your films do you consider most successful?

WF: Well, a few. I'm very happy with *Jade, Rules of Engagement, Killer Joe, Bug, The Exorcist* . . . I would have to say *Sorcerer*, and *The French Connection*. Those come immediately to mind. And *To Live and Die in L.A.* And it's not that I achieved them, or realized them perfectly, but I did come very close to my vision of them in the execution.

C&B: Mr. Friedkin, it's been a real pleasure to talk to you.
WF: I think your site is great and I was very happy to do the interview.

"I Never Thought My Films Would Find a Large Audience": William Friedkin Interviewed

A. J. Goldmann / 2016

From *The Spectator*, July 9, 2016. Reprinted by permission.

The last of the great American auteurs talks to A. J. Goldmann [of *The Spectator*] at this year's Cannes Film Festival about hits, flops, and how *Star Wars* destroyed independent cinema.

From the Oscar-winning classics of the early seventies—*The French Connection* (1971) and *The Exorcist* (1973)—to the southern trailer trash noir *Killer Joe* (2011), William Friedkin has been behind some of the darkest films ever to come out of Hollywood. He has also had a famously bumpy career, careening from great successes to big flops (does anyone remember *Jade*?). Somehow, he's always rebounded. Currently, the eighty-year-old director is developing *Killer Joe* into a television series, set to star Nicholas Cage as the cowboy hat–wearing detective/ hitman played so mesmerizingly in the film by Matthew McConaughey.

At the Cannes Film Festival in May, Friedkin was basking in the sort of adoration he hadn't known for half a lifetime. The man who reinvented the chase scene and showed how pea soup, under the right circumstances, can be the most frightening substance in the universe, was one of the festival's most prominent guests, dropping in to present restored versions of his films and to give the annual masterclass.

In a dark blue suit and a pinstripe shirt, Friedkin is sitting in a leather chair under this year's festival poster, an ethereal-looking still from the finale of Godard's *Le Mepris* that shows a man ascending majestic steps overlooking the Mediterranean. "I'm happy to present the films," he tells me. "And I'm happy that anyone still wants to see them, but I can't watch them. I've seen all of these films maybe a thousand times. They no longer have any allure for me." Friedkin tiptoes out of the theater before the movies begin.

He regrets, however, not having time to check out the other films. "The only way I would get to see the films is if I served on a jury. And I would never do that.

Never. Because I don't know that one film is better than another. People who run the track or racehorses or tennis or boxing—they're in competition. I'm not in competition with some guy from Iran or Uruguay."

That afternoon I catch Friedkin joking that the screening of his 1985 film *To Live and Die in L.A.* will be empty. While his French handlers seem nervous, not quite catching on to the self-deprecating humor, Friedkin himself is laughing like an endearing, somewhat crazy uncle. I found myself thinking: is this the guy who made *The Exorcist*? "You need to have a sense of humour," he says. "Otherwise you'd go absolutely crazy."

The second film Friedkin presented at the festival is his personal favorite, *Sorcerer* (1977). Its producers must have had a sense of humor: Friedkin's fresh take on Henri Georges Clouzot's 1953 classic *Wages of Fear* was shot in five different countries, went way over its projected $15 million budget (an unheard-of sum for a movie at the time), and faced numerous setbacks due to injury and disease (Friedkin caught malaria). To top it all, the film was a commercial and critical flop, savaged for being too dark, too complex, and too inaccessible.

Sorcerer is often seen as sounding the death knell of American auteur cinema, along with box office fiascos by the decade's other big indie directors, Martin Scorsese (1977's *New York, New York*), Michael Cimino (1982's *Heaven's Gate*), and Francis Ford Coppola (1981's *One from the Heart*). Most think that's how the wild *Easy Rider* generation of American directors came to a screeching halt in the early 1980s. Friedkin disagrees.

"I don't think [*Sorcerer*] had anything whatever to do with it," he tells me, adjusting his aviator shades. "The major studios in Hollywood could not allow so-called auteurs to take over the industry. The owners and managers of the studios demanded control. And what my generation did was we took the controls because they didn't know the audience and we did at the time."

Then came a little film called *Star Wars*, directed by George Lucas and released the same year as *Sorcerer*—its aftermath was the franchising of Hollywood movies that continues unabated to this day. Friedkin clearly has a distaste for this stuff, but he's not bitter. "The films being made today are seen by the widest audiences ever. But they're not for me," he explains, adding that he'd rather rewatch *Citizen Kane*, *The Verdict*, or MGM musicals.

The seventies was a decade when Hollywood was churning out sophisticated adult fare with the regularity that it now makes films about men in underwear and capes. In Friedkin's view, the end of auteur cinema in America wasn't about the fortunes of individual films such as *Sorcerer*, but a systemic choice by the studios to reap the sort of profits that were hitherto only dreamed of. Sure, films like *Network*, *Chinatown*, *Taxi Driver*, and *Deliverance* were all box office hits, but nothing close to the hundreds of millions that *Star Wars* generated (and continues to generate).

In 2013, Friedkin won a lawsuit against Paramount and Universal for ownership of *Sorcerer*, rescuing it from a legal limbo that had made it impossible for him to screen it. He also supervised the digital remastering that has since been made available on Blu-ray. Seeing the film as the director originally intended (rather than the poor-quality VHS that was the only way to access it for decades) has helped this brutally intense, utterly unique movie to emerge from both the critical slamming and from the shadow cast by *Wages of Fear*.

For his part, Friedkin doesn't consider *Sorcerer* a remake at all. "I love the film by Henri Georges Clouzot, but I never set out to imitate it. I love the story. I think the story was kind of vital, about four strangers at odds with each other, but if they didn't cooperate they would all die—and the whole idea of no matter how hard you strive, we all end up the same way. And all that is in that story." While he's glad to see *Sorcerer* finding an appreciative audience today, he remains somewhat uncertain whether a film he made out of personal conviction could gain a following. "I never thought any of my films would find a large audience. Never occurred to me. Especially the ones that were the most successful," he says with a shrug.

The following day, Friedkin addressed the packed house that had turned out for the festival masterclass. In the course of the interview, the French critic Michel Ciment made several references to the "commercial failures" of the director's career. "Look, Michel, I didn't come here to be insulted," he countered, jokily.

"Inside of every one of us who has ever created anything there is an almost constant record of failure," he told the festival audience. "That's what we think about. That's what involves our thought process. I know some of the most successful filmmakers and songwriters, and inside these giant talents is a little mouse." In Friedkin's case, the mouse hasn't stopped roaring for more than half a century.

We Need an Exorcist!

Maureen Dowd / 2018

When you've got a demonic child in Washington splattering dark stinking bile, croaking gibberish, spewing vulgar personal attacks, lying to sow confusion, whining about the unfairness of the attempts of righteous men to compel the diabolical behavior and head-spinning outbursts to stop, who do you call?

The demon-buster himself, of course, William Friedkin, the director of *The Exorcist*.

Before Donald Trump became president, the most frightening thing that happened in the capital was *The Exorcist*, which brags on its DVD cover that it's "the scariest film of all time."

It could well be, if the measure is moviegoers putting down their popcorn in unison when Linda Blair gushes green vomit.

"That was oatmeal—the pea soup was just for coloring," the eighty-two-year-old Friedkin tells me, as we have lunch at 1789 in Georgetown, a restaurant opposite the steep concrete steps where Jason Miller's tortured Father Karras fell to his death in a violent struggle with the demon.

Friedkin offers an eerie connection to the Trump White House, noting that he edited the film at 666 Fifth Avenue, the accursed Manhattan building with the Number of the Beast at the center of Jared Kushner's money problems.

The book and screenplay were written by William Peter Blatty, inspired by a news story he heard about in a religious class: the 1949 case of a fourteen-year-old boy in a Maryland suburb of Washington. Objects appeared to move around on their own in the boy's bedroom and he was violent and speaking Latin phrases. The boy, a Lutheran who grew up to be an engineer at NASA, underwent an exorcism, first with a priest from Georgetown University and then with priests in St. Louis.

After studying up on the case, Friedkin has decided it was "jive."

"It just doesn't hold water," he says, eating asparagus soup that looks enough like what came out of Linda Blair's mouth to make me a little queasy.

Friedkin's career peaked in the early seventies with two blockbusters, *The French Connection* and *The Exorcist*. Eventually he felt so out of touch with a Hollywood possessed by comic books and sci-fis that he began directing operas.

Now he has returned to the subject that haunts him with a documentary called *The Devil and Father Amorth*, opening this month.

Friedkin used a hand-held camera to film an interview with Father Amorth, the chief Vatican exorcist, who worried that "Satan rules the world" and was in the Vatican. He died in 2016 at ninety-one.

The director, who had never seen an exorcism, also talked the priest into letting him film the exorcism of an Italian architect named Cristina with whom he had done the ancient ritual many times.

"It was harrowing," Friedkin says. "These five strong guys are holding her down. They're sweating. Father Amorth told me that during one of the exorcisms, she accused him of his sins and they were real."

Friedkin took this footage to neurosurgeons and psychiatrists, and one psychiatrist challenged it, saying Cristina did not show "the classic symptoms" of possession, such as her head turning 360 degrees and her body levitating.

"I said, 'Doctor, we made that up,'" Friedkin recalls dryly. "Blatty invented what we think of as possession and exorcism today, and I had to find a way to film it. Father Amorth never encountered stuff like that, but he encountered other extraordinary occurrences and personality changes and voice changes. But there was no levitation or head spinning."

The filmmaker says that for his documentary he did nothing to amplify the guttural growl of Cristina, which evokes the terrifying voice used by Mercedes McCambridge, which was dubbed in for Blair's in the possession scenes.

"When she breathed into the mic, you'd hear five or six sounds come out at once, like John Coltrane playing the sax," he says. "When I first called her, she said, 'I'm in AA. I had a serious drinking problem. I am a lapsed Catholic, but I still have strong ties to the church. So in order to do what you want, I'm going to have to start drinking Jack Daniel's again and smoking cigarettes and eating raw eggs.' And she wanted to have her own two priests with her at all times."

Friedkin is chockablock with such tales.

He says the first of his four wives, Jeanne Moreau, installed a lifelong love of Proust in him by reading it aloud.

Happily married to Sherry Lansing for twenty-six years, Friedkin says, he wasn't really "Hollywood's most combustible director," as *The Telegraph* once called him.

"I don't drink," he says. "I've never done drugs. I've never tried grass. But I think Miles Davis is a reason to live." He does cop to slapping a couple of people to get the sad and angry performances he wanted, noting that another word for director is "manipulator."

He did not want Gene Hackman to play the iconic New York police detective Popeye Doyle in *The French Connection*.

He gave the role to Jimmy Breslin instead. "He had exactly the look I had in mind, a Black Irishman," Friedkin says. "The first day, he was great, great, great. The second day, he forgot what he did on the first day. The third day, he didn't show up. Comes Friday, he shows up and says, 'Hey, isn't there a car chase in this movie?' I said, 'Yeah.' He said, 'You know, I promised my mother on her deathbed I wouldn't drive, so I don't know how to drive.' I said, 'You're fired.'"

He gave Hackman the part, and they sparred so much during filming that at the end, he told a producer: "I may get away with this thing, but if I had to do *The Gene Hackman Story*, I wouldn't hire this guy." He acknowledges now that Hackman is one of the greatest American film actors.

After lunch, Friedkin makes me descend the Stairway to Hell, the seventy-five steps in the movie's climactic scene that I had avoided my whole life. I saw *The Exorcist* on my twenty-first birthday and was so unnerved, I went to bed and missed my own party.

Standing on the steps, Friedkin channels the demon, growling, "Your mother still rots in hell, Karras, you faithless slime." Tourists taking selfies on the stairs look around, startled.

And even all these years later, I still want to crawl under the covers.

No Sympathy for the Devil: *The Exorcist* Director William Friedkin Looks Back

Kory Grow / 2018

Filmmaker William Friedkin is leading a group of journalists around Georgetown, the Washington, DC, neighborhood that served as the setting for his 1973 blockbuster *The Exorcist* on a fittingly overcast April day. After a quasi-lecture about his history with the film in Georgetown University's Healy Hall, we've walked through classrooms, courtyards, and churches that all played significant roles in the making of the picture and the book that inspired it. Now we're on one of the streets that actress Ellen Burstyn, who played beleaguered mother Chris MacNeil, strolls down during the calm before the storm. "I cut to four or five different shots of her walking just to show what I believe is the beauty of this magnificent little town," he says. Our destination served a more sinister role.

"*The Exorcist* Steps," as they're officially known on a DC landmark placard, are where Jason Miller's character, Father Damien Karras, plunges to his death after the demon Pazuzu, which had been afflicting twelve-year-old Regan MacNeil, enters him. "We built a false front that came out to where those trees are," Friedkin says at the head of the stairs, pointing up. "The house had to be extended about twenty-five yards. The stunt man's jump could never have been possible, but this is the house that [author William Peter] Blatty wrote about, so I decided to make an extension and make it possible. It was an incredible jump. All the steps and corners were padded with rubber."

The stone stairwell—which is nearly 125 years old—consists of seventy-five steps that stretch three stories. "I'm told this is one of the five most visited sites in Washington," he says. And while TripAdvisor ranks its popularity lower, user-submitted photos mostly show multiple people gleefully posing dead on them. It's been a mecca for cinephiles ever since *The Exorcist* became a runaway hit nearly fifty years ago.

When the adaptation of Blatty's 1971 novel came out, it was a revelation. Horror, up to that point, was monster flicks like *Frankenstein* and *Dracula* and unsettling psychodramas like *Psycho* and *Rosemary's Baby*; Friedkin's film was gritty and visceral almost like a documentary. And it was over the top. Here was a jejune girl possessed by a demon, screaming, "Fuck me Jesus," while stabbing her crotch with a crucifix; her head spun 360 degrees; she spewed ropy pea soup like a fire hydrant, and, before any of that could happen, she was subjected to all sorts of bloody, watch-through-your-fingers medical tests.

It was shocking and—years before *Jaws* ratified the blockbuster we know—it had people lining up at the entrances of movie theaters while the exits were soppy with puke from the previous showing. The *New York Times* reported at the time that it was "the biggest thing to hit the industry since Mary Pickford, popcorn, pornography, and *The Godfather*." It inspired several sequels, including one by Blatty, and a TV series; it's been referenced in countless rock and rap songs; and Linda Blair even appeared in an *Exorcist* spoof, *Repossessed*.

Now Friedkin is revisiting the topic of possession in a new film, a documentary titled *The Devil and Father Amorth*, for which he filmed an authentic rite of demon purging carried out by a real-life, world-renowned exorcist, the late Father Gabriele Amorth. The director, who won Oscars for *The French Connection* and is also known for *To Live and Die in L.A.* and *Rules of Engagement*, returned to Georgetown today to bring his experience full circle, and he beams with pride as he visits his own personal stations of the cross.

Friedkin is now eighty-two. A man of average height, he has a big, commanding, friendly personality. When bystanders ask for selfies with him and the *Exorcist* steps, he positions their cellphone for them to frame the photo as cinematically as possible. He speaks in long, husky, staccato monologues. He has an inquisitive nature—when Italy comes up in conversation, he says he wanted to see the Leaning Tower of Pisa and has anyone seen it?—and it's that indefatigable questioning, that curiosity, that brought him back to the themes of possession and exorcism all these years later.

"I had serious doubts about making this documentary," Friedkin says, a hint of P. T. Barnum flare in his voice. "I did it because I was able to witness this, and I wanted to share it with people to make of it what they will. And you're not gonna see an exorcism in any other way."

In Healy Hall's wood-paneled Philodemic Room, where Georgetown's ancient Philodemic Society holds regular debates, Friedkin stands in front of a wooden throne at a university-branded podium. His arms are variously crossed, placed on his hips and outstretched in a Christlike pose as he speaks. Portraits on the walls of notable Philodemicians and alumni from the past two centuries gaze down on him as he recalls his history as it relates to *The Devil and Father Amorth*, a journey which began in the late sixties.

After telling the producer of TV's *Peter Gunn* to stuff it after he was asked to direct "the worst script I ever read," its screenwriter, one William Peter Blatty, approached him and thanked him for his honesty. "He said, 'We all know this script is no good,'" Friedkin recalls. "'I really admire what you did, turning it down, because you lost a job in there.'" A few years later, when Friedkin was doing prerelease press for *The French Connection*, Blatty sent him galleys of *The Exorcist* and asked if Friedkin would direct a film of it. Several filmmakers had come and gone from the project, including Stanley Kubrick ("He wanted to only develop his own stories," Friedkin says), Arthur Penn ("He did not want to do any other stories that had violence after *Bonnie and Clyde*"), and Mike Nichols ("He said he will never be able to find a twelve-year-old girl who can carry this movie").

"Why me?" Friedkin asked. The author replied, "Because you're the only director who has never lied to me." Blatty had directorial approval, leading to several disagreements with the producers. Once *The French Connection* became a hit, the studio stopped fighting him on Friedkin. It was a victory for Blatty, for whom *The Exorcist* was a very personal story.

It was in one of Healy Hall's classrooms where, while earning a bachelor's degree in English, he heard about a case of possession in a nearby Maryland town. The story was so unusual it had even made the front page of the *Washington Post*, which reported, "In what is perhaps one of the most remarkable experiences of its kind in recent religious history, a fourteen-year-old Mount Rainier boy has been freed by a Catholic priest of possession by the devil, Catholic sources reported yesterday." The boy was a Protestant but was referred to a Catholic priest, after furniture started moving of its own accord, things flew across the room, and the walls made scratching sounds. Blatty researched the incident as much as he could, hoping to write a nonfiction account, but hit wall after wall with little to go on and turned the story into a novel. (A *New York Times* search for the word "exorcism" between 1940 and 1959 turns up only thirty results with only one reporting on a specific instance of exorcism, which took place in England.)

Friedkin took the subject matter seriously. Although he was born Jewish ("Yes, I was bar-mitzvahed," he later tells *Rolling Stone* glibly), he says he believes in the teachings of Jesus Christ. "I made the film with that belief, and, of course, Mr. Blatty wrote it with not only that strong belief, but his deep faith in the church."

To both Friedkin and Blatty, who died last year, *The Exorcist* was not a horror story, but one of the "mystery of faith." It's a loose term Friedkin refers to frequently both in Georgetown and in a later interview that doesn't so much mean, "How could God forsake people by allowing possession?" so much as, "How does the nature of faith lead people to believe in things like possession?" With *The Devil and Father Amorth*, Friedkin doesn't attempt to solve the mystery of faith. Instead, he indulges it.

Friedkin and Blatty first became aware of Father Gabriele Amorth around the time the priest published in 1990 the book *An Exorcist Tells His Story*. Amorth mentioned the movie in a paragraph, writing, "It is thanks to the movies that we find a renewed interest in exorcisms." He also quoted another Jesuit priest who said of *The Exorcist*, "Save some special effects, the film had dealt very soberly with the problem of evil, reawakening an interest in exorcisms that had been all but forgotten." Amorth was grateful for the film.

By the time of his death in 2016 at the age of ninety-one, Amorth is said to have performed some seventy thousand exorcisms over twenty-nine years, as the practice has a certain prevalence in Italy due to the influence of Catholicism. Some five hundred thousand people reportedly request exorcisms a year in a country of sixty million, according to *USA Today*.

A Pauline priest, Father Amorth become famous through media appearances and once claimed that both Hitler and Stalin were "certainly" possessed by the Devil, according to the National Catholic Register, though he said they were still both responsible for their deeds as individuals; he also declared "ISIS is Satan." Armchair diagnoses aside, Amorth would see a possessed person only after he or she had met with a medical doctor or a psychiatrist and were told they were untreatable. He founded the International Association of Exorcists in 1990 and served as its president for a decade. Friedkin calls him "the most spiritual man I think I've ever met outside of William Peter Blatty."

In 2016, the director met Amorth for the first time while on a trip to Italy where he was receiving a lifetime achievement award at the Lucca Film Festival. Exploring his touristing options while there, he asked a theologian friend if he could meet either the Pope or Father Amorth while in Rome. The pontiff was out of town, he was told, but Amorth would meet him.

Friedkin later relayed his story to then–*Vanity Fair* editor Graydon Carter who asked him to write about Amorth. "I wrote a sixty-five-hundred-word article that they printed and at the end of the interview, I asked [Amorth] if he would ever allow me to witness an exorcism," Friedkin tells everyone gathered in the Philodemic Room, just as a cell phone goes off, playing Mike Oldfield's "Tubular Bells," the eerie theme music from *The Exorcist*. "I didn't plan that," he says to a room of laughs. (The phone belongs to Julie Blatty, the author's widow.)

The filmmaker expected a "no" when he asked to see an exorcism, but Father Stefano Stimamiglio of the Pauline order told him Amorth would allow it. Friedkin asked to film it. Again, to his amazement, he got a yes with the stipulation that he alone could film it with a small camera. (Father Stimamiglio did not return a request for comment about how and why the approval to film was granted in time for publication.)

On May 1, he documented Amorth's ninth exorcism of a forty-six -year-old woman named Cristina. Although it's not in the film, Friedkin's *Vanity Fair* article states that her family believed she'd been cursed by her brother's girlfriend, whom the filmmaker later says belonged to something called the Pyramid Cult.

For about seventeen minutes, as shown in *The Devil and Father Amorth*, the priest sits next to the woman. He literally thumbs his nose at the Devil and begins to pray at which point Cristina's voice drops significantly, sounding very much like Regan's demon voice in both the movie *The Exorcist* and how it was described in Blatty's book as "deep and thick with menace and power." Cristina shouts "Stop it" in Italian.

"Surrender to the will of God," Amorth commands as several men restrain her as she attempts to leap forward. "Surrender to the will of the Virgin Mary. Surrender to the will of Jesus. . . . The Virgin Mary will destroy you, Satan." It's not quite "The Power of Christ compels you" with Linda Blair floating in the air as Holy Water rips her skin apart, but it's still arresting. Cristina's demon tells Amorth that it is Satan Himself but also that there are many demons inside her. "We are legion." When it's done, Cristina appears to return to normal until Amorth exorcises her parents in case the demon moved to another person and she lashes out again. "Something I cut from the film is that Father Amorth told me that during the course of the exorcism, the woman, in her altered personality, had cited to him some of his actual sins," Friedkin says. "I had the good sense not to ask him what these sins were and mention them."

Friedkin attempted a follow-up interview with Cristina without Amorth present but, upon learning she was acting irrationally, he left his camera in the car and did not film the encounter. He tells the camera in the movie that her boyfriend threatened his life and demanded the film as she slithered her body around a church like a snake and bellowed in her demon voice. "No, I want it shown," Friedkin says Cristina shouted in her demon voice. "I certainly would have turned the camera on, had I brought it," he says later, "but I didn't want to upset her by putting a camera in her face because of the way she sounded on the phone."

Amorth contracted pneumonia and died without liberating Cristina, whom Friedkin says, he's told is still seeking exorcisms. "I'm convinced Father Amorth was authentic," Friedkin tells the hall, "and this woman had a complete transformation of personality." *USA Today* reports that requests for exorcisms have tripled since the priest's death.

A couple of days after the Georgetown visit, Friedkin welcomes *Rolling Stone* into his plush suite at New York City's high-end hotel, the Carlyle. He's dressed comfortably in a black button-up, beige slacks, and sneakers. A copy of the thriller *Fear: A Novel*, by Dirk Kurbjuweit, a bowl of fruit, and an empty bag for Manolo Blahnik shoes sits next to a stack of CDs by his late friend, Miles Davis. "I showed the film *The French Connection* to him, and his comment after was, 'Hey, Billy, how come two guys to chase one guy?'" Friedkin laughs. "Later, when I did *To Live and Die in L.A.*, I showed it to him and he said, 'Two guys to chase one guy.'" He laughs again.

Friedkin retrieves a bottle of Fiji water to share and we settle into a table in the corner of the room next to windows that overlook East 76th Street where he reclines in his chair and crosses his legs. The conversation naturally gravitates to the mystery of faith. "It's the fact that people believe in somebody [Jesus Christ] who left no writings of his own. We have no recording of his voice," he explains. "We have no image of him that we can rely on. He lived for a very short thirty-three years, of which twelve years nothing is known. Yet people by the billions have believed that he was the son of God. There's something more to that that I can't dismiss."

Now that he's made two films about the mystery, he says he doesn't understand it any better. "I was absolutely terrified [during the exorcism] because I saw someone become completely unhinged and I had no idea why," he says, recalling that it was freezing cold in the room while warm outside. "Unlike the film *The Exorcist*, she wasn't in that state when I met her. *The Exorcist* suggest that once this happens, it's a permanent state but that wasn't true. She would go in and out of these fits and had had numerous exorcisms. It was just really disturbing and terrifying. She was in such extreme pain.

"It was her pain that finally got to me, and I wondered, 'Why is this directed at this woman? What did she ever do to deserve this?'"

When Friedkin reedited *The Exorcist* in 2000, he included a scene where the two priests attempted to answer that. "I think the point is to make us despair," the elder priest, played by Max von Sydow, says. "To see ourselves as animal and ugly. To reject the possibility that God could love us." When he hears that today, the director says, "Blatty wrote that line, and it's beautiful."

The Bible describes possession, whether literal or metaphoric, in simpler terms. "Your adversary, the Devil, prowls around like a roaring lion, seeking someone to devour," reads 1 Peter 5:8. And in Mark 5, a group of impure spirits who identified themselves as Legion were so craven that they begged their exorcist, Jesus Christ, to send them into a herd of two thousand pigs. Once the sows were theirs, they drowned themselves. When you look at the source material, so-called "possession" appears to be a kind of confusion.

To understand it all better, Friedkin took his home-movie exorcism to various experts—brain surgeons, psychiatrists, representatives of the church—and interviewed them for the second half of *The Devil and Father Amorth*. Dr. Neil Martin, then the chair of neurology staff at UCLA, described Cristina as experiencing a "major force within her." He added that Cristina seemed to be suffering delirium, and, when Friedkin asks if she would be better helped by brain surgery than this ritual, the doctor says, "unlikely." "I haven't seen this kind of consequence from any [regularly treatable] disorders," he explains.

A group of shrinks referred Friedkin to their bibles: the American Psychiatric Association's *Diagnostic and Statistical Manual of Mental Disorders* and the World Health Organization's *International Statistical Classification of Diseases and Related Health Problems*. Dissociative Identity Disorder, as defined in DSM-V, is "an experience of possession." It explains: "Possession-form identities in D.I.D. typically manifest as behaviors that appear as if a 'spirit,' supernatural being or outside person has taken control, such that the individual begins speaking or acting in a distinctively different manner. . . . An individual may be 'taken over' by a demon or deity, resulting in profound impairment, and demanding that an individual or a relative be punished for a past act, followed by more subtle periods of identity alteration." Moreover, it says, "The identities that arise during possession-form D.I.D. . . . are not a normal part of a broadly accepted cultural or religious practice," dovetailing even deeper into Friedkin's mystery of faith. One of the doctors compared exorcism to "placebo response"—"If you believe something is more likely to work, it's more likely to work." To that point, it's worth noting, too, that because the diagnosis is faith-based, people who aren't Christian, such as Muslims or Jews, are unlikely to be seeking a Catholic exorcist.

Reflecting on his interviews, the filmmaker agrees that it's uncommon that a doctor would make a recommendation based on a video with no examination. He says, "You're right, that was unusual. But they saw the whole thing and they made comment." (An attempt to reach Dr. Martin for comment was unsuccessful.)

A Catholic leader he interviewed, Bishop Robert Barron, who serves for the Archdiocese of Los Angeles, told Friedkin he never met anyone he felt needed an exorcism, but he believed in the phenomenon of possession. But he added that he would never be able to speak to the Devil the way Father Amorth did because he did not feel he was holy enough. "It was the most shocking thing I had heard through the whole thing," Friedkin says. "What do you mean? You have the power of Christ." (A request for comment from Bishop Barron was not returned in time for publication. Similarly, requests for general comment on the film from the Vatican and the Archdiocese of New York were not returned.)

His documentary is rough and personal, but he stands by it. When questioned about Cristina's voice, which sounds manipulated or double-tracked because there appear to be multiple levels to it, he asserts he did not alter it. "She had never seen *The Exorcist* movie and there are certain similarities to the way Regan and [voice actress] Mercedes McCambridge sounded in the film," he says. "I thought that Cristina's voice was remarkably similar. McCambridge's voice was due to having started drinking again to do this and swallowing raw eggs and stuff. So when she'd breathe into a microphone"—he makes a wheezing sound—"you would hear four or five different sounds. It's like when Coltrane played. You'd hear overtones. We recorded [Cristina] at a normal level and . . . we did not mess with the tracks."

He doesn't want to color people's opinions by trickery, he says. He wants people to draw their own conclusions about faith and possession from the picture. "It was a home movie, and then it occurred to me, 'Is there anything that could be done with it?'" he says. "It's a document by the Vatican exorcist, which had never been filmed. 'Why should just I see it?'"

When Friedkin watches *The Exorcist* these days, it's usually to approve of a print. But he's still impressed by what he sees. It's not his favorite movie he's made (that's *Sorcerer*) but the mystery of faith—the connecting thread to today—is still strong.

"Some of the scenes are amazingly well done," he says with a laugh. "The fact that we had no digital in it. We had to achieve all of that. But what still holds me are the performances." He's also proud of the way audiences suspended their disbelief while watching. "I'm sure a lot of people are skeptical about the real thing when it comes to exorcism," he says, "but the movie scared the hell out of them."

He remembers James Cagney requesting his audience during a taping of *The Merv Griffin Show*, and the actor told him, "I've got a bone to pick with you, son. I had the greatest barber in the world for more than thirty years. He saw your movie and he left the profession to become a priest. I'll never find a barber that good again."

"I thought that was wonderful," Friedkin says.

In 1974, the film was nominated for ten Academy Awards. It won two, for sound mixing and for Blatty's screenplay adaptation of his book. It did not earn Friedkin Best Picture or Best Director Oscars as he had won two years earlier for *The French Connection*. "There was a campaign against *The Exorcist* led by Robert Aldrich and George Cukor," he says. "The guy who produced the awards show that year told me they were going around saying, 'If *The Exorcist* wins Best Picture, it's the end of Hollywood as we know it.' Fuck them. I think there was a lot of resentment and jealousy. Robert Aldrich wanted to direct *The Exorcist*. And I think what bothered Cukor was that the film was disturbing and blasphemous, as well as the fact I had recently won it for a little fucking documentary about two cops."

Nevertheless, the movie's cultural impact is undeniable and far greater all these decades later than that year's winner, *The Sting*. Just look at the way people flock to the *Exorcist* Steps. "When the film first opened, I went back to Georgetown and there were thousands of people on the steps around the house and that continued for years," Friedkin says. "I saw kids sitting on every step for years, eating sandwiches, smoking, hanging out. It really disturbed the owner of the house and we had to build her that terrible black fence."

Those stairs—and steps in general—are a defining metaphor in both *The Exorcist* and Friedkin's latest film. When we walked through Georgetown, Friedkin kept pointing out stairways he shot—one in Healy Hall that Jason Miller's character ascends to ask for the extension, one out front where Burstyn's character led a student protest, another in a courtyard that led to the Jesuit residence, another outside where two priests discuss obtaining the Roman ritual of exorcism and then two minutes away those famous seventy-five steps that ended in a pool of blood. In *The Devil and Father Amorth*, Friedkin explains that the priest used to perform his exorcisms in the Scala Sancta atop a staircase—the Holy Stairs that lead to the praetorium of Pontius Pilate—that can only be climbed on one's knees.

"It all represented the idea of ascension," Friedkin says.

It's something he won't be doing anytime soon, at least on the *Exorcist* steps. Back in Georgetown, he'll only go up a few to take photos before coming back down. "I used to regularly go up those seventy-five steps," he says. "I tried it last week here, and it almost claimed my life. I actually had the thought on the last landing that it would not only be fitting but poetic for me to die on these steps."

Index

About the Editor

Christopher Lane is an acclaimed film and television writer, director, and producer. He is also an award-winning educator and lecturer, film and media curriculum developer for various educational institutions, and former Film Production Program Coordinator. He regularly sits on national and international film and arts discussion panels and film festival juries and currently curates and archives a large silent film ephemera and materials collection intended for exhibition.

Printed in the United States
By Bookmasters